AF335239

RIVER CROSSINGS
CONTEMPORARY ART COMES HOME

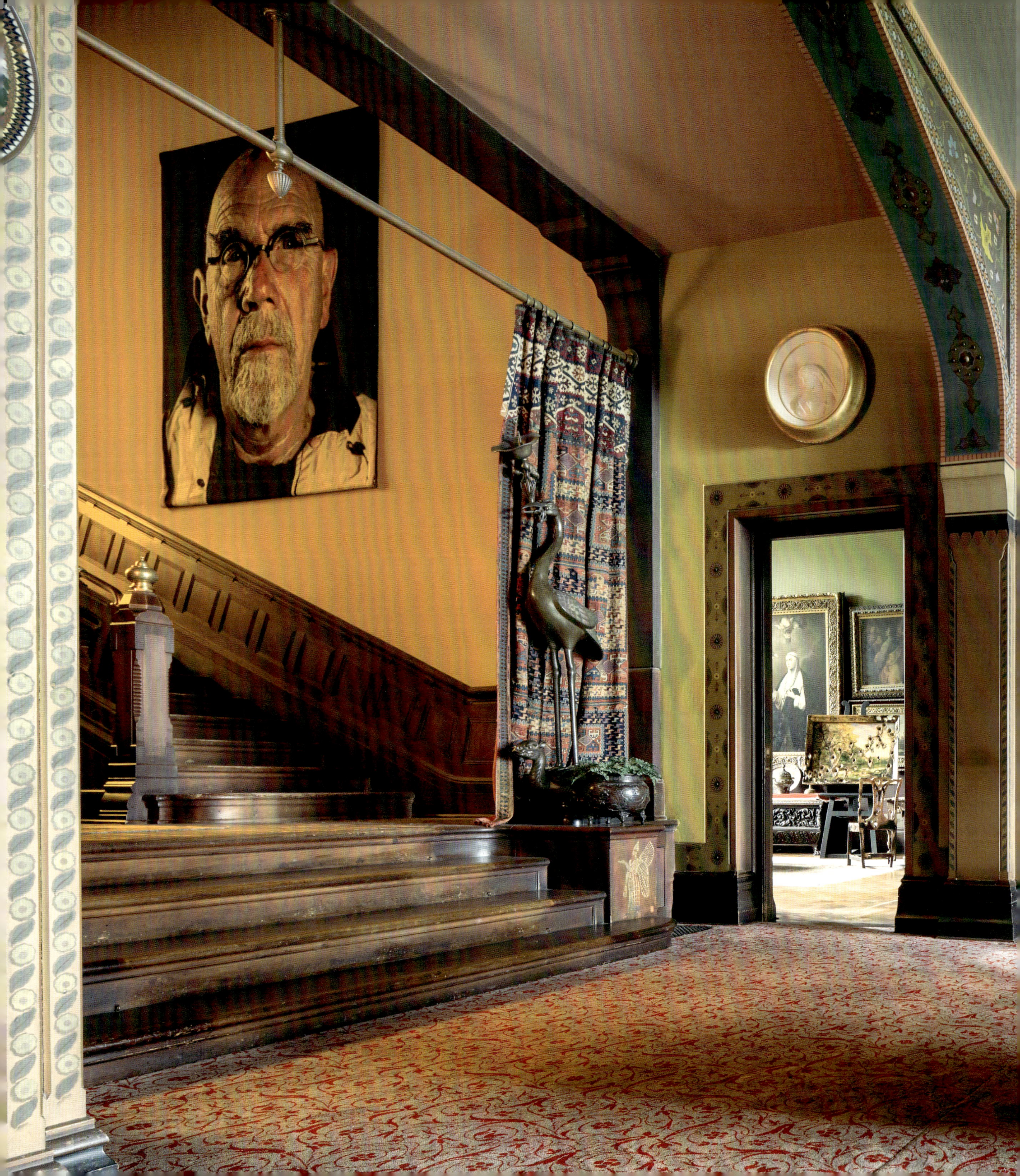

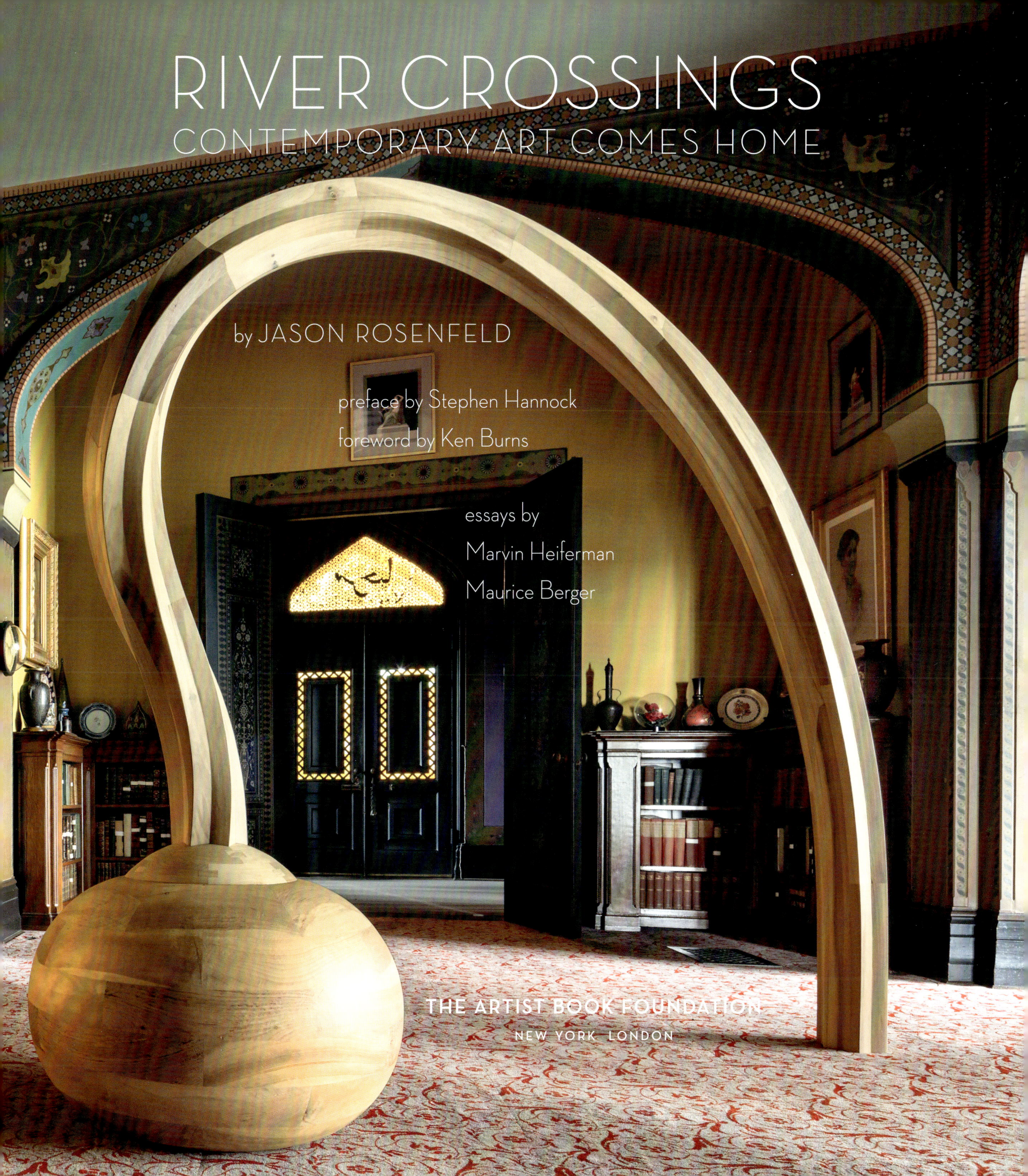

RIVER CROSSINGS
CONTEMPORARY ART COMES HOME

by JASON ROSENFELD

preface by Stephen Hannock
foreword by Ken Burns

essays by
Marvin Heiferman
Maurice Berger

THE ARTIST BOOK FOUNDATION
NEW YORK LONDON

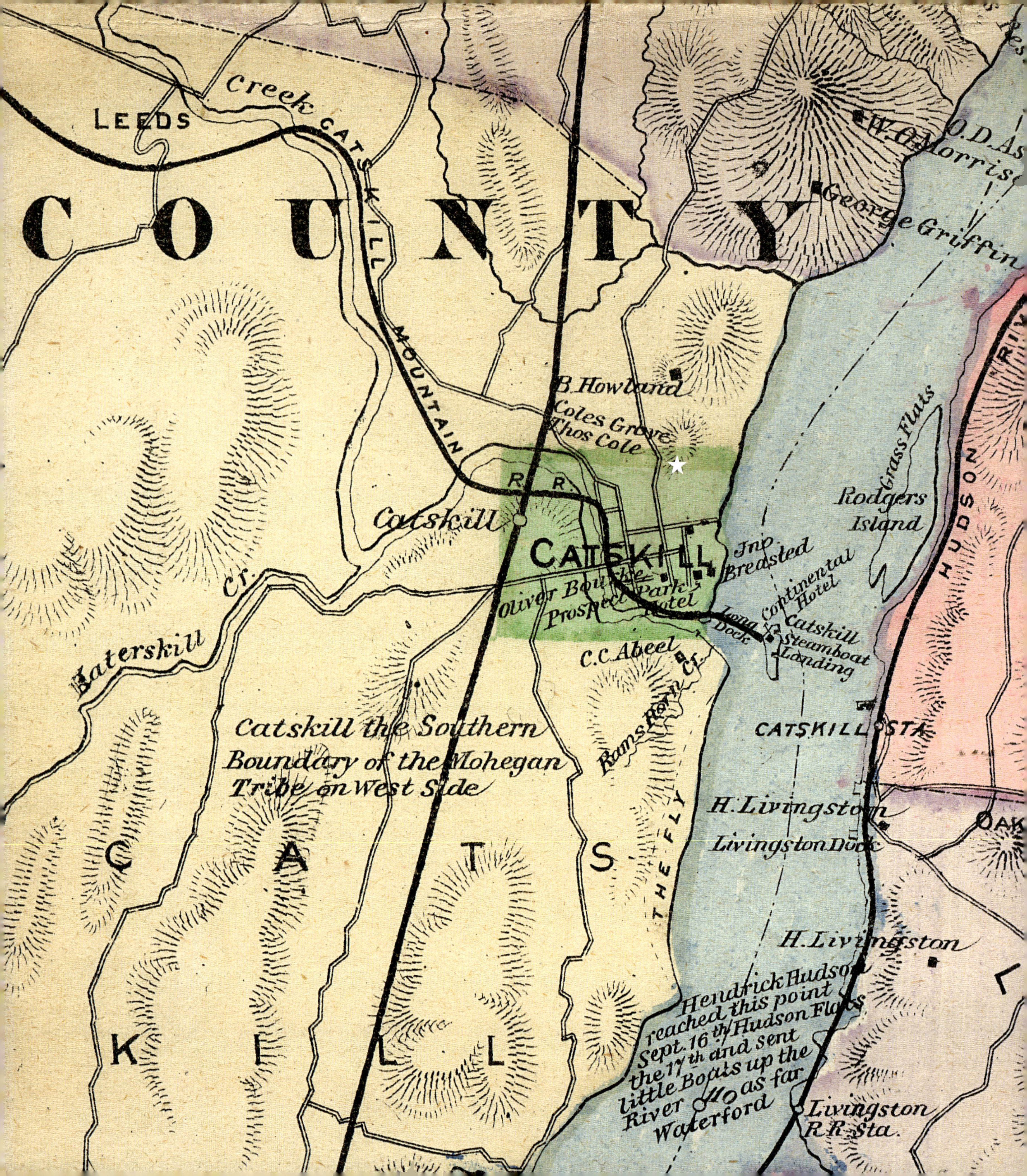

LEEDS
Creek CATSKILL
COUNTY
CATSKILL MOUNTAIN
W.G.Morris
O.D.As
George Griffin
HUDSON RIVER
B. Howland
Coles Grove
Thos Cole
Grass Flats
Rodgers Island
R. R.
Catskill
CATSKILL
Jno Breasted
Continental Hotel
Oliver Bouck
Prospect Park Hotel
Catskill Steamboat Landing
Long Dock
Baterskill
Cr.
C. C. Abeel
Catskill the Southern
Boundary of the Mohegan
Tribe on West Side
Rams Horn Cr.
CATSKILL STA.
CATSKILL
H. Livingston
Livingston Dock
THE FLY
OAK
H. Livingston
Hendrick Hudson
reached this point
Sept. 16 th Hudson Flats
the 17 th and sent
little Boats up the
River as far
Waterford
Livingston
R. R. Sta.

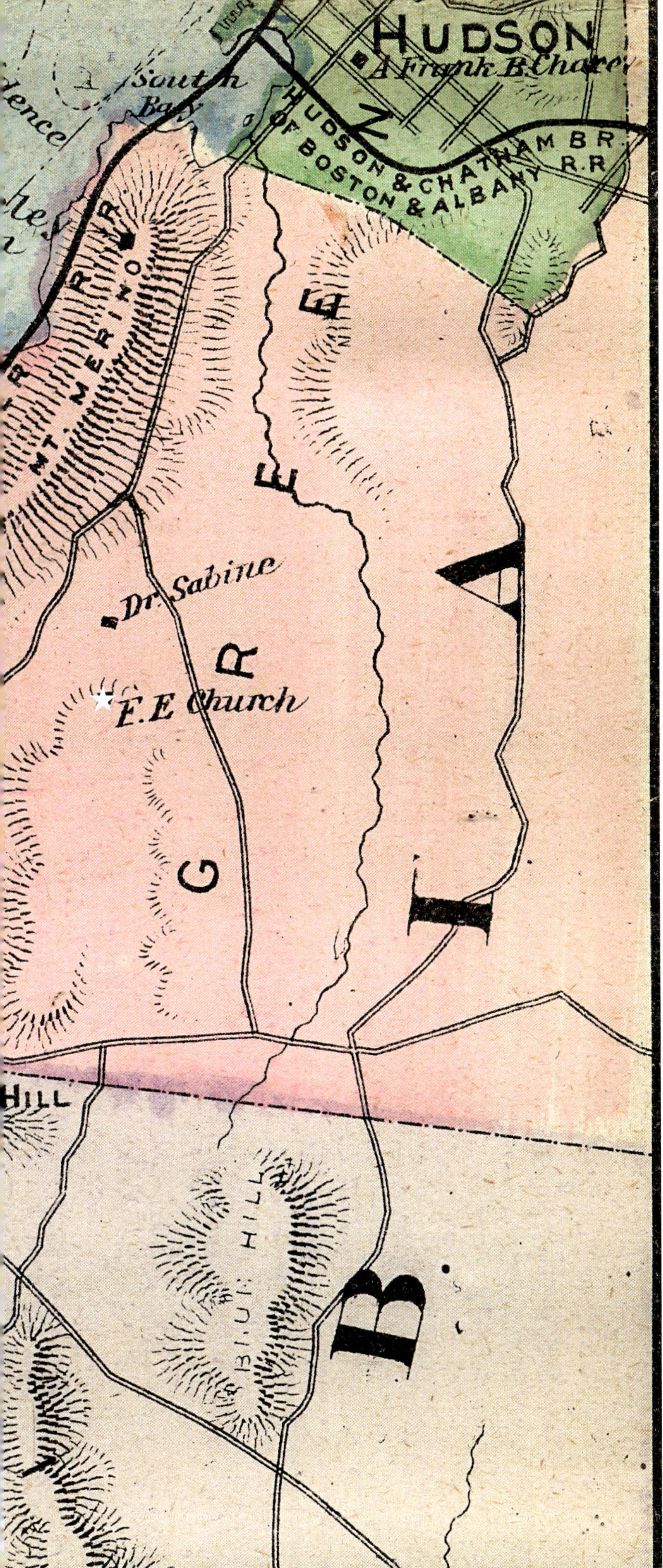

CONTENTS

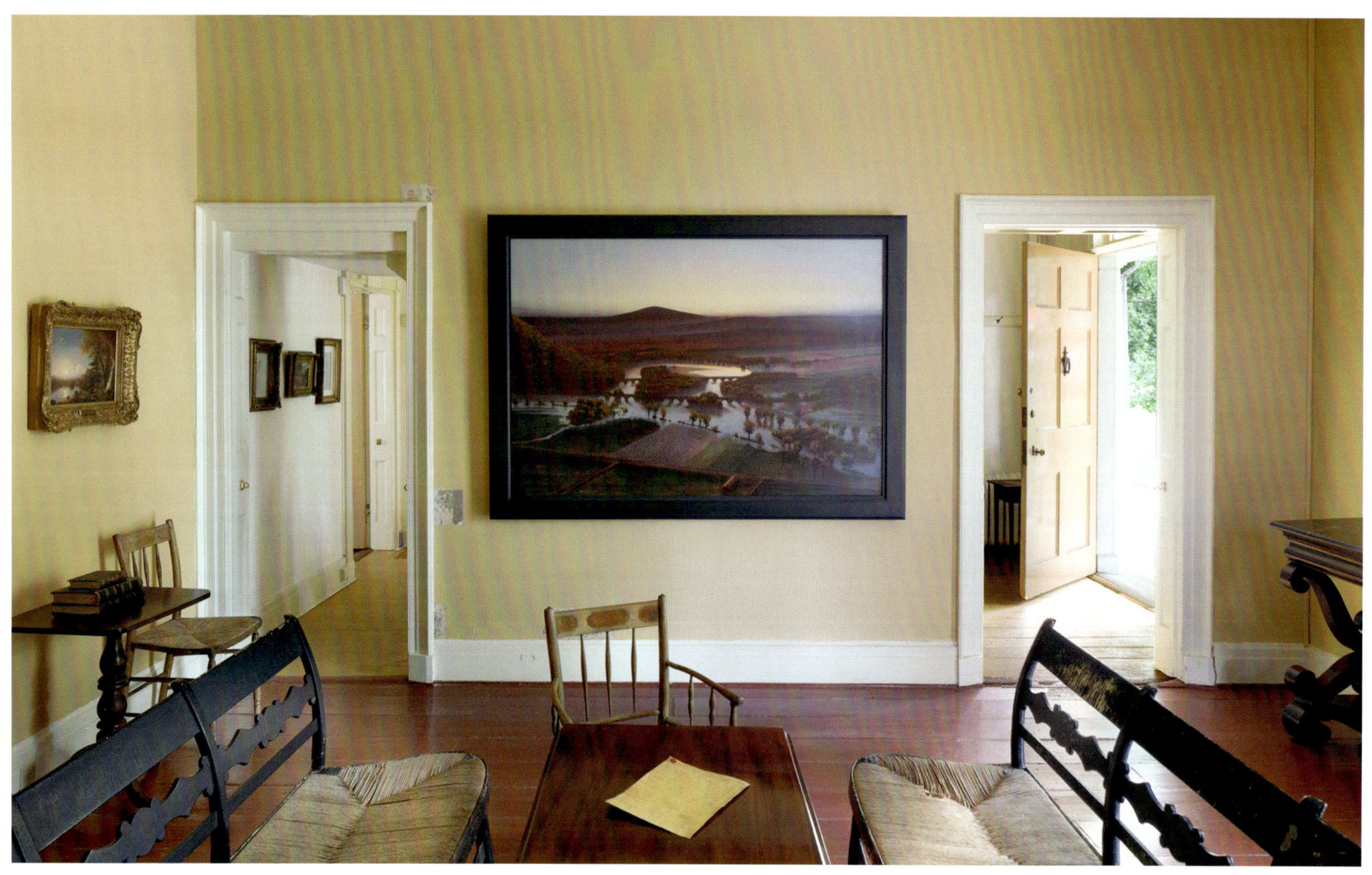

Stephen Hannock, *The Oxbow, Flooded, for Frank Moore and Dan Hodermarsky (Mass MoCA #196)*, 2013 (plate 15) at Thomas Cole National Historic Site.

I HAVE ALWAYS BEEN a fan of Kurt Vonnegut. The work and the man. His simple but profound observations have come to my rescue on many occasions. But it is perhaps his facility with time travel that I have employed most frequently.

I have never visited Tralfamadore, but important conversations have taken place between my painter-self and the likes of Rembrandt van Rijn, J.M.W. Turner, Arthur Dove, Michelangelo Merisi da Caravaggio, and Jacob Lawrence. . . . And then Thomas Cole and Frederic Edwin Church.

If Cole and I were on the west porch of his house in Catskill 150 years ago, along with his teenage student Church, we just might muse on the art we would find on his walls and dotting his lawn in the third millennium. Would the paintings and sculptures be "landscape" in nature? Would the new phenomenon of photography be dominant?

As an artist who has been motivated by the Tonalists, Luminists, and earlier nineteenth-century American painters, the obvious place to start might be with the art that excites me now. For an artist who paints compositions with a horizon, I'm actually not inspired by many "landscape paintings." I see my work more as set designs or cinematic "establishing shots" for diaries that will be written throughout a given composition. Artists of my generation and beyond frequently find their way into these diaries. Who is to say it wouldn't be these artists occupying the walls of Cedar Grove and Olana in 2015?

This is where Jason Rosenfeld and I began our effort to introduce the nineteenth-century American painters to works of art in 2015. Along the way, artists' referrals and an appreciation for recent history helped fill in the rest (that is, before the Civil War it would have been impossible to convince Cole and the young Church, et al., that the slaves in America would be freed…and then in the early twentieth century that this little community downriver called Harlem would spawn a culture that would impact the entire world).

I would personally like to thank Jock Reynolds for allowing the Yale University Art Gallery's recently acquired *Oxbow* of mine to be loaned for this show with only a couple of months' notice. This painting was the first domino in our succession of choices for both houses. *The Oxbow, Flooded, for Frank Moore and Dan Hodermarsky (Mass MoCA #196)* (plate 15) shows the same nook in the Connecticut River that was first drawn by Thomas Cole in 1833 and then painted by him in 1836 (fig. 1). And it was from this familiar starting point that the art was selected.

A special note: Frank Moore (plates 30 and 31) to whom my *Oxbow* painting in the show is dedicated, was one of the most renowned artists to assemble a major body of work while afflicted with full-blown AIDS. It was Frank who designed the AIDS ribbon. He is also the reminder that any discussion of art in the third millennium *has* to include recognition of the devastating impact that AIDS has had worldwide, and specifically on American culture. The kitchen alcove servants' quarters in the basement of Cedar Grove struck us as an eerie reminder of the cots in Greenwich Village cold-water flats that were offered to sick friends early on in the 1980s. It is in this space that we set up our installation that includes two pieces by Frank Moore and Duncan Hannah's *Little Swing* (plate 29)

Last, profound thanks to Sara Griffen, now the retired director of The Olana Partnership, and to Betsy Jacks, the director of the Thomas Cole National Historic Site. It was their persistent velvet headlocks that left me with no other choice than to notify friends and acquaintances that this exhibition was an idea that should be brought to life. Henry Geldzahler used to tell us that there was no such thing as a good idea for a painting or a bad idea for a painting. Just good paintings and bad paintings. After too many years of chatter about whether contemporary art in these particular nineteenth-century homes is a good idea or a bad idea, the show is here. Let the discussion begin.

Stephen Hannock
North Adams, Massachusetts
June 2015

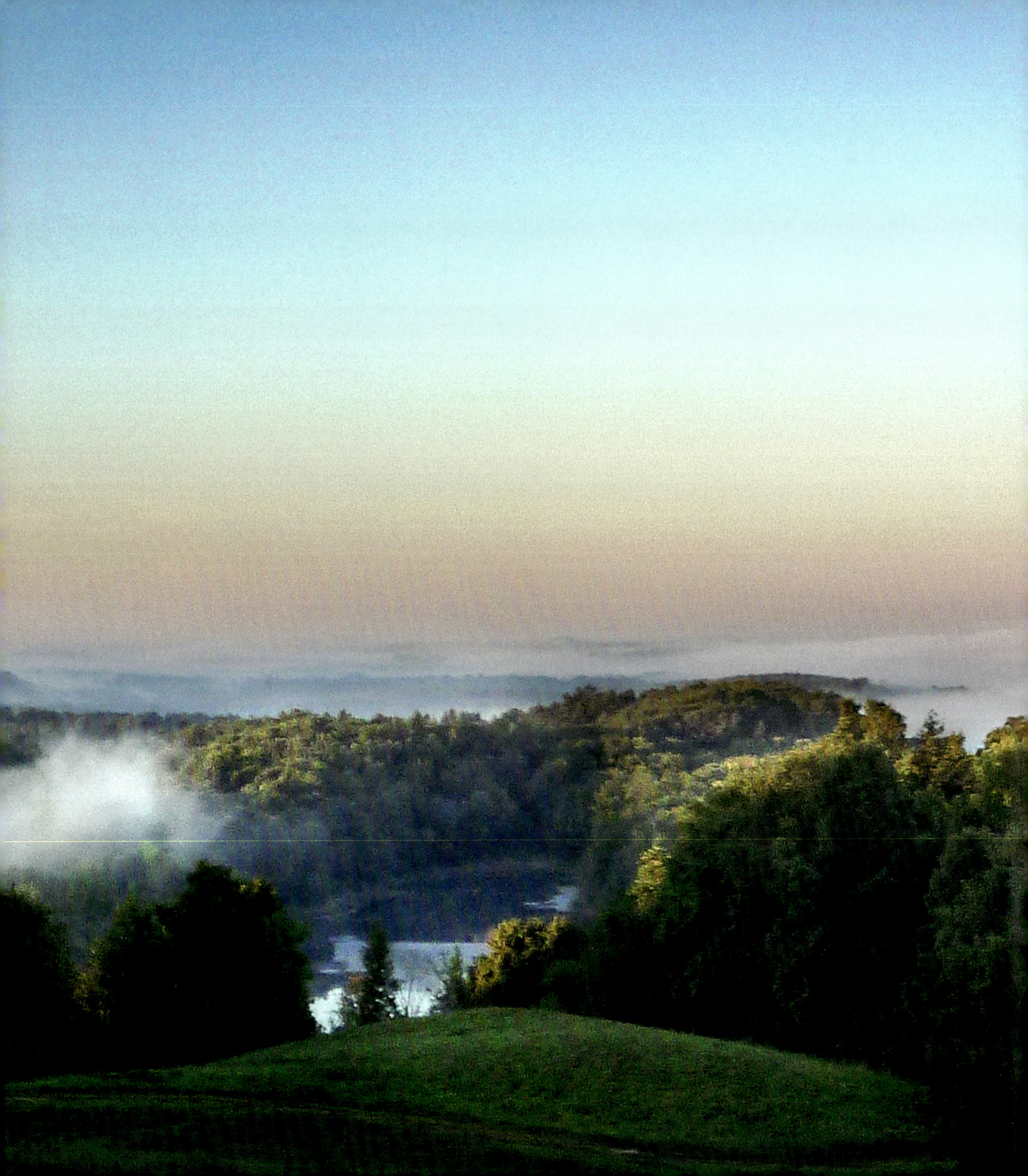

FOREWORD

The Snake, the Clearwater, the Columbia.
The Green, the Tampa, the Colorado.
The Yellowstone, the Missouri, the Mississippi.
The Ohio. The Tennessee. The Cumberland. The Hudson.

WE ARE A CONTINENT OF RIVERS; they are the avenues of our
early advancement and aspirations in a new world. On this continent
we could begin anew, liberated from the bonds of European tyranny,
smallness, certainty.

Here we would find our own way, improvising as we went. It would
be an act of faith. We would trust people—for the first time—to govern
themselves. We would allow people to worship God as *they* saw fit.
In this new American catechism we would find ourselves, and God, in
a Nature not (yet) spoiled. We would worship in cathedrals made by
Nature, not by the hand of man. Our "transcendentalism" would fit our
individuality—an individuality that seemed to effortlessly merge the
civic and the political with the spiritual and the mysterious.

In no short time, our art would follow, shunning the formalized
dogma of Religion and State. Our art would be liberated *by* and *in*
Nature, an ecstatic expression of possibility and renewed faith. And
here on the banks of the Hudson River, we would invent this new artistic vocabulary to accompany our political and religious revolutions, a
set of manners and assumptions and aesthetics that comes down to
us today as wholly us, ourselves—naïve, earnest, inquisitive, restless,
scared, lonely, uplifted, and corrupt. Those first baby steps created an
American art that continues to this day, manifested in new urges and
impulses. . . .

And that is why the sullied old River still inspires.

Ken Burns
Walpole, New Hampshire
April 2015

View across the Hudson River from Olana.

RIVER CROSSINGS

CONTEMPORARY ART COMES HOME

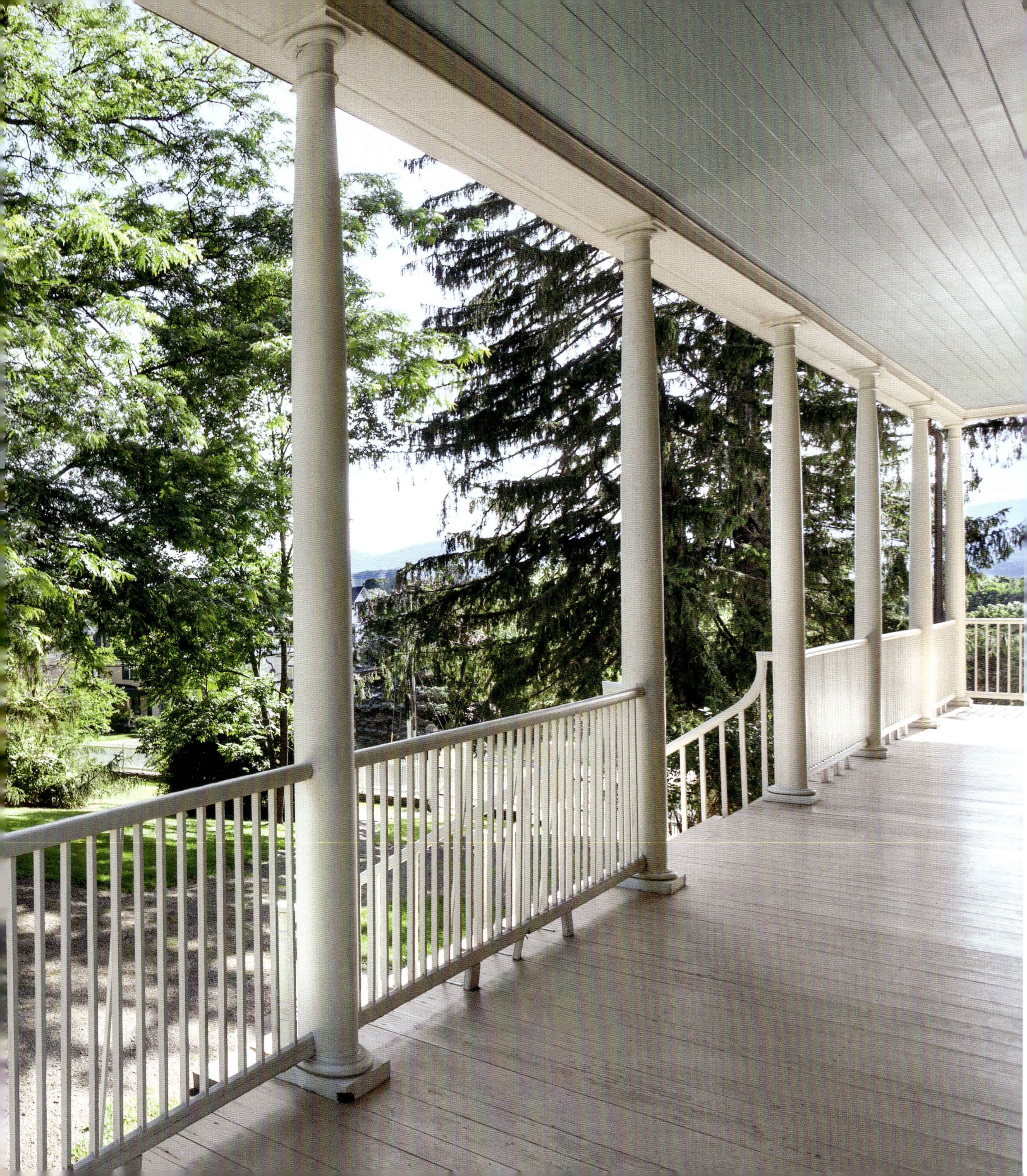

RIVER CROSSINGS
"AN UNBOUNDED CAPACITY FOR IMPROVEMENT BY ART"

Origins

IN 1836, in his "Essay on American Scenery," the Lancashire-born progenitor of American landscape painting, Thomas Cole (1801–1848), in elevated language that betrayed his twin aspirations to be an artist and a poet, imagined the possibilities for the Hudson River to be lined someday with edifices to match those beside the great rivers of Europe, where he had grown up:

> The Rhine has its castled crags, its vine-clad hills, and ancient villages; the Hudson has its wooded mountains, its rugged precipices, its green undulating shores—a natural majesty, and an unbounded capacity for improvement by art. Its shores are not besprinkled with venerated ruins, or the palaces of princes; but there are flourishing towns, and neat villas, and the hand of taste has already been at work. Without any great stretch of the imagination we may anticipate the time when the ample waters shall reflect temple, and tower, and dome, in every variety of picturesqueness and magnificence.[1]

Only a quarter-century after Cole's death in 1848, his most important pupil, Frederic Edwin Church (1826–1900), would do much to fulfill his master's prediction in building Olana across the Hudson from Cedar Grove, Cole's property in Catskill. *River Crossings* extends Cole's description of the future of the Hudson River and its valley to the present. This exhibition seeks to expand Cole's architectonic and aesthetic mandate at both these historic properties, and to trace the "improvement by art" wrought in the Hudson Valley since the Church family decided to give up Olana, in 1964, and for the first time to employ these two great pilgrimage sites of American art history together to reveal this continuous story of novel and complex artistic creation.

The Thomas Cole National Historic Site and Olana were ground zero for advanced contemporary art in America in the mid-to-late nineteenth century. Cole showed his latest works in the public rooms of Cedar Grove in the hopes of attracting patrons, and Church reserved space in his neo-Persian domestic temple to display his own art. Prior to Cole, advanced artistic endeavors in America hugged the Atlantic coastline and congregated in urban centers: Boston, New York, and up the Delaware River in Philadelphia. It was the particular innovation of the initial members of what has become known as the Hudson River School to head deep into the countryside in search of subjects, and to settle in those same environs. For Cole, and then Church, as for artists in the present, it was essential not only to be away from New York City and its din, but also to be able to get back to

it swiftly. Cole and the young Church were dependent on the steamboat. Later in life, Church took to the rails, as one does today, up the main Albany trunk line. But that seemingly paradoxical accessibility and removability has proved a fundamental necessity in the making of great art.

Art historian Robert Storr has written that the point of a museum retrospective "is not to historicize the new but to refresh the historical, in the process giving the public a chance to see where the art of their time really went, regardless of where it was supposed to go."[2] *River Crossings* is not a retrospective on a single artist—in its broad selection of artists it does just the opposite. It is not a comprehensive exploration of the art of Cole and Church; in fact, they are secondary players, in an aesthetic sense, in the display. It is an attempt to "refresh the historical," as all exhibitions, even contemporary art shows, must do. It aims to think anew about these Hudson River School artists, members of what Angela Miller has called, more appropriately and in less geographically narrow terms, the first New York School, and to trace their legacy not in a literal way, but in terms of the broader aims of their practices, in the art of the present.[3] The selection includes only a few artists whose works pay direct homage to that of Cole and Church, artists who by no means simply retread earlier landscape traditions. *River Crossings* acknowledges the importance of the two titanic inceptors of American art, and the houses that they crafted and lived in, and seeks to illuminate a continuity of spirit with contemporary artists who live and work in the region, or have a connection to its byways and towns.

Most of the artists in this exhibition are geographically linked to the broadly defined Hudson River region. Some, like Cindy Sherman (plates 17–20) and Elizabeth Murray (plate 14), had connections to Buffalo early in their careers. The Erie Canal, which formed a newly sprouted tendril of the Hudson snaking west upon its opening in 1825, the year Cole began to spend time upstate, provides an aqueous connection to the Buffalo region. And Buffalo is of course near to Niagara, an important subject for both of these nineteenth-century artists, and accessible by rail for Cole, who went there in 1847. Some, like Stephen Hannock (plates 15 and 16), Gregory Crewdson (plate 12), Chuck Close (plate 35), Stephen Petegorsky (plates 8–11), and Joel Sternfeld (plate 2), have connections with the Pioneer Valley in western Massachusetts, in particular the run of the Connecticut River near Mount Holyoke made famous in the history of art and the American popular imagination in Cole's *View from Mount Holyoke, Northampton, Massachusetts, after a Thunderstorm—The Oxbow* of 1836 (fig. 1).[4] A presiding theme in this exhibition is the connection between New York City and the migration of artists north in search of remove, new

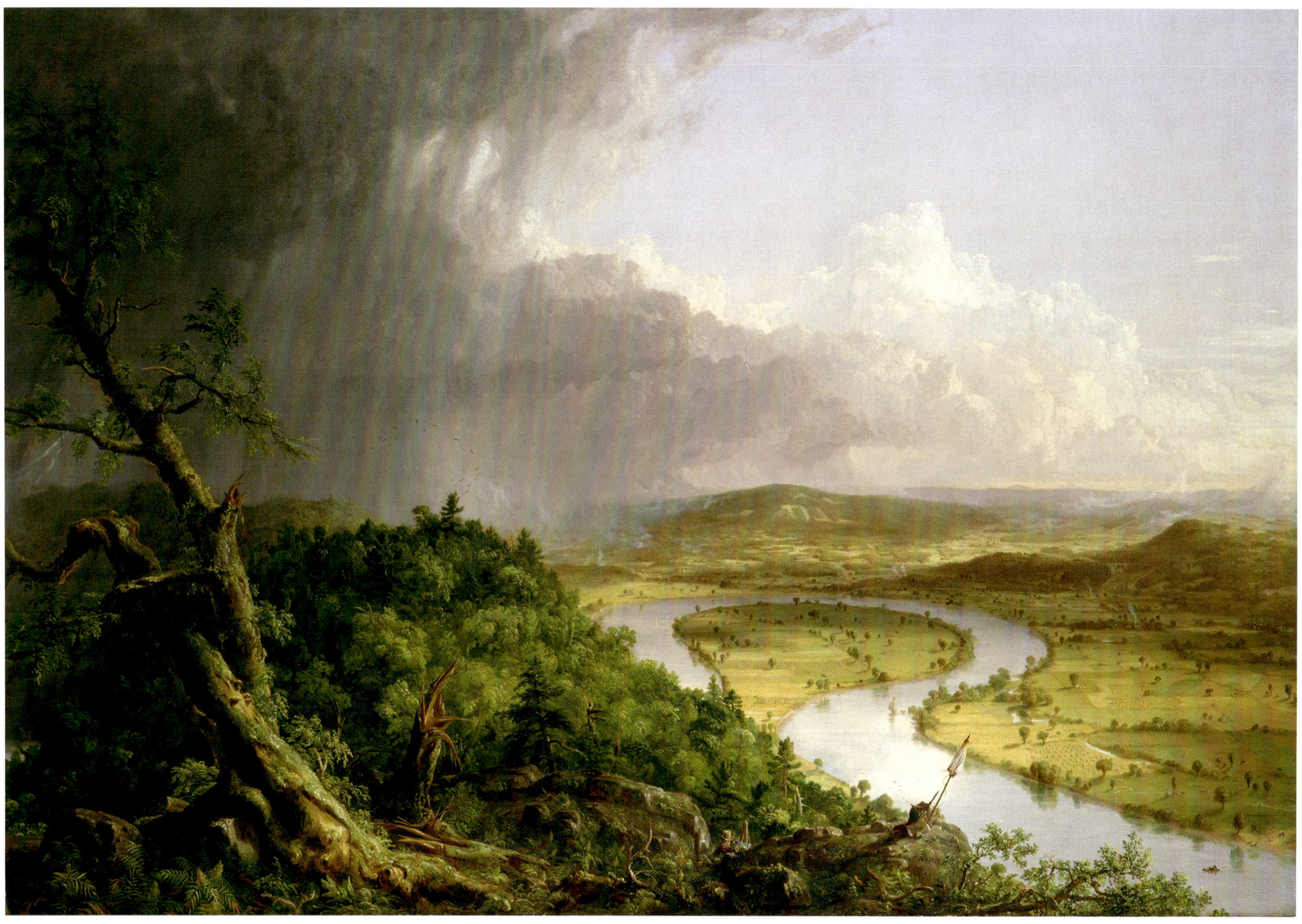

Fig. 1. Thomas Cole (1801–1848), *View from Mount Holyoke, Northampton, Massachusetts, after a Thunderstorm—The Oxbow*, 1836. Oil on canvas, 51½ x 76 in. (130.8 x 193 cm). Gift of Mrs. Russell Sage, 1908 (08.228). The Metropolitan Museum of Art, New York, NY. Image copyright © The Metropolitan Museum of Art. Image source: Art Resource, NY.

sites of inspiration, studio space, and cheaper rents. After Cole and Church and their followers, the next generation of artists to move upriver were those of the Harlem Renaissance, who populated the northernmost extremities of Manhattan and often took the river and the railway as theme, as represented in the art of Romare Bearden (plate 26), who also advanced the aesthetic of collage and assemblage in a manner that has had a great impact on succeeding artists such as Rashaad Newsome (plate 32), Sienna Shields (plate 27), Kianja Strobert (plate 25), and Jerry Gretzinger (plate 13). In more recent times, artists have felt the lure of the Hudson Valley once again, as rents have risen in New York City's artist enclaves both traditional and new in Soho, Williamsburg, DUMBO, and Bushwick.

Cole's call for improvement by art was an aim shaped by the idea of the United States' national construction—that the hand of human endeavor is necessary for the transformation of wilderness by culture, for the establishment of a history, and the evolution of a civilization. Cole's point of view in "Essay on American Scenery" in 1836 was

steeped both in the romantic and the picturesque. Sensitive to environmental change, Cole's opposition to the railway and deforestation has been well documented.[5] But while Church put Cole's ideas into practice, as the dramatic sight of turreted Olana looming atop what was then called Sienghenberg ("Long Hill") and inching closer as it is approached from the river can attest, neither artist anticipated improvement as a veer into despoilment, and the ecological disasters perpetuated by industry and development in the mid-twentieth century. Our unfortunate collective inheritance has been taken up pointedly by a number of artists in *River Crossings*, such as Maya Lin (plate 40) and Valerie Hegarty (plate 36). And Angie Keefer and Kianja Strobert in their modestly scaled but powerful *Empire State* (plate 24) address the same mid-twentieth-century period's predilection for high modernism, and its often deleterious and dehumanizing effects in the design of the Governor Nelson A. Rockefeller Empire State Plaza in Albany. As Cole readily acknowledged in his ambitious painted series *The Course of Empire* (1833–1836), now at the New-York Historical

Society, the pursuit of civilization has its drawbacks. Human vicissitudes intervene despite the best aesthetic intentions. The artists in this exhibition well continue Cole's social and cultural inquiry.

Concept

The striking centerpiece of the segment of *River Crossings* at Olana is Martin Puryear's *Question* (plate 37). Form notwithstanding, this work crystallizes this central idea of the art in this exhibition, which is to see Puryear's title not as a description of his tulip poplar, ash, and pine sculpture's curvaceous resemblance to a punctuation mark, or as identifying an interrogative or an expression of doubt. Rather, it should be interpreted as a directive. Question. Always. Question tradition, authority, primacy, materials, vision, reasoning, motivation, validity, history. This is what Puryear's elegant and elevated art has always done, and the artists in this exhibition do just that, in the spirit of their professional forebears, Cole and Church, who questioned the low status of landscape painting in aesthetic culture, who objected to the hegemony of European traditions, who challenged the economic structure of the art market and contemporary modes of display. Who settled in an Elysian landscape and advocated for its preservation, just as The Olana Partnership allied with conservation groups does today. The artists in *River Crossings* have taken as a prime directive the need to question our world and its received aesthetic canons; they see the drive to make art as equally fulfilling an innate impulse and a desire to communicate. Their openness to expansive readings of their art is indicated by their collective agreement to have their works shown in spaces never conceived for contemporary art as defined in the present era, in natural light levels that challenge the modern eye's need for saturation and growing preference for LEDs, on walls that may be neither plumb nor stark white, and in environs that might include an old guitar, nineteenth-century sombreros, old and heavily framed landscape sketches, stenciled doors, a monkey skull, and low ceilings. On carpets, below moldings, above mantelpieces, around doorways, amidst beds, steamer trunks, majolica, cabinets of curiosities, bitumen-marred works after old masters, and in the basement.

Witness: in Thomas Cole's cramped bedroom at Cedar Grove, Charles LeDray's whimsical, compelling, locally engaged, and unexpected installation. *Village People* consists of 73 delicately fabricated, miniature caps that flow in an unimpeded and gently undulating line around the upper section of all four walls (plate 28). One ball cap reads "Araxes" in stately seriffed gold on deep blue. The name is Greek for the Persian "Aras" and denotes a river in ancient Asia Minor and present-day Turkey, Armenia, Azerbaijan, and Iran. In book eight of Virgil's Augustan-era epic, *The Aeneid*, this waterway assumes a personality: It is angry at human attempts to span it, and the poet described it as *pontem indignatus Araxes*: "Araxes chafing under his bridge."[6] The text forms a description of the shield, forged by Vulcan, that Venus gives her son Aeneas, and upon whose surface is depicted "the story of Italy and the triumphs of the Romans"—events that will

occur to the Trojan prince's progeny in Italy. Araxes comes at the end of the description, listed amongst conquered tribes and lands including rivers such as the Euphrates. Araxes represents a river, and a region, not yet conquered by Rome, a river still unbridged, though apocryphally Alexander the Great had built one across it, and in battle Mark Antony was said to have crossed it twice. Thus Aeneas's shield looks into the future, beyond the events of Virgil and Augustus's present, and at Araxes, the river that prides itself on resisting being crossed.[7]

LeDray's wordplay in his hats is a measure of the commitment to context that so many of the artists who have collaborated on this show have demonstrated. For Araxes is not just a river of antiquity, but it flowed past "Olane," described in book eleven, chapter fourteen of Strabo's *Geographica* (first century BC/first century AD) as a "strong fortress" near the city of Artaxata in contemporary Armenia, that supposedly overlooked the river and the Garden of Eden.[8] In the second century BC, Polybius also mentions an "Olana" in northern Italy, one of the mouths of the River Po emptying into the Adriatic with, like the town of Hudson, a safe anchorage harbor.[9] Rivers are a consistent element in these historical references. It is uncertain where LeDray unearthed the obscure name Araxes; if not in Virgil, then perhaps it refers to the private biopharmaceutical company, in a doff to corporate culture commonly found on his hats, or maybe to Karl-Heinrich Ulrichs' *Araxes: Call to Free the Nature of the Urning from Penal Law*, a publication in 1870 that was an early call for lesbian and gay rights. On the wall in Cole's bedroom the "Araxes" hat hangs in a stretch between caps reading "Karnak 19 Flashing Cement" and "Athens Generating Plant" to the left, and at right "Marcellus" followed by "Afrodite Nassau," forming a run of classically inspired names. History, however, is blended with locality in LeDray's work: the Athens power plant is less than four miles from the Thomas Cole Site on Route 9W; Marcellus may refer to the town in Onondaga County, New York; and Afrodite is the name of a Hudson River oil and chemical tanker registered in the Bahamas.

Araxes: the river that resists being crossed. For a long time, the broad Hudson below Albany, similarly, would not be crossed by any structures except railway bridges, until the rise of the automobile led to the construction of the Bear Mountain Bridge in the Highlands, opened 1924, then the Mid-Hudson Bridge at Poughkeepsie in 1930, then finally the Rip Van Winkle Bridge at Catskill in 1935, 110 years after Cole first came north. This replaced the more aquatic and less aerial transit that had persisted from Cole's day. *River Crossings* celebrates the efforts of artists not only to cross the river east and west, but also to navigate it north and south, up and down from New York City. Hudson and Catskill, towns separated by this broad and deep river, part of the trunk of the ancient Hudson fjord, were linked first by ferries. Transport was ever key to the evolution of these towns. Hudson bears the oldest continually operating rail station in the state (1875). In Church's day four rail lines converged there, and the artist could, and did, take a fairly direct train to Boston, an impossibility today.[10]

Hudson's vibrant shipping industry has long vanished, although its manufacturing heritage of ironworks and ready-to-wear clothing and Catskill as a brick-production center are reimagined and perpetuated in both of LeDray's works in the exhibition, *Village People* and *Empire* (plate 46) on the Round Verandah at Olana. Cole and Church were in the vanguard in their day in terms of seeking to leave the metropolis to both pursue their subjects more readily and with more focus, and to establish roots in new locales. They used their respective houses as showpieces for their still-wet paintings, and also their collections of contemporary art, largely works by their family members and peers. And it is critical that Cole was able to get back to New York City via steamboat and Church via the railway—they did not wish to be far from the place that supported them. The Pre-Raphaelites and the Impressionists would do the same, in London and Paris, respectively, in the later nineteenth century, and this is the story of the evolution of modern Western art in the period. In fact, understanding systems of production and transport that allowed for the efflorescence of modern art in the late-nineteenth century is critical for a fuller comprehension of the art of the early Hudson River School.

As noted above, many of the artists in this exhibition call the Hudson Valley their home, or their art reflects their experiences in the region, as in the way that LeDray mines local history and establishments for his hats. Angie Keefer and Kara Hamilton's *Heavy Fixture* (plate 23) installation incorporates multiple elements: Herkimer diamonds that Hamilton herself surface excavated farther upstate and crafted into a floor lamp; one of only two extant daguerreotypes of Cole; and Cole's own mineral collection. Much of the power of *Heavy Fixture* comes from being in the presence of this unique daguerreotype photograph, a polished plate that was itself in the presence of Cole when his image was captured, and peering into it today in the East Parlor of Cole's own house, the room where Cole's wife Maria's uncle Sandy, who owned the house, lived, and which the Coles later used as a dining room.[11] The impact of photography on art, aesthetic experience, and lived life is a thread running through the exhibition, and the state of that newish art form in the lifetimes of Cole and Church is laid out in Marvin Heiferman's enlightening essay in this volume (pp. 22–27). Just as Cole and Church reinvented landscape painting in the mid-nineteenth century, artists working with photography such as Joel Sternfeld (plate 2) and Stephen Petegorsky (plates 8–11), who shoot in the Connecticut River valley, where Cole worked and Church grew up, and Gregory Crewdson (plate 12) and Letha Wilson (plates 43 and 44) enthusiastically reject any characterization of landscape photography as cliché and have productively rethought the tension between humanly constructed and natural landscapes, and between "growth and decay, the cycles of civilization" that are the themes of Cole's most trenchant landscapes, such as *The Oxbow* (fig. 1).[12]

Relatedly, Valerie Hegarty's installation in the Dining Room at Olana (plate 36) responds specifically both to such themes in Cole's art and local fauna, as the woodpeckers that are hacking at the paintings and furniture in her installation are indigenous to the Catskills, and one, the pileated woodpecker, suffered loss of habitat and was hunted to near extinction by the time of Church's death in 1900 and is now a protected species. Maya Lin's *Silver River—Hudson* (plate 40) is part of an ongoing project to convey the world's great rivers in cartographic art, like Gianlorenzo Bernini (1598–1680) depicting the four great waterways of Catholic hegemony for the Pamphilj family Pope, Innocent X, in the Piazza Navona in Rome. But while Bernini's was an act of Counter-Reformation fervor and political posturing, Lin's rivers including the Hudson, Thames, Seine, and Niagara sound an ecological and environmental counter-pollution clarion call. In her related and ongoing project titled *What is Missing?* Lin is documenting changes in habitat over time due to human intervention. It exists in the form of a website, a growing archive, and various sculptural and multimedia installations.[13] Lin has written that she sees rivers as "complex systems that are so great in length that we tend to understand them only in their direct relationship to us at the moment."[14] This is dramatized at Olana with the view south out the arched window in the Sitting Room of the river proper. Lin used recycled silver in casting her Hudson bas-relief, and the afternoon light, slanting across the southernmost Catskill Mountains and glittering along the sculpture's metallic finish, enhances the idea of river as reliquary.

Following more literally in the footsteps of Cole and Church, longtime local resident Thomas Nozkowski has spent decades hiking through the landscape around his Ulster County base. The results are paintings that, more often than not, are hardly recognizable as landscapes in a traditional visual sense, or even as vestigial natural forms, but instead exhibit a level of refinement in abstract painting unmatched by any of his peers (plates 3–7). To a degree, Nozkowski's project is a conceptual one—like the date paintings by the recently deceased On Kawara (1933–2014) from that Japanese artist's *Today* series (1966–2014), which were limited to a narrow range of three colors and to eight sizes. Nozkowski uses a limited number (three) of identical formats in his abstractions and rigidly adheres to them. *Untitled (9-25) (Sam's Point)* (plate 6) is a rarity; he produces this larger 30-by-40-inch size at a rate of less than one canvas a year. The tertiary title refers to a preserve along the Shawangunk Ridge in Ulster County. This painting initially seems more literal than others in terms of its tripartite horizontal composition, the sense of a craggy foreground commensurate with the geologic formations of the preserve, its mass of deep mid-range sky, and then the primary-colored crystallizations of lowering cloud above. But as with all of Nozkowski's paintings, close looking rewards, in the form of layers upon layers of glazes and vibrating swatches of submerged colors in the trunk section, treated with the delicacy of Paul Klee's (1879–1940) early watercolors, with an interloping blue-stepped pyramid edging in toward center from the lower-right edge, and a solitary golden brick at the bottom, seemingly deposited from above. For Nozkowski, as with Cole and Church, the true landscape becomes but a template for the artist's imagination. Inspiration comes from all directions. And like Kawara in his *I Went* series (1968–1979), wherein he traced in red paint his movements over the full course of a given day on photocopied maps, or the typographic recitations of walks in the work of Richard Long (b. 1945), or Andy Goldsworthy's (b. 1956) documentation of his ephemeral site-specific creations in the landscape, Nozkowski's work reveals his interest in particularities of experience conveyed via art, but in an undecodable visual language, encouraging a spirit of discovery for the viewer commensurate with the artist's own rapt absorption in nature.

In the upper Sitting Room at the Cole Site, Nozkowski's paintings hang hard by those of Elizabeth Murray (plate 14) and Sienna Shields (plate 27), wherein abstraction and landscape further intertwine, and they are all joined by Cole's preferred view out the southwest window toward the northernmost ridges of the Catskill Mountains. The intensity of Murray's surface in this early painting is in contrast to Nozkowski's precise and less boisterously textured canvases, but closer looking is, again, required. While Murray's *Untitled (After Golden Delicious) II* may superficially resemble the undulation of a hillock, and bear an evident horizon, her art instead is concerned with "the transformation of the picture plane into the picture surface," as Storr has written.[15] The low and wide panoramic landscape format, like that of a decorative overdoor picture, is less about a translated view of nature than a response to the groundbreaking geometric abstractions of Frank Stella (b. 1936) in the late 1950s and 1960s. Stella's was an attempt to make his sole subject the flat picture plane, a gambit promoted in modernist writing by Clement Greenberg and formalist critics. But Murray added crucial innovations in this glowing work: emphasizing surface and thus unsettling Stella's grids, applying the paint more vigorously, and denying depth with blazing color as a response to the smooth, perpendicular, and darkly colored experiments of Stella and Ad Reinhardt (1913–1967). Nozkowski, similarly, plays with finish and especially the pulsing edges of forms, but using more subtle effects and more sheer surface. Shields's massive collages engage color as form itself and seem derived from the plane view of maps, overlaid with squares of pure hues in a kaleidoscopic topographical and pulsing grid.

Assemblage and collage in the work of Shields and postwar American artists owe much to the remarkable innovations of Romare Bearden. As the novelist and critic Albert Murray noted, Bearden approached "his subjects not as a portrait painter might, or a landscape artist of, say, the Hudson River School, but in the manner of a jazz musician."[16] That is to say, in an improvisational and exploratory manner, instead of the presumed formulaic and academic approach of artists like Cole and Church. It is interesting that Murray chose the Hudson River School as a foil. Cole and Church both collaged elements of observed natural scenery from either multiple locations or their imaginations, along with flora and fauna, in making their seemingly seamless views. But Bearden's rich use of collage and the fragmented, distorted, layered, yet still recognizably figurative results allowed him to develop his own personal style, one that collapsed time and so seems continually fresh today, and one that, like the similarly musically inflected art of the slightly-older painter, Bearden's

friend Stuart Davis (1892–1964), produced a resolutely new American aesthetic. The amplified historical power of the work, as made by an African American and situated in this exhibition in a Federal-style farmhouse built before the Civil War, is well elucidated in Maurice Berger's essay in this volume (pp. 28–31).

The dialogue between Bearden in late explosively colored and assuredly composed works such as *Prelude to Farewell* (plate 26) and Rashaad Newsome (plate 32) is strong, in terms of process and subject. Both artists expanded the collage tradition in Modernism as established first in the *papiers collé* of Pablo Picasso (1881–1973) and Georges Braque (1882–1963), and then in the Dada and Surrealist eras in Raoul Hausmann (1886–1971), Hannah Höch (1889–1978), George Grosz (1893–1959), Max Ernst (1891–1976), and Salvador Dalí (1904–1989).[17] Both Bearden and Newsome developed processes and imagery that reflect a mode of working outside of the fine arts, involving music and movement and performance. Bearden's works employ avant-garde techniques and are about the human condition, read through the filter of African American experience over the course of the twentieth century. Newsome is concerned with conflating an aesthetic of aristocratic privilege from European medieval to Baroque culture with contemporary hip-hop culture. Both developed a style that was personal in reference and individually distinctive in form. In 1963, in the midst of the national grappling with civil rights issues, Bearden proposed to the Spiral Group of African American artists that they work collectively to create collages to respond to current events, in the spirit of utopian and socially minded artist collectives stretching back to the late-nineteenth century. They rented space on Christopher Street in the West Village, but no one joined him in the aesthetic wing of this endeavor, so he set out to make such works on his own. Newsome appears symbolically to have taken on Bearden's invitation, and in his recent collages continues in the vein of the earlier artist's historically grounded, socially engaged practice.

This evolution and establishment of a self-identity through subject is a key trope in the history of American art, in the history of this nation comprised of peoples bearing traditions from all over the world, who found themselves inhabiting a landscape ripe for self-invention and redefinition. The British-born Cole understood this and channeled it as a strength in the development of his American-based art that traded in the European tradition, but whose traditional narratives and allegories were reinvented for a nascent nation.[18] Church followed suit, and his career is not so much a challenge to Cole's legacy, but an amplification of its aims.[19] It represents a respectful, collaborative seeking of the new across generations that is characteristic of advanced American art. The story in the modern era is not much different. This does not make it repetitive. On the contrary, it is precisely this rapidity of innovation that American postwar artists took up from the Cubist–Dadaist–Surrealist generations of European artists, to spur international artistic innovation for the next half-century.

This establishment of an identity best emerges in *River Crossings* in the work of Chuck Close, Cindy Sherman, Elijah Burgher, Stephen

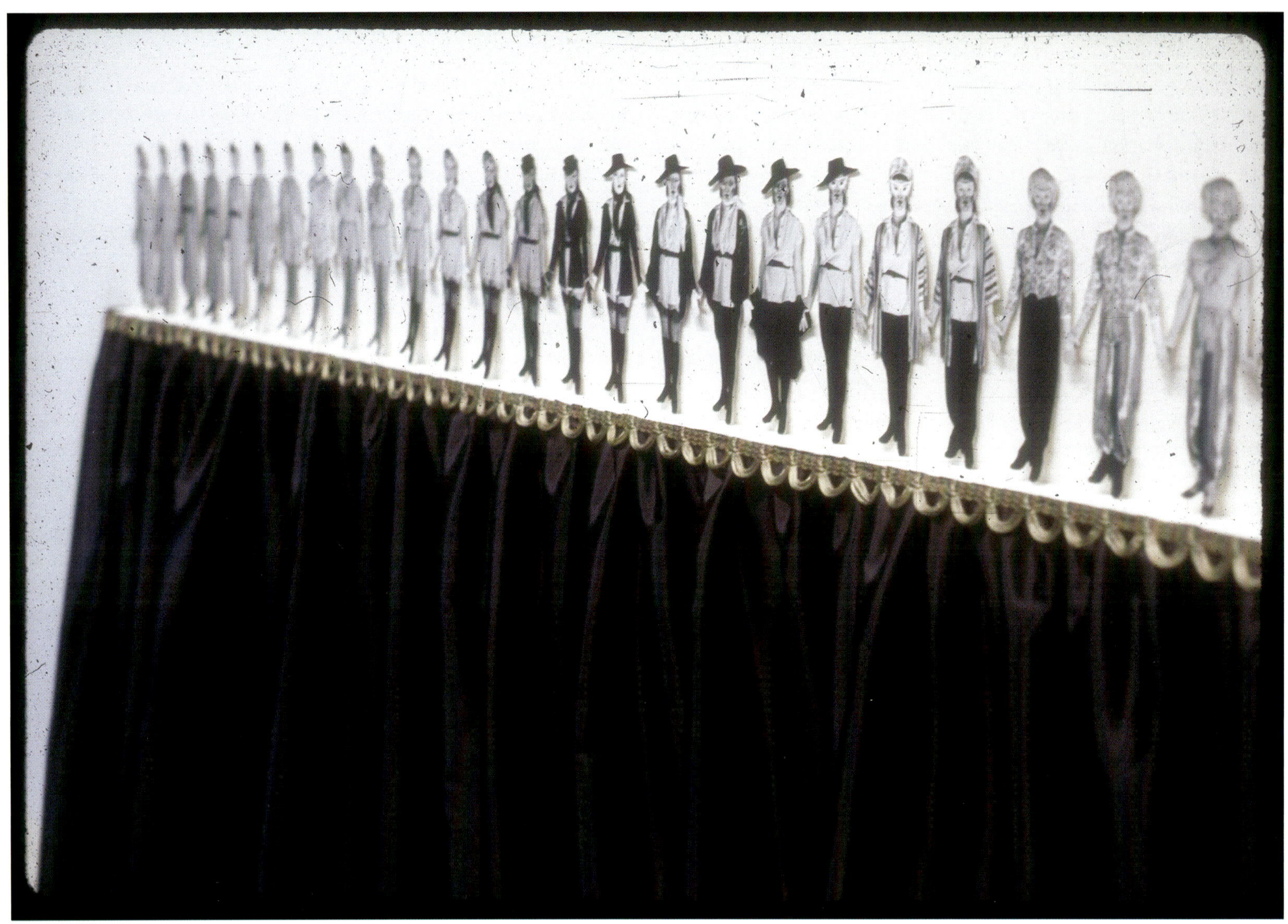

Fig. 2. Cindy Sherman, installation view, *Line-up for Linda from Robert*, from *In Western New York*, Albright-Knox Art Gallery, Buffalo, NY, 1977. Color slides, 15/16 x 13/8 in. (2.4 x 3.5 cm). The Hallwalls Collection at the Poetry Collection of the University Libraries, University at Buffalo, Buffalo, NY.

Hannock, and Will Cotton. Close has made himself, and his ever-growing coterie of friends and associates the subject of his penetrating portraiture since his art-school days, and at Olana his most recent self-portrait presides over the entire affair, from an airy perch on the vast Stair Hall wall (plate 35). In Church's day a large, early-nineteenth-century Japanese temple scroll titled *Nehan-Zu: Buddha Attaining Nirvana* occupied this privileged position, a work presently in need of conservation and not on view.[20] In his yellow rain slicker, with his characteristically level but concentrated gaze, Close, who perhaps more than anyone active in the New York City art world today represents an engaged, visible, and venerable presence on the scene, achieves his own measure of pictorial transcendence. Unlike Close's unsparing presentation of his changing features over the past half-century, Sherman's art is remarkable in how it assumes an idea of multiple identities while establishing a distinctive personality all its own. Sherman's *Line-up* series of twelve prints made in 2011 was derived from the last

works she made before moving to Manhattan from Buffalo in 1977, a set of 35 cut-out images of herself in character with hands touching, titled *Line-up for Linda from Robert* (fig. 2).[21] Four images are included in the exhibition (plates 17–20), and they serve notice that her now-familiar role-playing and questioning of gender distinctions in her art was present from the 1970s. Elijah Burgher's subject is similarly societal constructions of personas, but he works in the realm of queer identity and has developed a personal language of what he terms "sigils," rune-like scripts bearing symbolic meaning in a variety of genres, including landscape, portraiture, and geometric/symbolic abstraction. His precise drawings in colored pencil can, like his works from sketching around Ashokan Reservoir in Ulster County, bear a Ruskinian intensity in their response to local color in nature. And his rainbow-hue anthropomorphic drawings seem to channel the proto-Dadaist work, and humor, of Francis Picabia's (1879–1953) mechanomorphic portraits from the period when he was working closely with Alfred Stieglitz

(1864–1946) in New York. Hannock's identity, and history both personal and artistic, are merged, literally, in the surface of his works, in the forms of pasted materials and block capital script telling stories across the landscape and exploring his web of connections, encompassing many of the artists on display (plate 15).[22] And Cotton, like Hannock, draws on art history in giving the superficial impression of borrowing the portraiture conventions of the Baroque, with its tenebrist back-grounds and spotlit effects, or cloudy aerial confections worthy of Giovanni Battista Tiepolo (1696–1770), but seen through a painterly scrim that is more akin to Gerhard Richter (b. 1932) than Caravaggio (1571–1610). The evolution of a signature style redolent of perpetual self-discovery in American art, by using oneself as subject, or by trans-forming the aesthetics and expectations of old master paintings, is a running theme in the work of these artists. And Olana itself, in particu-lar, fully fits into this mode—for few artists' houses and grounds so bril-liantly encapsulate the aspirations and interests of its progenitor as Church's modern "castled crag."

Artists' homes will always be seen as reflections of self, and the preservation of them as museums, filled with what their inhabitants selected, collected, or created, promotes this conception. They can feel like jewel boxes that contain the sparklings of an artist's life, encased in amber. But Olana is remarkable in expanding from period interiors to embrace the landscape that Church spent the last decades of his life perfecting and seeding to eventually reach mature form after his death. LeDray's *Empire* is installed on the Round Veran-dah in the transitional space between Church's studio, where artificial natures were fabricated on canvas, to the true natural environment and prospect view west across Church's carefully designed forest to the Hudson and Catskill Mountains beyond. Don Gummer's large sculptures make the leap and sit in the actual landscape. They have been installed around the ornamental lake at Olana (plates 47–50), and also on the front lawn at the Cole Site (plates 33 and 34), to expand the exhibition experience to outside these houses, in emulation of Church's and Cole's engagement with nature. Gummer's upright metal sculptures derive from a tradition stretching back to Picasso, Julio Gonzáles (1876–1942), David Smith (1906–1965), and Louise Bourgeois

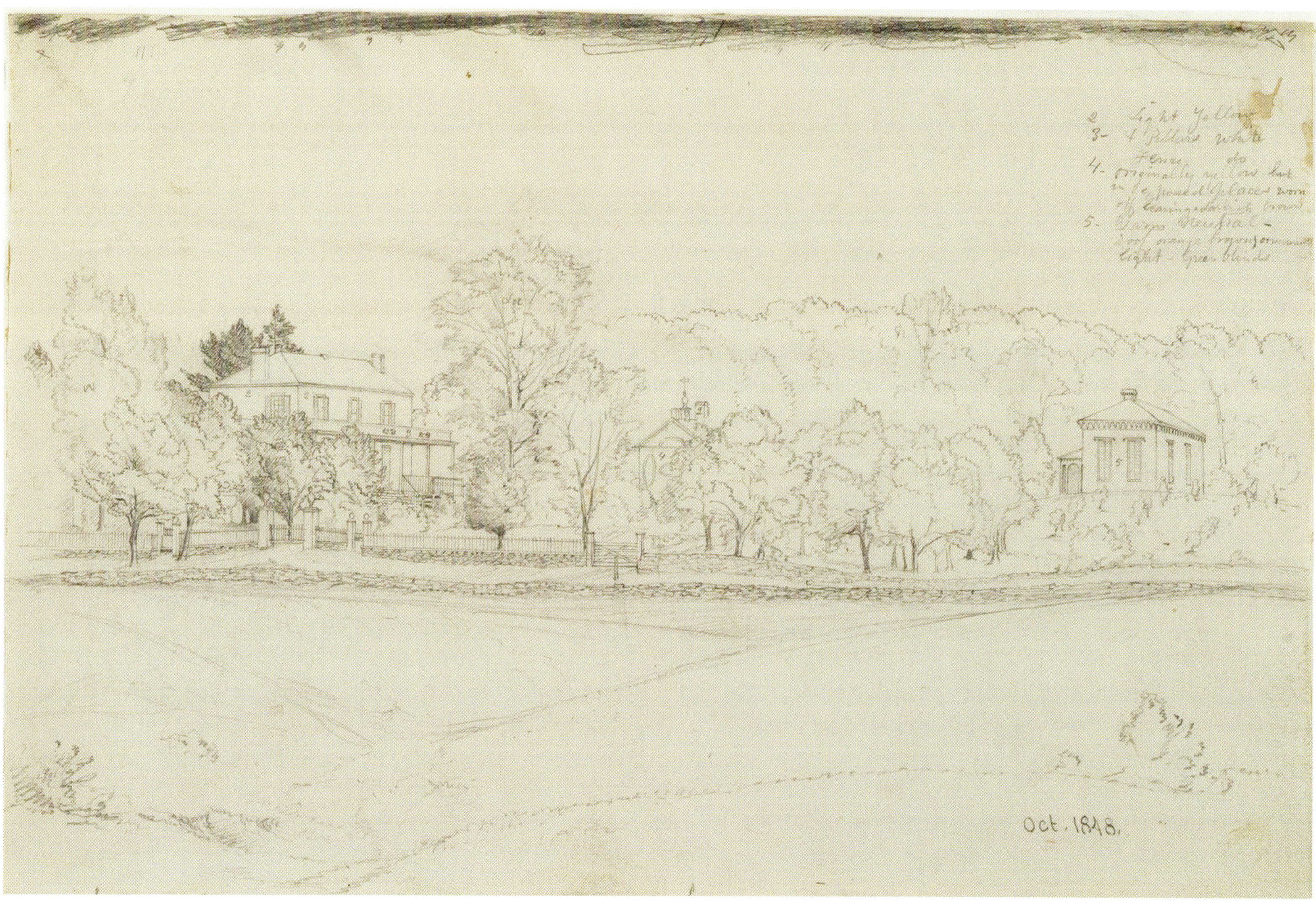

Fig. 3. Frederic Edwin Church (1826–1900), *View of Cedar Grove (Thomas Cole's House and Studio), Catskill, NY, 1848*, 1848. Graphite on buff paper, 6¾ x 10¼ in. (17.1 x 26 cm). Olana State Historic Site, Hudson, New York, Office of Parks, Recreation, and Historic Preservation, OL.1980.1413.

(1911–2010), but unlike the recent demonstrative essays in magnitude and iron mass by Richard Serra (b. 1939), Gummer's works provide a beautiful and responsive interplay with the environs of the Cole Site and Olana. They convey a sense of centripetal motion and antigravitational lift, making their industrial materials seem light. Seen over the run of *River Crossings* against hints of green and in the crisp air of early spring when first installed, then the lushness of summer in the valley, and finally in polychrome fall followed by brittle early winter, they well respond to the variety of landscape Church sought to devise in Olana's realm. At Cedar Grove, Gummer's two sculptures (plates 33 and 34) lie in a path leading from house to detached studio, allowing visitors to reenact Cole's daily pilgrimage from the domestic to the artistic, and back again. They follow a line traced in Church's invaluable drawing of a section of Cedar Grove's 88-acre estate including house and studio, from 1848 (fig. 3).

Realization

The challenge of installing contemporary works at the Cole Site and Olana was twofold: first, to get permission from each institution's board of trustees and state overseers to remove works temporarily and change the existing display; and second, to safely place art of an unfamiliar character in the houses using available installation materials. For example, at Olana innovative solutions needed to be devised to install pieces on walls that could not be drilled into, necessitating using nails already in place or the existing nineteenth-century picture rail with its consequent weight limitations. The presence of a nail, hammered in the wall decades ago, could determine the placement of a work. Lin's *Silver River—Hudson* (plate 40) is 7 feet high, made of cast recycled silver, and could not be affixed to the wall, so Hannock prepared a canvas, painted it the color of the walls of the Sitting Room, and rigged it so that it could hang just off the picture rail. The result is a complex interplay between Church's magisterial oil *El Khasné, Petra* (1874), Lin's glittering relief, and the spectacular prospect view south along the Hudson out of the huge Islamic-style window. LeDray, for his site-specific installation *Empire* on the Round Verandah outside Church's studio, actually built a second floor layer to cover the existing wood planks and painted it the heritage shade to match so that his bricks and cinderblocks would not harm the permanent fabric of the site. Puryear's grand *Question* sits in the center of the famed "Court Hall," which has been denuded of any material that sat on the floor, and it has been displayed without roping it off, so visitors can walk around and under it. It is a very different way to conceive of the experience of viewing art in this magnificent, Persian-style, hand-built house.

Cole's Cedar Grove is a federal-style home built in 1815. It turns out that it is surprisingly receptive to all kinds of art, with plentiful wall space and a sparseness of architectural detailing, outside of some fine woodworked mantelpieces that delighted, on his visits, Mr. Puryear, a man who knows a thing or two about the manipulation of woods. The

minimalist walls may change soon, as an exciting initial investigation of paint layers on the walls has revealed decorative painting done by Cole, for which the Cole Site recently received a major NEH grant to restore. But at Cedar Grove there are paintings, sculptures, photographs, and multimedia works involving projection and small monitors and lights keyed to motion sensors in almost every available space; there are 32 new works in the house and 2 outside. The walls of the entire second-floor landing are covered with Gretzinger's *Jerry's Map* (plate 13), the product of more than 50 years of labor and a richly immersive environment results. While some artists in the exhibition have been responding directly to the work of Cole and Church, as noted above, the others also have been seen to harmonize with what those nineteenth-century landscape painters were after in these environs long ago. There is an affinity with artists who have carried on this tradition, though their subjects may not be the environs of upstate New York, but who represent a continuity of innovative artistic production some 190 years since Cole first sketched on nearby Catskill Creek.

These two houses are accessible to and preserved on behalf of the public and this exhibition enhances the sense of ownership and expands it, if only for a short time, to include gems of contemporary art. It is an opportunity to see such American works of recent vintage in domestic environs, under low light or natural light conditions, to experience them in a manner far removed from the blazingly illuminated galleries, museums, and institutions where they are normally displayed. And the result has been that the paintings, sculptures, photographs, and videos have a sense of renewed animation; they breathe and exist in our own space and they seem, in these two handmade nineteenth-century houses, remarkably and comfortably, at home.

*   *   *

In "Essay on American Scenery," Thomas Cole wrote of the subject of the title as "almost illimitable," though of course he could not have had knowledge even of what lay west of the Ohio River, let alone the Mississippi, and the motifs and themes that his student Church, and Church's own progeny such as Albert Bierstadt (1830–1902) or Thomas Moran (1837–1926), would later assay in terms of the expanding American scene. But Cole knew the immediate vicinity west of the Hudson, and even that restricted geographical domain seemed brimming with the infinitely possible to him. Ultimately, he sought improvement by art in his environs and life, but it is Cole's work, and that of his successor Church, that has also allowed for continual improvement of art itself, in a capacity that continues to find an almost illimitable dialogue in the present.

New York, NY
May 2015

1. Thomas Cole, "Essay on American Scenery," *American Monthly Magazine* 1 (January 1836), given as a lecture in 1835 at the American Lyceum, New York; web: csun.edu/~ta3584/Cole.htm.

On Cole's literary aspirations, see Marshall B. Tymn, *Thomas Cole's Poetry* (York, PA: Liberty Cap Books, 1972).

2. Robert Storr, *Elizabeth Murray* (New York: The Museum of Modern Art, 2005), 20.

3. Angela Miller, *The Empire of the Eye: Landscape Representation and American Cultural Politics, 1825–1875* (Ithaca, NY: Cornell University Press, 1996), 3.

4. On Hannock's connections to Cole and the Hudson River School, see Jason Rosenfeld, *Stephen Hannock: Imaginary Realism, Meaningful Contradictions*, exh. cat. (New York: McKenzie Fine Art Inc./Los Angeles: Michael Kohn Gallery, 2002).

5. See William H. Truettner and Alan Wallach, eds. *Thomas Cole: Landscape into History* (New Haven: Yale University Press, 1994).

6. J. W. Mackail, *Virgil's Works* (New York: The Modern Library, 1950), 166–168 [8: 726–728]. Robert Fagles' recent translation reads "Araxes River bridling at his bridge" (2006).

7. Andrew Feldherr, "Viewing Myth and History on the Shield of Aeneas," *Classical Antiquity*, vol. 33, no. 2 (October 2014), 19–20.

8. As determined in Gerald Carr's research. See John Ashbery's essay, "Frederic Edwin Church at Olana: An Artist's Fantasy on the Hudson River," republished in Eugene Richie, ed., *Selected Prose: John Ashbery* (Ann Arbor: University of Michigan Press, 2004), 266. Isabel Church gave her husband a copy of this Roman-era text in 1879. There are also links to the supposed resting site of Noah's Ark in the region. http://www.perseus.tufts.edu/hopper/text?doc=Perseus:text:1999.01.0198:book=11:chapter=14&highlight=olane.

9. Polybius, *The Histories*, book 2, chapter 16, lines 11–12. http://penelope.uchicago.edu/Thayer/E/Roman/Texts/Polybius/2*.html.

10. See Anne Mazlish, ed., *The Tracy Log Book 1855: A Month in Summer, Charles Tracy's Diary on Mount Desert Island* (Arcadia Pub. Co., 1997), for details of one such trip, with illustrations by Church. I am grateful to Kimberly Flooks for this reference.

11. See David Seamon, "Thomas Cole and Cedar Grove," 2000, web: http://www.arch.ksu.edu/seamon/Thomas_Cole.htm.

12. See Truettner and Wallach, 3.

13. http://whatismissing.net/#/home.

14. Maya Lin, "Here and There," in *Maya Lin: Here and There* (New York: Pace, 2013), 13.

15. Robert Storr, *Elizabeth Murray: Painting in the '70s* (New York: The Pace Gallery, 2011), 6.

16. Murray quoted in Ruth Fine and Jacqueline Francis, eds., *Romare Bearden: American Modernist* (New Haven: Yale University Press, 2011), 64, from *The Blue Devils of Nada: A Contemporary American Approach to Aesthetic Statement* (New York: Vintage Books, 1996).

17. See Pepe Karmel, "The Negro Artist's Dilemma: Bearden, Picasso, and Pop Art," in Fine and Francis, eds., *Romare Bearden: American Modernist* (New Haven: Yale University Press, 2011), 249–268.

18. See Tim Barringer, "The Course of Empires: Landscape and Identity in America and Britain, 1820–1880," in Andrew Wilton and Tim Barringer, *American Sublime: Landscape Painting in the United States 1820–1880* (London: Tate Publishing, 2002), 38–65.

19. See John Wilmerding, *Master, Mentor, Master: Thomas Cole & Frederic Church* (Catskill, NY: Thomas Cole National Historic Site, 2014).

20. I am grateful to Evelyn Trebilcock for information on this object, OL.1980.1259.

21. See Gabriele Schor, *Cindy Sherman: The Early Works 1975–1977* (Ostfildern, Germany: Hatje Cantz Verlag, 2012), 78–80.

22. See Jason Rosenfeld, *Stephen Hannock. Recent Paintings: Vistas with Text*, exh. cat. (New York: Marlborough Fine Art Ltd 2012), and "Stephen Hannock: New England/New York," in *Stephen Hannock* (Manchester, VT: Hudson Hills Press, 2009), 35–47.

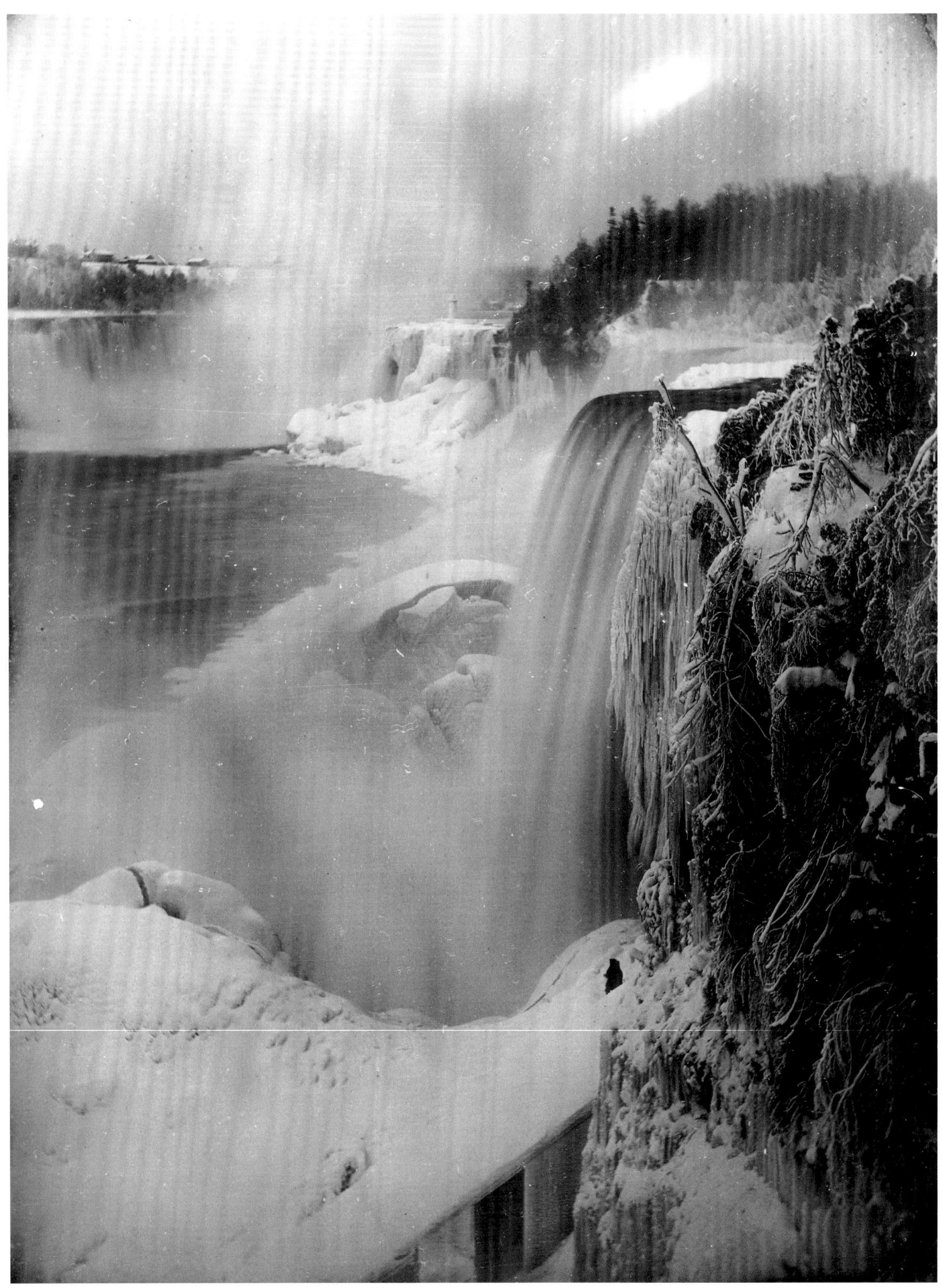

Fig. 4. Platt D. Babbitt (1823–1879), *Niagara Falls, Winter View*, 1850–1859. Daguerreotype, 8¼ x 7¼ in. (21 x 18.4 cm). Acc. no. OL.1981.604. Collection Olana State Historic Site, Hudson, New York, New York State Office of Parks, Recreation and Historic Preservation.

IT WAS IN THE EARLY 1850S, just a few years after Thomas Cole's death, that a town 65 miles south of his home in Catskill, New York, became known as Daguerreville, forever linking New York and the Hudson River Valley's imaging culture as firmly to photography as it was to painting and the fine arts. Members of the Lewis family made their fortune there after building a factory on Quassaic Creek, a tributary of the Hudson between Newburgh and New Windsor, to manufacture the compact and accordion-bellowed cameras that enabled the era's camera-operating entrepreneurs to keep up with the public's demand for photographic images of themselves and the landscapes they moved through.[1]

Nearby in Orange County, the Reverend Levi Hill was among the first to experiment with the hand-coloring of daguerreotypes.[2] Farther north, the enterprising Platt D. Babbitt leased a retail perch at the edge of Niagara Falls where, in 1853, he sold souvenir daguerreotypes (fig. 4) that miniaturized the colossal cascades, establishing a marketplace for tourist images that helped nineteenth-century Americans to more conveniently commune with nature and consider the sublime.[3] If Thomas Cole, founder of the Hudson River School of painting, died before photography's allure and popularity became widespread, Frederic Edwin Church, one of Cole's star pupils, was among the first generation of artists to mature in an image world driven by photography.

Church is not believed to have taken photographs himself but he assembled a substantial collection of approximately 2,000 of them during his lifetime. That archive—which still exists and is largely intact—served as a source of research and inspiration for Church's own artworks, proved useful in the design and construction of Olana, and fueled his wide-ranging interests in the history of civilization, the sciences, and the spiritual, as well as the natural world.

Throughout his career, Church produced abundant drawings and studies, picking and choosing from their carefully observed details to create the spectacular landscape paintings for which he became so widely celebrated. He was known, too, to work from photographs and even, in some instances, to paint on top of them to create working sketches. "Church in many respects was the most remarkable painter of the phenomena of nature I have ever known," wrote William James Stillman, one of his former students who later abandoned painting to become a journalist and photographer.[4] Church's powers of observation and precise draftsmanship contributed greatly to the impact and popularity of his work, as Stillman went on to critically note:

His mind seemed a camera obscura in which everything that passed before it was recorded permanently, but he added in the rendering of its record nothing which sprang from human emotion . . . . The primrose on the river's brim he saw with a vision as clear as that of a photographic lens, but it remained to him a primrose and nothing more to the end. All that he did or could do was the recording, form and colour, of what had flitted past his eyes, with unsurpassed fidelity of memory; but it left one as cold as the painting of an iceberg.[5]

Even if that awesome chilliness were the case, as mid- to late-nineteenth century taste began to shift from the romantic and lyrical toward a greater appreciation of scientific precision and industrial spectacle, Church's clear vision reflected and even helped to reinforce a new and photographically defined cultural zeitgeist. In the spring of 1859, the public display of Church's huge and panoramic painting, *Heart of the Andes* (fig. 5), drew more than 12,000 enthusiastic viewers to the Studio Building on West 10th Street to see what was widely acknowledged to be the most popular display of a single artwork in Manhattan.[6] Each of them paid a 25-cent admission fee. Many used opera glasses to take in the startling details in a landscape painting that measured nearly 6 feet high and 10 feet wide and looked even larger, theatrically installed in a huge, curtained frame and dramatically lit by filtered skylight. Men and women alike reported becoming dizzy and faint in the painting's presence, simultaneously exhilarated and terrified as they felt themselves becoming immersed in its epic sweep and specificity.[7]

New Yorkers flocking to see Church's majestic painting were not, however, unfamiliar with spectacle, the overwhelming nature of representational detail, and the thrill of image immersion. Not far from Church's studio in lower Manhattan, visitors to P. T. Barnum's American Museum and to Mathew Brady's photographic portrait studio were similarly awed and impressed by displays of unusual "natural" attractions and images depicting greatness of various kinds. By 1859, the collecting and viewing of stereographic photographic images had become so widespread that, one month after Church's painting was displayed, Oliver Wendell Holmes noted:

The mind feels its way into the very depths of the picture . . . . Then there is such a frightful amount of detail, that we have the same sense of infinite complexity which Nature gives us. A painter shows us masses; the stereoscopic figure spares us nothing—all must be there, every stick, straw, scratch, as faithfully as the dome of St. Peter's, or the summit of Mont Blanc, or the ever-moving stillness of Niagara.[8]

Not surprisingly, Church—the creator of other and equally impressive landscape paintings such as *Niagara* (1857) and *The Icebergs* (1861)—owned a number of Babbitt's daguerreotypes of the Falls, numerous albumen prints of icebergs, and stereographic cards

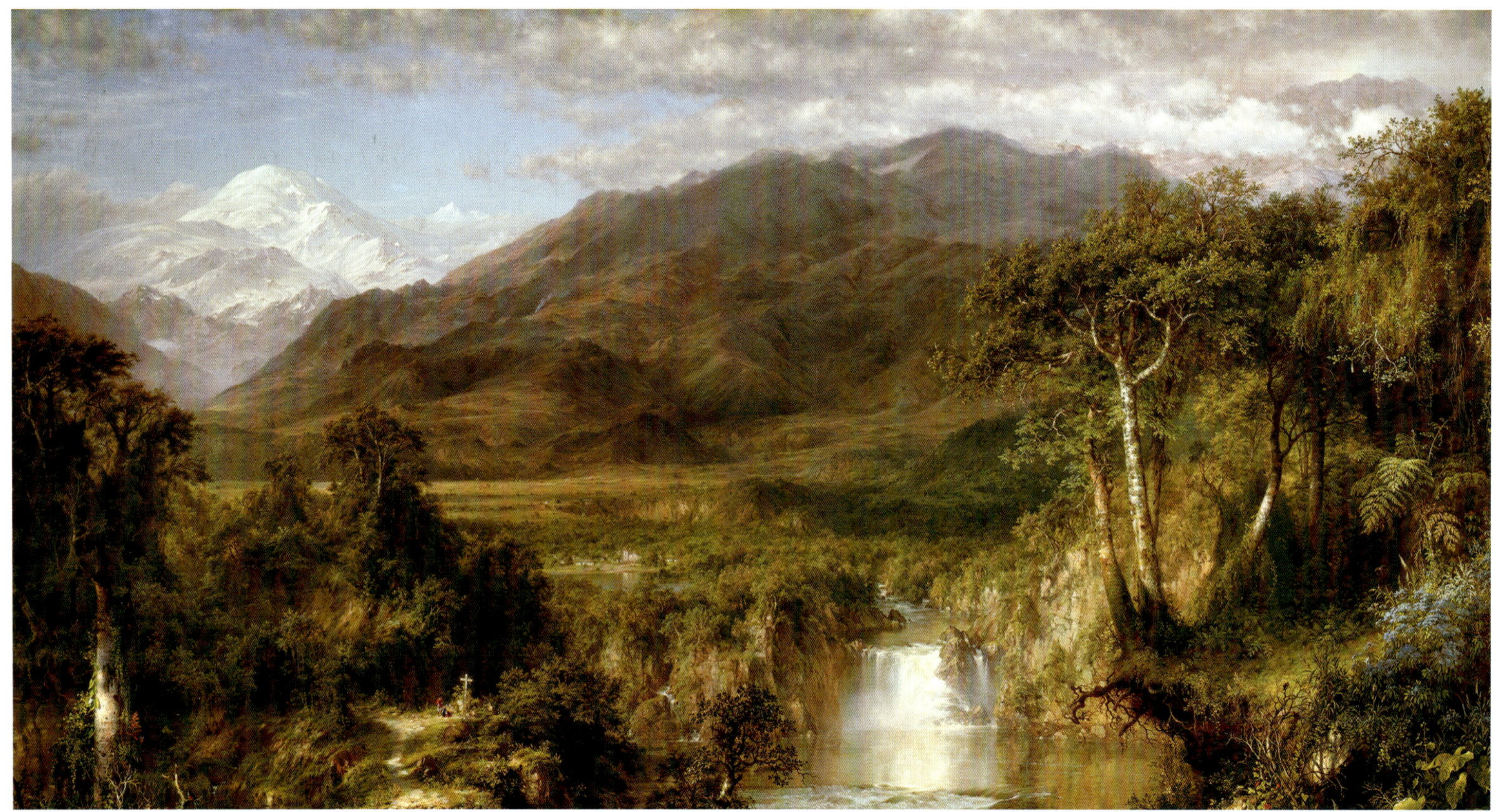

Fig. 5. Frederic Edwin Church (1826–1900), *Heart of the Andes*, 1859. Oil on canvas, 66⅛ x 119¼ in. (168 x 302.9 cm). Bequest of Margaret E. Dows, 1909 (09.95). The Metropolitan Museum of Art, New York, NY. Image copyright © The Metropolitan Museum of Art. Image source: Art Resource, NY.

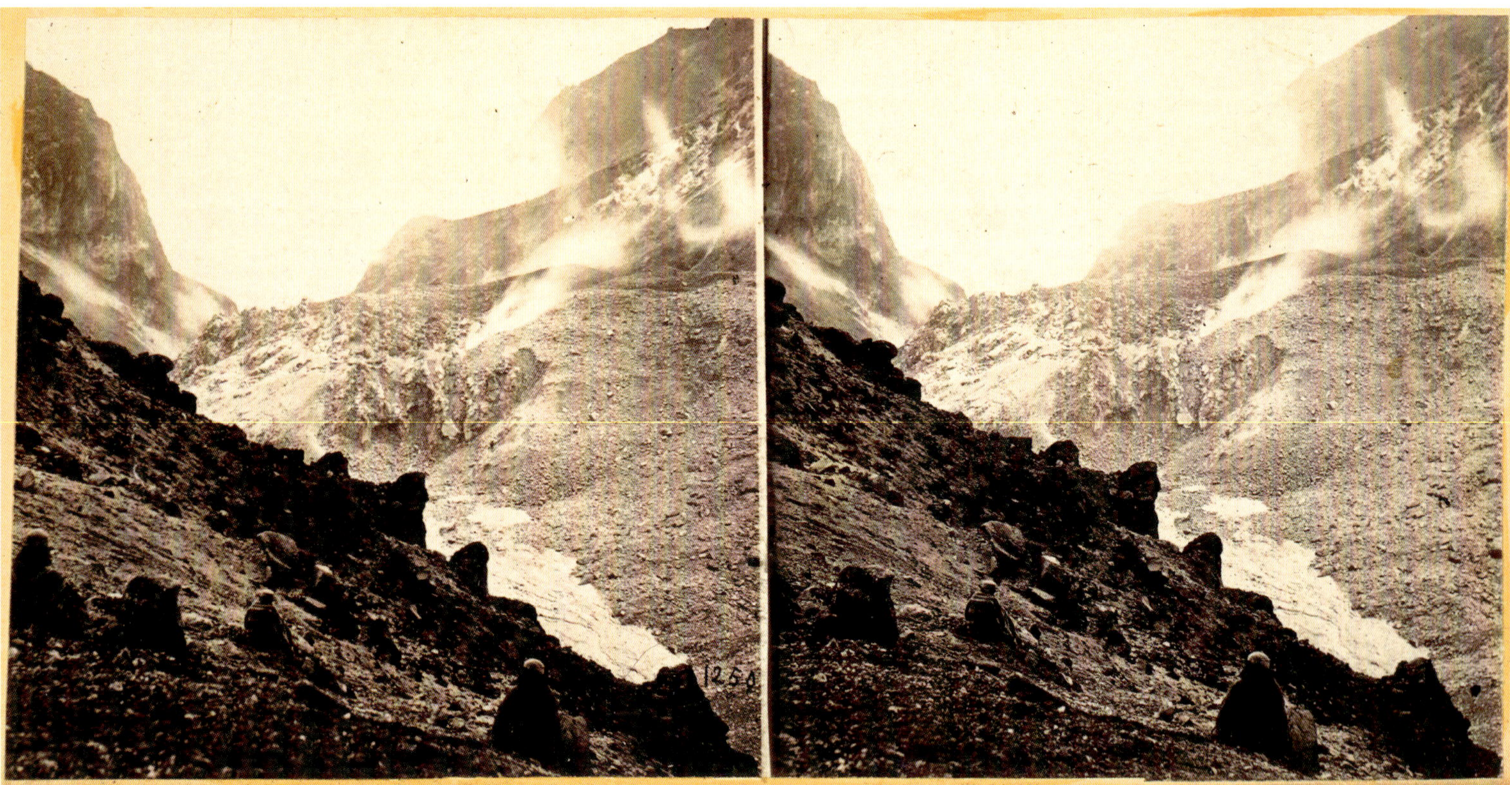

Fig. 6. Camillus Farrand (published by E. & H.T. Anthony and Company, New York), *View Within the Crater of Pinchinca, Looking Down from the Side of the Great Eastern Wall*, c. 1860. Stereograph, 3 x 6 in. (7.6 x 15.2 cm). Acc. no. OL.1986.218. Collection Olana State Historic Site, Hudson, New York, New York State Office of Parks, Recreation and Historic Preservation.

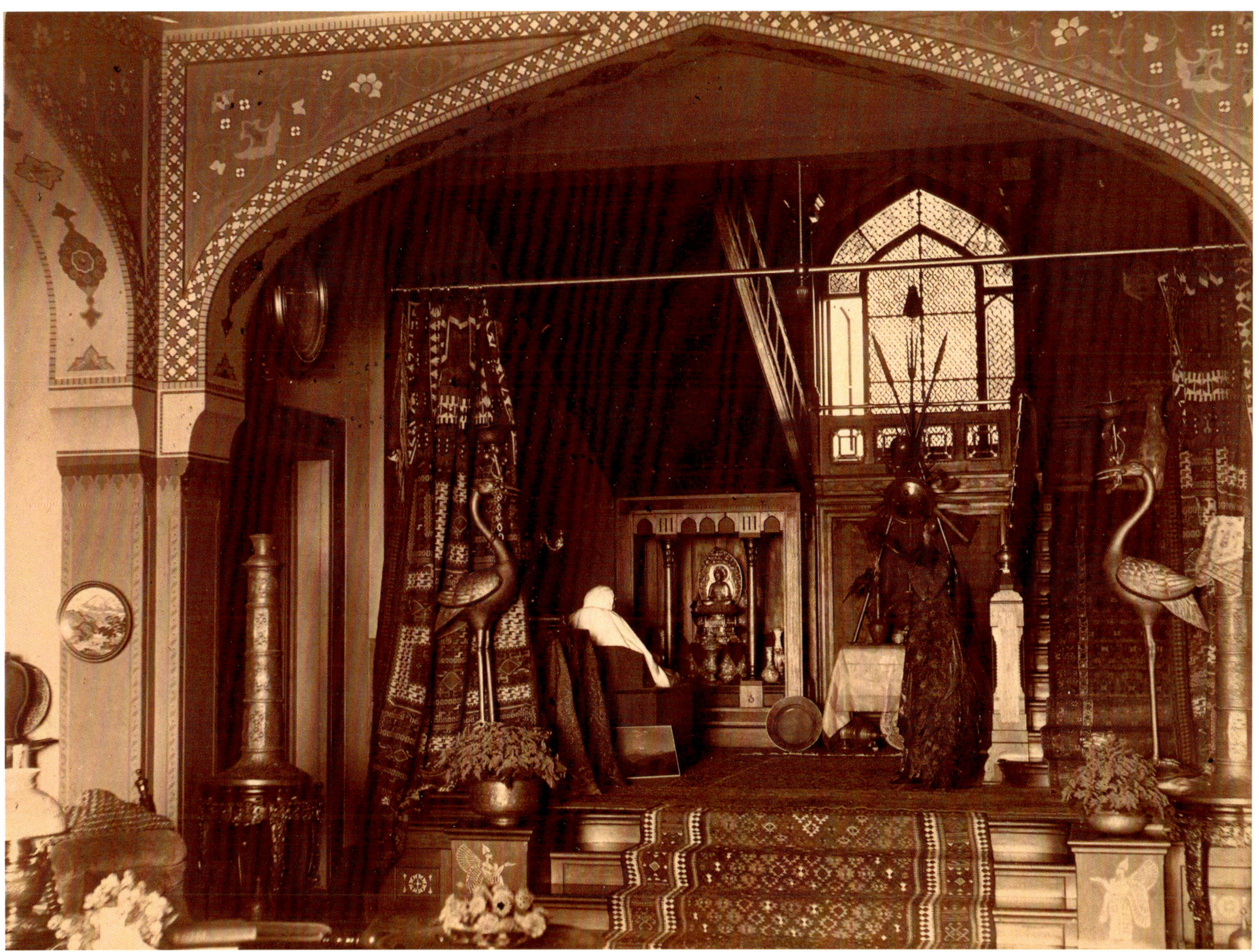

Fig. 7. Unidentified photographer, *Court Hall, Main House at Olana*, 1880–1890. Albumen print, 6⅛ x 8⅜ in. (15.6 x 21.3 cm). Acc. no. OL.1993.7. Collection Olana State Historic Site, Hudson, New York, New York State Office of Parks, Recreation and Historic Preservation.

mass-produced on Lower Broadway by E. & H. T. Anthony and Company (fig. 6), all of which suggest that he, too, was transfixed by and valued all varieties of photographic illusion. As Thomas Weston Fels documented in *Fire & Ice: Treasures from the Photographic Collection of Frederic Church at Olana*, Church purchased these photographs, and others, during his travels to South America, Mexico, the Caribbean, Europe, and the Middle East. He collected works by some of the medium's early pioneers, including Eadweard Muybridge, Carleton Watkins, Désiré Charnay, Francis Frith, and Samuel Bourne. The photographic images in Church's collection were, in comparison to the bravura of his painted work, humble in their materiality, but served as "a source of inspiration and armchair travel, offering reminders of favorite locations, details of architecture, culture, and nature and supplementing his actual travels with images of places he was unable to visit himself."[9]

The grand scale, hyperrealism, and far-flung geographic sites featured in Church's acclaimed works underscore the nineteenth cen-

tury's growing desire to contextualize humanity's place in the physical world based upon new perspectives provided by science's most up-to-date findings. Church himself was deeply influenced by the research of Alexander von Humboldt, the German naturalist and geographer. Charles Darwin's *On the Origins of Species* was published and widely discussed the same year Church's *Heart of the Andes* was exhibited. Darwin's subsequent volume, *The Expression of the Emotions in Man and Animals* (1872), was among the first books to be illustrated with photographs. Not surprisingly, in the following decades the public's taste for allegorical art would give way to an omnivorous hunger for photographic fact and proof.

It was William Henry Jackson's majestic photographs of Yellowstone that helped convince the United States Congress of the need to establish the first of the country's national parks in 1872. In 1889, *National Geographic* magazine, which would soon introduce twentieth-century audiences to lush landscapes unimaginable and unattainable in Church's time, published its first photographic image, a halftone engraving of a topographic map of North America.[10] In 1900, the year of Church's death, the shrewd marketing of the inexpensive and easy-to-use Brownie cameras manufactured at Kodak's Rochester, New York, headquarters irrevocably transformed public engagement with the landscape and expectations of the images made both of and in it.

If, in twentieth-century America, it would be Ansel Adams who assumed Church's place as the masterful interpreter and popularizer of environmental splendor, it would be far less stentorian, but edgier image-makers who could more critically reassess the landscapes of the modern era to acknowledge our increasingly uneasy relationship to them. The starkly elegant photographs that Dorothea Lange and Robert Frank each took of asphalt highways stretching far into the distance, for example, made it clear that the landscape had become something to pave over and move through as quickly as possible as much as it was something to be admired. By the 1970s, Robert Adams, Lewis Baltz, Ed Ruscha, Stephen Shore, and Joel Sternfeld, among others, challenged the scope and course of landscape photography by focusing in on the everyday and the mundane, not on the sublime, to picture how nature inevitably seemed destined to turn into real estate.

Among the artists in this exhibition, Lynn Davis's luminous photographs of Niagara's Horseshoe Falls and of an iceberg (plates 38 and 39) are among those that most directly harken back to Church's subject matter and appreciative stance. Gregory Crewdson's photograph, from a project shot on deserted movie sets in Cinecittà's backlots outside of Rome (plate 12), reminds us of the pull of atmospheric images that purposefully evoke a nostalgic sense of place by bridging fact and fiction. In response to Thomas Cole's celebrated painting, *View from Mount Holyoke, Northampton, Massachusetts, after a Thunderstorm—The Oxbow* (fig. 1), Joel Sternfeld made the large color photograph, *April 20, 2007, The East Meadows, Northampton, Massachusetts* (plate 2). That work, one from an extended series he made between 1976 and 2006, documents and reminds us of changes to the terrain that Cole depicted. In works that are startling and theatrical, but reflect pictorial strategies quite different from Church's, Letha Wilson disrupts the serenity and materiality of landscape images by literally folding, punching holes in, and covering over sections of them with cement (plate 44).

If, during Church's lifetime, landscape paintings and photographs regularly paid homage to higher spirits and forces, contemporary artists wandering through and exploring the landscape have different sets of environmental issues and interests. Today, it is hard to extol or portray the Edenic in light of the mounting evidence of climate change,

assertions of corporate development rights, and the erosive wear and tear that even the best-intentioned of travelers enact upon the sites of wonder they visit. Thomas Cole and Frederic Edwin Church sought out singular vantage points for their interactions with nature. We—in response to wide-screen movies, images shot from mobile phones and with wearable cameras, and given our easy access to surveillant, God's-eye-views of the globe's surface from services like Google Earth—conceptualize and experience the landscape quite differently in the twenty-first century. Viral videos online—of rock climbers and skydivers, and some shot from minicams strapped on the backs of animals—are more likely to cause us to question our place in the natural world than traditional paintings and photographs are. Perhaps what is called for, now, is simply patience—as the computational and sensory kinks of virtual reality imaging get worked through—until we are once again able to immerse ourselves in the stateliness and thrill of nature as personally and intensely as the Hudson River School of painters once did.

New York, NY
April 2015

1. Beaumont Newhall, *The Daguerreotype in America* (New York: Dover Publications, 1975), 35.

2. Michelle Anne Delaney, "Photography Changes the Work Curators Do." *Photography Changes Everything* (New York and Washington: Aperture and Smithsonian Institution, 2012), 218.

3. Anthony Bannon, "Photography Changes What Tourists Expect to See." *Photography Changes Everything*, 192.

4. William James Stillman, *The Autobiography of a Journalist in Two Volumes* (London: Grant Richards, 1901), vol. 1, 95.

5. Ibid., 96.

6. Heilbrunn Timeline of Art History, The Metropolitan Museum of Art: http://www.metmuseum.org/toah/hd/chur/hd_chur.htm.

7. Deborah Poole, "Landscape and the Imperial Subject: U.S. Images of the Andes, 1859–1930." *Close Encounters of Empire: Writing the Cultural History of U.S.-Latin American Relations* (Durham, NC: Duke University Press, 1998), 107–138.

8. Oliver Wendell Holmes, "The Stereoscope and the Stereograph." *The Atlantic*, June 1, 1859. http://www.theatlantic.com/magazine/archive/1859/06/the-stereoscope-and-the-stereograph/303361/.

9. Thomas Weston Fels, "Fire & Ice: Observation on the Photographic Collection of Frederic Church." *Fire & Ice: Treasures from the Photographic Collection of Frederic Church at Olana* (New York and Ithaca, NY: Dahesh Museum of Art and Cornell University Press, 2002), 13–14.

10. "First Photograph Published in National Geographic." http://photography.nationalgeographic.com/photography/photographers/first-photo-article.html.

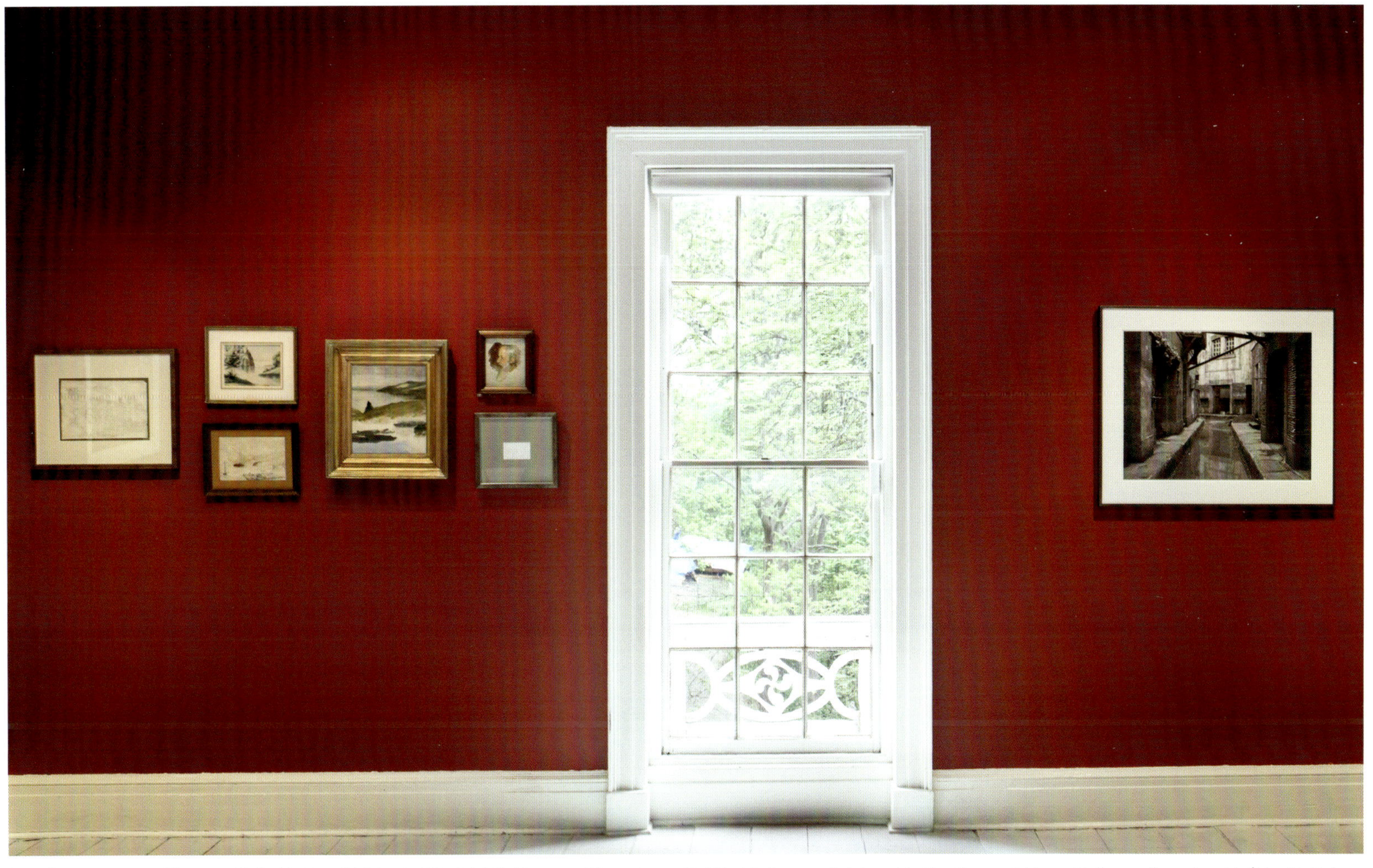

Installation view at Thomas Cole National Historic Site (right), Gregory Crewdson, *Untitled (21)*, 2009 (plate 12) in the Second-Floor Gallery, all works at left by T. Cole.

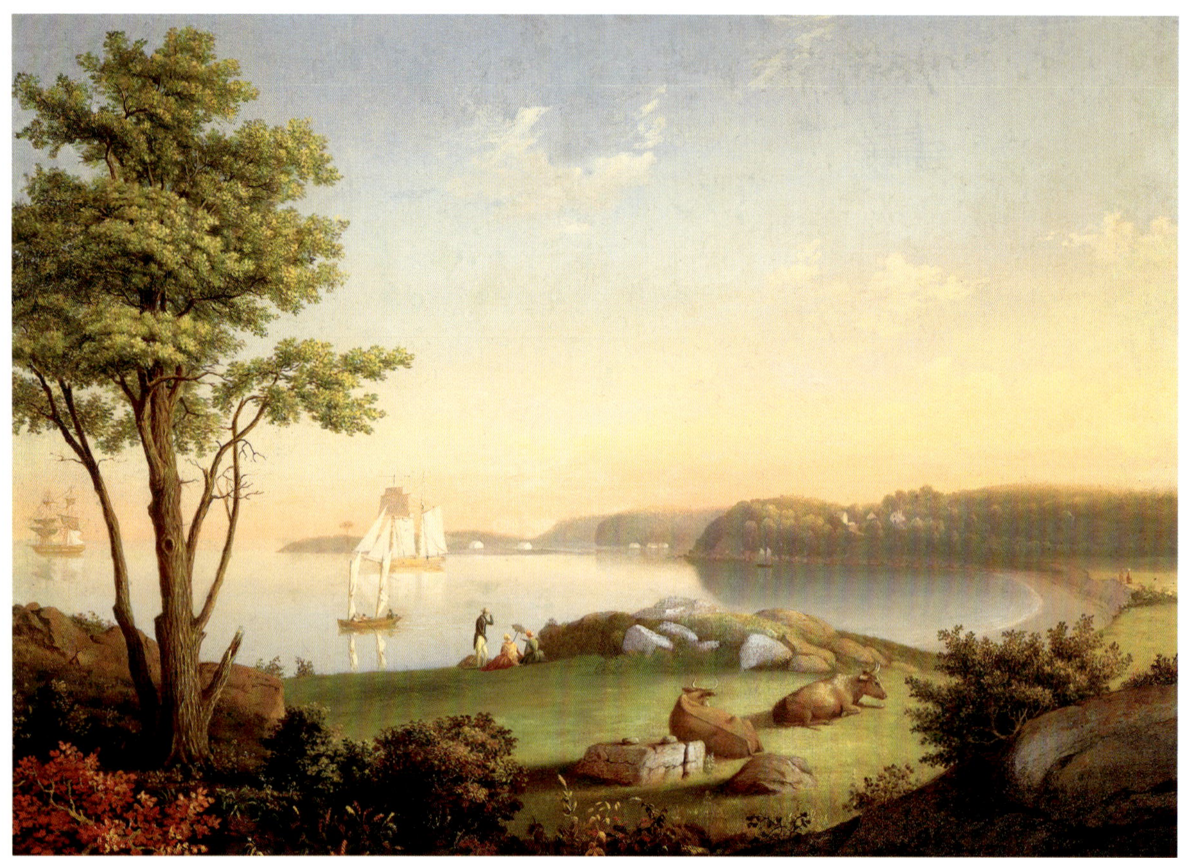

Fig. 8. Mary Blood Mellen (1819–1885), *Field Beach*, c. 1850s. Oil on canvas mounted on board, 24¼ x 33¹⁵⁄₁₆ in. (61.6 x 86.2 cm). Collection of the Cape Ann Museum, Gloucester, MA, gift of Jean Stanley Dise, 1964.

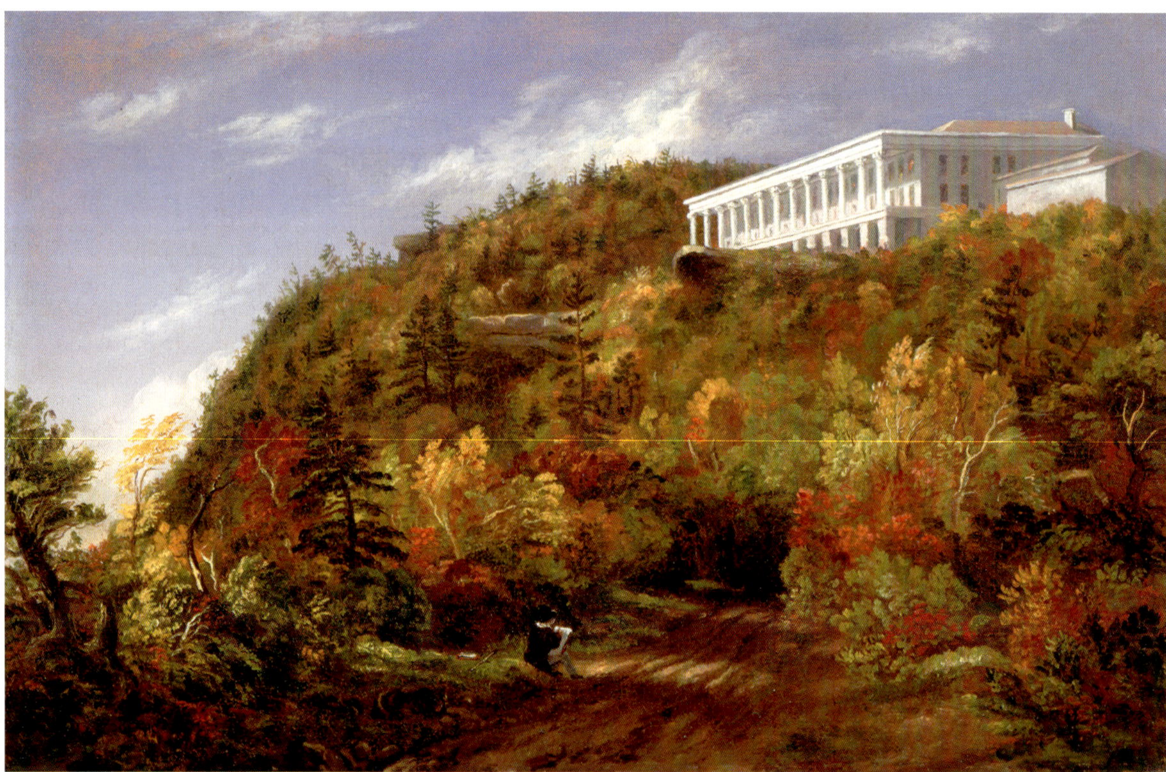

Fig. 9. Sarah Cole (1805–1857), *A View of the Catskill Mountain House*, 1848. Oil on canvas, 15⅛ x 23⅜ in. (38.4 x 59.4 cm). Albany Institute of History & Art, Albany, NY purchase, 1964.40.

ROMARE BEARDEN'S COLLAGE, *Prelude to Farewell*, 1981 (plate 26), assumes its temporary place in the North Room in the main house at The Thomas Cole National Historic Site in Catskill, New York. It is one of numerous works in the site-specific exhibition of contemporary art, *River Crossings*. Bearden, a renowned African American artist, art historian, social worker, and cultural commentator, created a vast body of work, typically collages that melded the sensibilities of Dada photomontage and Cubism with southern folk traditions and African art. In *Prelude to Farewell* we witness a woman bathing, "a train (which Bearden said represents departures and arrivals), contrast between exterior and interior space, and an aura of constrained yearning and desire."[1]

The work's sense of transition and longing is particularly fitting in the context of the Thomas Cole Site, a relic of an era when African Americans in the North, living in social limbo between outright enslavement and full enfranchisement, yearned for freedom. The presence of Bearden's work in the home and studio of the founder of the Hudson River School of nineteenth-century painting invites a range of interpretations, not just about what is missing from history, but also the potential of art to retrospectively alter the way we see and understand the past.

The central conceit of *River Crossings*—the juxtaposition of art and artifacts created a century and a half apart—creates a dialogue between past and present. Its historic and contemporary works would seem to represent two polarities in art, one innovative and conceptual, the other conventional and realist. But the artists of the Hudson River School—exemplified by Thomas Cole and Frederic Edwin Church, whose home and studio in Hudson, New York, the Olana State Historic Site, serves as the exhibition's other venue—were once as vanguard as the contemporary artists with whom they are paired.[2]

River Crossings does more than remind us of the revolutionary status of these historical figures in their time. Its makes us rethink this history. The introduction of contemporary women artists and artists of color into the story of a nineteenth-century movement that was largely male and almost exclusively white, for example, motivates us to acknowledge its biases and omissions.

The imposing paintings of the Hudson River School expound on quintessentially American themes at the dawn of the Industrial Age: the wonder of discovery and exploration as well as the imperatives of settlement and expansion. They depict their majestic and picturesque settings from afar. What is usually not visible in their mythic, panoramic worldview is the intricate reality of life on the ground, a world beset by the banal necessities, struggles, conflicts, and prejudices of everyday existence.

From this standpoint, the Hudson River School was a political and moral product of its time. Many art historians and curators have accepted its allegorical and exclusionary perspective, without acknowledging what is missing from it, especially the immediate concerns of the countless others of the Hudson Valley: the poor who lacked political or cultural authority, the women who were ceaselessly subjugated, and the African Americans who experienced unspeakable prejudice.

Despite this, the Hudson River School, as an artistic movement, was not entirely insular. During the latter half of the nineteenth century, female artists "played pioneering roles in the exploration of the American outdoors."[3] They endured in spite of numerous obstacles, from routinely being denied admission to art academies and clubs, principal outlets for learning, networking, and career building, to social biases that viewed them as incapable of withstanding the rigors of painting in the rugged outdoors.[4]

Undeterred by these barriers and prejudices, women made their mark on the Hudson River School. As art historians Nancy Siegel and Jennifer Krieger documented in their 2010 exhibition at The Thomas Cole Historic Site, *Remember the Ladies: Women of the Hudson River School*, it was possible for them to sustain careers as artists. This groundbreaking project amended the historical record, bringing to light an impressive roster of esteemed female painters including Susie M. Barstow, Julie Hart Beers, Sarah Cole (fig. 9), Josephine Chamberlin Ellis, Eliza Greatorex, Elizabeth Gilbert Jerome, Mary Blood Mellen (fig. 8), Evelina Mount, Harriet Cany Peale, Jane Stuart, and Laura Woodward. As Krieger observes:

> These artists managed to make their way through vast, unexplored stretches of the American landscape and to shimmy up trees (for better views) in spite of their long skirts. . . . Rather than complain about all that society had placed in their way, women artists pushed forward to accomplish their goals. As a result of their determination, our own cultural topography has been immeasurably enriched."[5]

The potential for artists of color to rise above the biases and restrictions of their time was considerably more limited. In our collective imagination, the North is often understood as a place of racial benevolence. But history tells a different story. If slavery and segregation in the South have come to exemplify the reality of white entitlement and supremacy in the United States, the North, too, shared this legacy.

In New York, for example, slavery was both common and legal in the eighteenth and early nineteenth centuries. Like several other northern states, New York ended the institution incrementally. The process took half a century, beginning in 1777, when abolitionist sentiment began to take hold, to 1827, when New York passed the last of many antislavery laws. Compared to most other northern states, slavery in New York, which was essential to many sectors of its economy, remained relatively durable as an institution. As the historian Patrick Rael writes:

> In contrast [to New York], Vermont outlawed slavery entirely in its state constitution of 1777, while Massachusetts's Supreme Judicial Court abolished chattel bondage with the stroke of a pen in 1783. Even states such as Rhode Island and Pennsylvania, which, like New York, ended slavery through gradual measures, began and ended the process earlier. The only Northern state to outlast New York in preserving slavery was New Jersey; the last slaves were freed there in 1865.[6]

The abolition of slavery in the North was not a panacea for African Americans, who continued to experience discrimination, both on a personal and an institutional level. Ultimately, full enfranchisement was not possible in the era of the Hudson River School. As late as 1869,

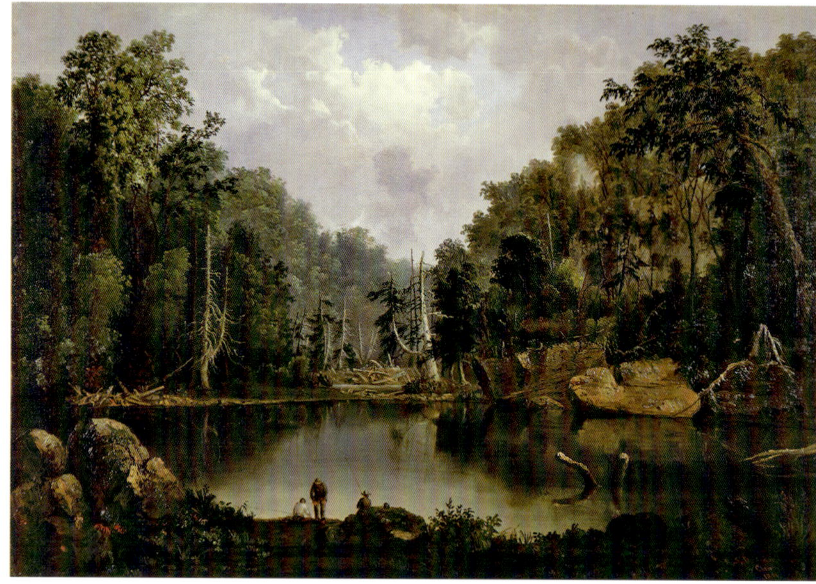

Fig. 11. Robert Duncanson (ca. 1821–1872), *Blue Hole, Flood Waters, Little Miami River*, 1851. Oil on canvas, 28½ x 41½ in. (72.4 x 105.4 cm). Cincinnati Art Museum, gift of Norbert Heermann and Arthur Helbig. Acc. no. 1926.18.

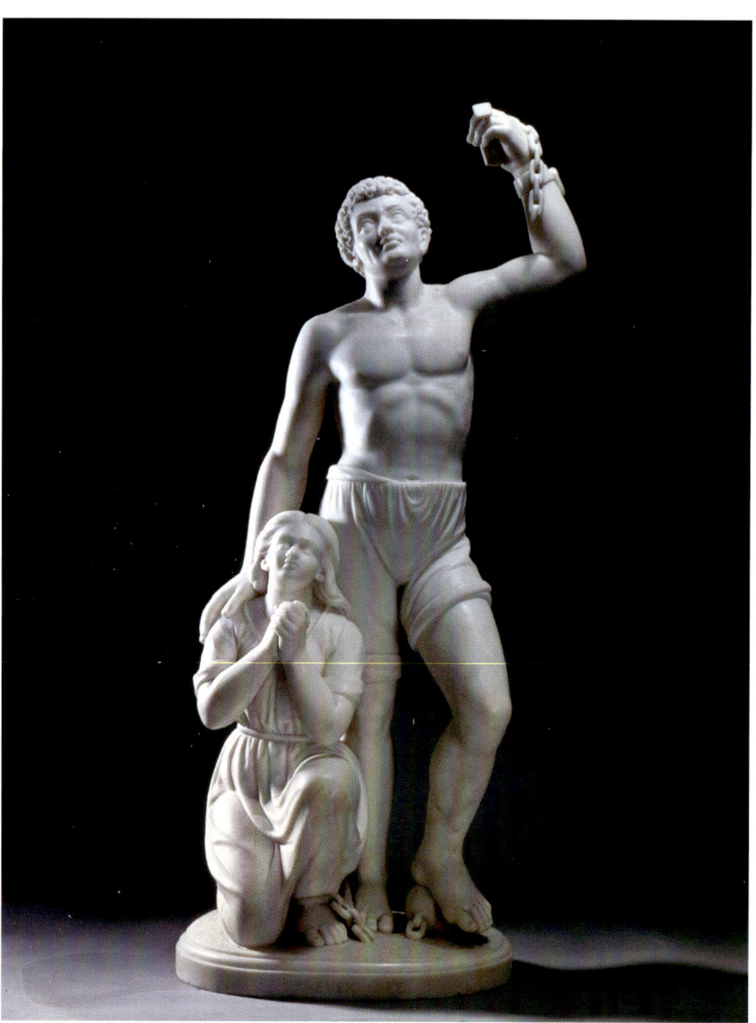

Fig. 10. Edmonia Lewis (ca. 1844–1907), *Forever Free*, 1867. Marble, 41 x 11 x 17 in. (104.1 x 27.9 x 43.2 cm). Howard University Gallery of Art, Washington, DC.

for example, a majority of voters supported the retention of property qualifications that effectively denied many African American men the right to vote in the state. It was not until ratification of the Fifteenth Amendment to the U.S. Constitution in 1870 that black men fully obtained that right in New York.

Well into the twentieth century, African Americans in the North continued to struggle with myriad indignities and prejudices, from formal segregation and unequal accommodations to poor living conditions and a range of social restrictions, both legal and de facto. Racial discrimination, institutional or otherwise, also extended to the institutions of culture, including the world of visual art. While a small number of talented African American artists achieved success in the nineteenth century—painters Charles Ethan Porter and Henry Ossawa Tanner, for example, and sculptor Edmonia Lewis (fig. 10)—Robert Duncanson remains one of the few with a connection to the Hudson River School.

Born in Seneca County, New York, in 1821 to an African American mother and a Scottish Canadian father, Duncanson lived in Canada as a child. He later relocated with his mother to Ohio, then traveled to Glasgow, Scotland, to study painting in 1853. Returning to the United States a year later, Duncanson established himself as a portraitist of prominent abolitionists. But it was his majestic landscape paintings (fig. 11), influenced by the Hudson River School and depicting locations in North Carolina, Pennsylvania, England, Canada, and Scotland, that brought him international recognition.[7] In keeping with its mandate to broaden the art historical lens for study of the Hudson River School, The Thomas Cole National Historic Site mounted a groundbreaking exhibition of Duncanson's paintings in 2011: *Robert S. Duncanson: The Spiritual Striving of the Freedmen's Sons.*

The contemporary artists of *River Crossings* counter the heady, ethereal imagery of the Hudson River School with work that embraces a century and a half of cultural revisionism and activism. The Modernist ethos, which blossomed in the late nineteenth century and dominated much of the twentieth, brought with it more than a formal commitment to abstraction and conceptualism in literature, visual art, architecture, design, music, dance, and film. It also helped inspire and abet notions of personal freedom and expression, as well as liberation movements committed to social justice, equality, and overcoming the dehumanizing forces of industry and social conformity.

River Crossings resonates with contemporary art committed to these cultural and social ideals—from Cindy Sherman's masquerading as women of different historic eras (plates 17–20), deconstructing the social codes and mores that defined and limited them, to Martin Puryear's sculpture, *Question* (plate 37), a massive, energetic swirl of wood that jettisons pedestals or other distancing devices to invite an immediate and joyful interaction with viewers. By pairing these works with paintings and decorative art from the nineteenth century, *River Crossings* has much to say about where we were as a nation, where we are now, and the work that still needs to be done as we contemplate a future as uncertain as it was at the dawn of the Industrial Age.

New York, NY
April 2015

1. Mary Schmidt Campbell, "Romare Bearden's *Conjur Woman*," Studio Museum in Harlem, http://www.studiomuseum.org/studio-blog/reading/mary-schmidt-campbell-romare-beardens-conjur-woman.

2. As Jason Rosenfeld, the co-curator of *River Crossings*, observes, the artists of the Hudson River School were in the "vanguard in terms of seeking to leave the metropolis to both pursue their subjects more readily and with more focus, and to establish roots in new locales." Correspondence with the author, January 26, 2015.

3. Jennifer C. Krieger, "Women Artists of the Hudson River School," *Antiques & Fine Art* (Spring 2010), 140.

4. For more on the obstacles that these women faced and the ways they triumphed over them, see ibid., 140–145.

5. Ibid., 144.

6. Patrick Rael, "The Long Death of Slavery," in Ira Berlin and Leslie M. Harris, eds., *Slavery in New York* (New York: The New Press, 2005), 114.

7. While the landscape paintings of black artist Edward Mitchell Bannister were also influenced by the Hudson River School, Duncanson was the first African American artist to achieve acclaim in both Europe and the United States.

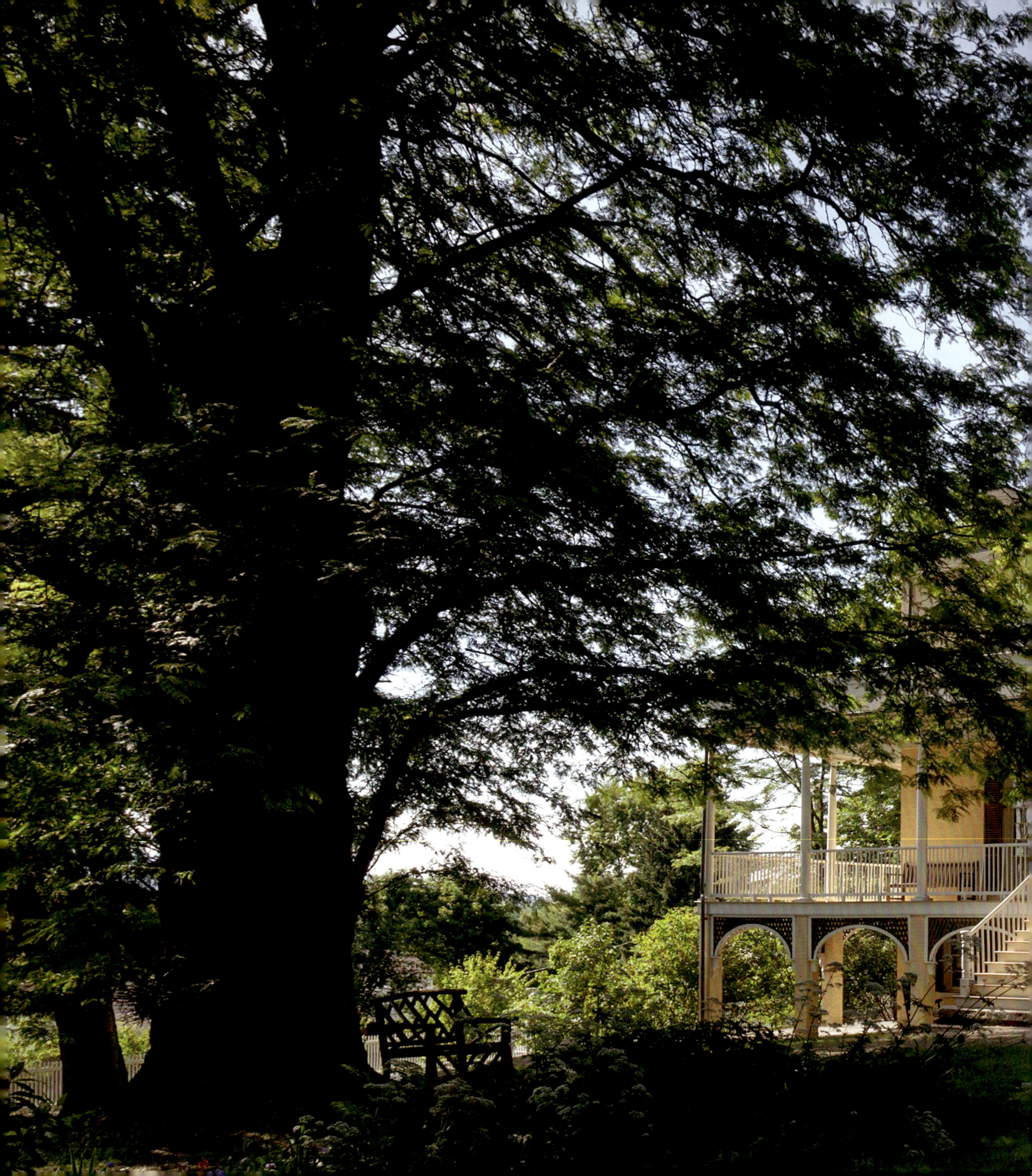

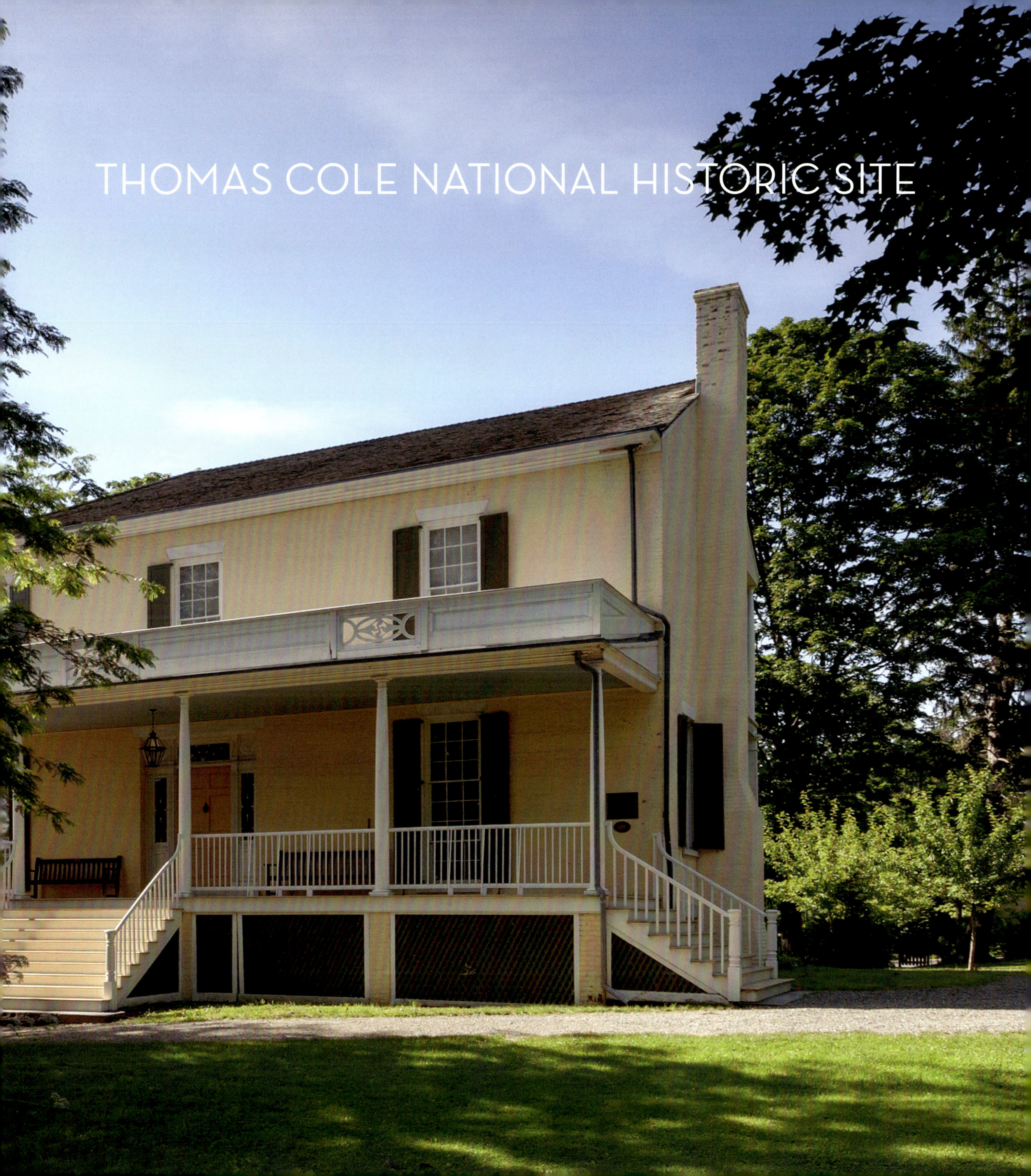
THOMAS COLE NATIONAL HISTORIC SITE

THOMAS COLE NATIONAL HISTORIC SITE PROFILE

"I must wait for time to draw a veil over the common details, the unessential parts, which shall leave the great features, whether the beautiful or the sublime, dominant in the mind."

—Letter from Thomas Cole to Asher B. Durand, January 4, 1838, in Louis Legrand Noble, *The Life and Works of Thomas Cole* (1853; ed. Elliot S. Vesell, Cambridge, MA, Belknap Press of Harvard University Press, 1964), 185.

THOMAS COLE'S DESCRIPTION of the effects of the passage of time as to "draw a veil" over his memory of things he had seen is an apt metaphor for the way his art is perceived today—through a veil of our own cultural norms and expectations. For each visitor to the Thomas Cole National Historic Site or Olana, and for each artist in *River Crossings*, what pierces the veil is personal and unique. The two historic sites have frequently hosted curators and scholars who expound on what aspects of the nineteenth-century artists' work are relevant today, but in 2015 it is artists from our own time who are exploring that question. This exhibition is an opportunity to see that visual conversation between artists across centuries.

The Thomas Cole National Historic Site is the former home of the artist Thomas Cole (1801–1848), the founder of the art movement known as the Hudson River School, and Olana is the home of Frederic Edwin Church (1826–1900), one of the movement's most celebrated artists. Church, who first traveled to Catskill to study with Cole, later built Olana directly across the river from his mentor. Today the two sites stand two miles apart on either side of the Hudson, linked by the Rip Van Winkle Bridge. Together these historic homes and studios tell the story of the origin and the apex of the Hudson River School of landscape painting, considered to be the country's first major art movement. In recent decades, the Thomas Cole site and Olana have placed increased emphasis on the connections between their nineteenth-century stories and the issues and themes that are relevant today. In addition, the two historic sites have sought to strengthen the connection between the two organizations, presenting themselves as a single destination and resource. *River Crossings* is one of the largest and most visible initiatives that fulfills these goals, uniting the two historic sites as well as connecting the past and the present.

This exhibition breaks new ground in many ways, but it is not the first time that new and innovative art has been shown at the residences of Thomas Cole and Frederic Church. It began with Cole himself, who would have hung his latest works, probably still wet from the studio, on the walls of the East and West Parlors in his Catskill home. As an artist, poet, essayist, and architect, Cole's vision of wild and untouched scenery with majestic mountains and tangled forests stood in contrast to the gentle landscape images that had come before. Critics, patrons, and fellow artists embraced his work enthusiastically, and Cole became the leader of an informal alliance of artists that included Church, Asher B. Durand, Sanford Gifford, Jasper Francis Cropsey, and other painters, as well as literary figures such as William Cullen Bryant and James Fenimore Cooper. Together they established a notion of America as a new Eden, a concept that still resonates with artists, environmentalists, and landscape enthusiasts to this day.

The exhibition's co-curators, Stephen Hannock and Jason Rosenfeld, have selected artists and artworks that shed light on the connections between nineteenth-century American art and contemporary times, and that speak to the historic environments in which they are installed. That dialogue takes on a special significance because the artworks will be placed into the very spaces where, it can be argued, a uniquely American art began. The juxtaposition of, for example, Frederic Church's formal rooms, complete with original nineteenth-century furnishings and a dramatic view of the Hudson River, with Maya Lin's *Silver River–Hudson* (plate 40), seemingly dripping down the wall, invites reflection on the issue of loss and our associations with the great waterway then and now. The goals of the project are to engage both current and new audiences with a presentation that differs from the traditional house museum tour, enabling visitors to access the historic spaces from a different angle, to provoke new ideas about the meaning of the art and history of the mid-nineteenth century, and to encourage audiences to confront the vast cultural shifts that distinguish Cole and Church's time from our own.

Throughout his life, in both writing and painting, Cole expressed a deep fascination with the passage of time. Perhaps his best-known work on this topic is the epic series entitled *The Course of Empire*, but in 1838 the artist created two other works that invite consideration of the present as a redolent scene of what has happened in the past. In one painting, two knights on horseback duel in front of cheering spectators near a luminous castle. In the second, the same castle is depicted in ruins, abandoned and overgrown. Cole titled the festive scene *Past* and the ruin *Present*.[1] The 2015 exhibition *River Crossings: Contemporary Art Comes Home* invites a similar consideration of the scenes before us—the homes of Cole and Church—where the past is everywhere in evidence. Nearly 170 years after Cole's death, his home provides the visitor with historically accurate settings where the stories of history can be told. At its core, the purpose of the Thomas Cole National Historic Site is to facilitate the connection between Cole's vision and the people and ideas of our own time. It is perhaps by looking at the present that we might best deepen our understanding of Cole and his import today, and perceive our moment not as ruinous, as in Cole's painting of 1838, but celebrate it as resurgent.

In this unique exhibition, location matters, as does the fact that it is
an artist-initiated exhibition. Artists, including Cole himself, have continu-
ually mined history to activate new ways of thinking about what history
means in the present moment. One can look to precedents by artists
who re-invent the space of a museum or shine new light on historic
artifacts, such as Fred Wilson's *Mining the Museum* at the Maryland
Historical Society in 1992, Mark Dion's numerous projects, and Andy
Warhol's *Raid the Icebox* at Rhode Island School of Design Museum in
1970. Equally appropriate is the vision of venues that have animated
historic sites with contemporary projects such as those realized at the
Eastern State Penitentiary in Philadelphia, the Tenement Museum in
New York City, the Isabella Stewart Gardner Museum and the Paul
Revere House in collaboration with the Institute of Contemporary Art
in Boston, to name only a few. Presenting contemporary works within a
historic site can refreshingly break conventions of seeing work on the
blank walls of the white cube.

So what will it mean to place contemporary artworks into the homes
and landscapes of two of the most innovative and influential painters of
nineteenth-century America? What new conversations will be initiated
in this juxtaposition and how will it enable us to see both historic and
contemporary works anew? For instance, how might a series of Cindy
Sherman's images of herself from the 1970s (plates 17–20) seem on the
gold walls of Cole's 1830s parlor, as compared to seeing these works on
the white walls of a gallery, a context that is now supposed to be the
newly traditional way to display art (see p. 56)? The historic rooms will
be enriched by the artworks themselves, such as Stephen Hannock's
Oxbow (plate 15), which pays homage to Cole but also includes writing
and collage that reference events that are important to Hannock's own
life. Is this entire exhibition not a rich landscape of relationships and
ideas across time and space?

One of the most compelling questions this exhibition poses is what
mattered most in Cole and Church's time, and what persists in importance today. It is hoped that *River Crossings* will give artists a central
role in the discussion, provoke a renewed interest in history, and shed
light on the unexpected and meaningful ways in which past and present
remain inextricably linked.

Elizabeth B. Jacks and Kate Menconeri
Catskill, NY
April 2015

1. Both were painted for P.G. Stuyvesant and are now in the Mead Art Museum, Amherst
College, Massachusetts. See William H. Truettner and Alan Wallach, eds., *Thomas Cole:
Landscape into History* (New Haven and London: Yale University Press, 1994), 94–96.

ON EXHIBIT AT THE THOMAS COLE SITE

KIKI SMITH

JOEL STERNFELD

THOMAS NOZKOWSKI

STEPHEN PETEGORSKY

GREGORY CREWDSON

JERRY GRETZINGER

ELIZABETH MURRAY

STEPHEN HANNOCK

CINDY SHERMAN

ANGIE KEEFER

KARA HAMILTON

KIANJA STROBERT

ROMARE BEARDEN

SIENNA SHIELDS

CHARLES LEDRAY

DUNCAN HANNAH

FRANK MOORE

RASHAAD NEWSOME

DON GUMMER

KIKI SMITH (b. 1954)

Kiki Smith grew up in New Jersey, crossing the Hudson to New York City in the late 1970s. More recently she has moved to Catskill, New York, and has become a valued supporter of the Thomas Cole Historic Site. She is the daughter of the American sculptor Tony Smith (1912–1980), who is associated with the Minimalism movement. Her father's preference for bronze is evident in *Wolf with Birds III* (plate 1), although this is not her most familiar medium. It is a bas-relief composition with a small wolf in right profile and two doves, in identical poses, flitting from lower left to upper right across the mammal's body. Smith cast this sculpture in bronze with gold leaf, and tiny specks of red and other colors dapple its matte surface. Since the 1990s, Smith has been interested in depicting nature in her work, often in the form of finely designed etchings, woodcuts, photographs, and lithographs, among other media, and as in the art of Valerie Hegarty (plate 36), Maya Lin (plate 40), and Letha Wilson (plates 43 and 44) there is an environmental imperative in her productions. Birds have a symbolic resonance for the artist, linked to the soul, "with associations ranging from the Holy Spirit to the fragility of the environment," and the use of white birds that recall the image of the dove in Catholic art are consistent with a strain of religiosity that runs through her oeuvre.[1] Fragility is less evident in the form of the wolf, whose claws are sharp and pronounced, and whose depicted hide is striated to convey a sense of coursing fur, but rough and metallic to the core, like a magnified etching. The sensitivity of the exquisitely naturalistic depiction is belied by the boldness of execution and expression in this prideful creature, calmly moving through space.

---

1. See material related to her exhibition at MoMA, New York, NY, in 2003–2004, *Kiki Smith: Prints, Books & Things*: http://www.moma.org/interactives/exhibitions/2003/kikismith/flash.html.

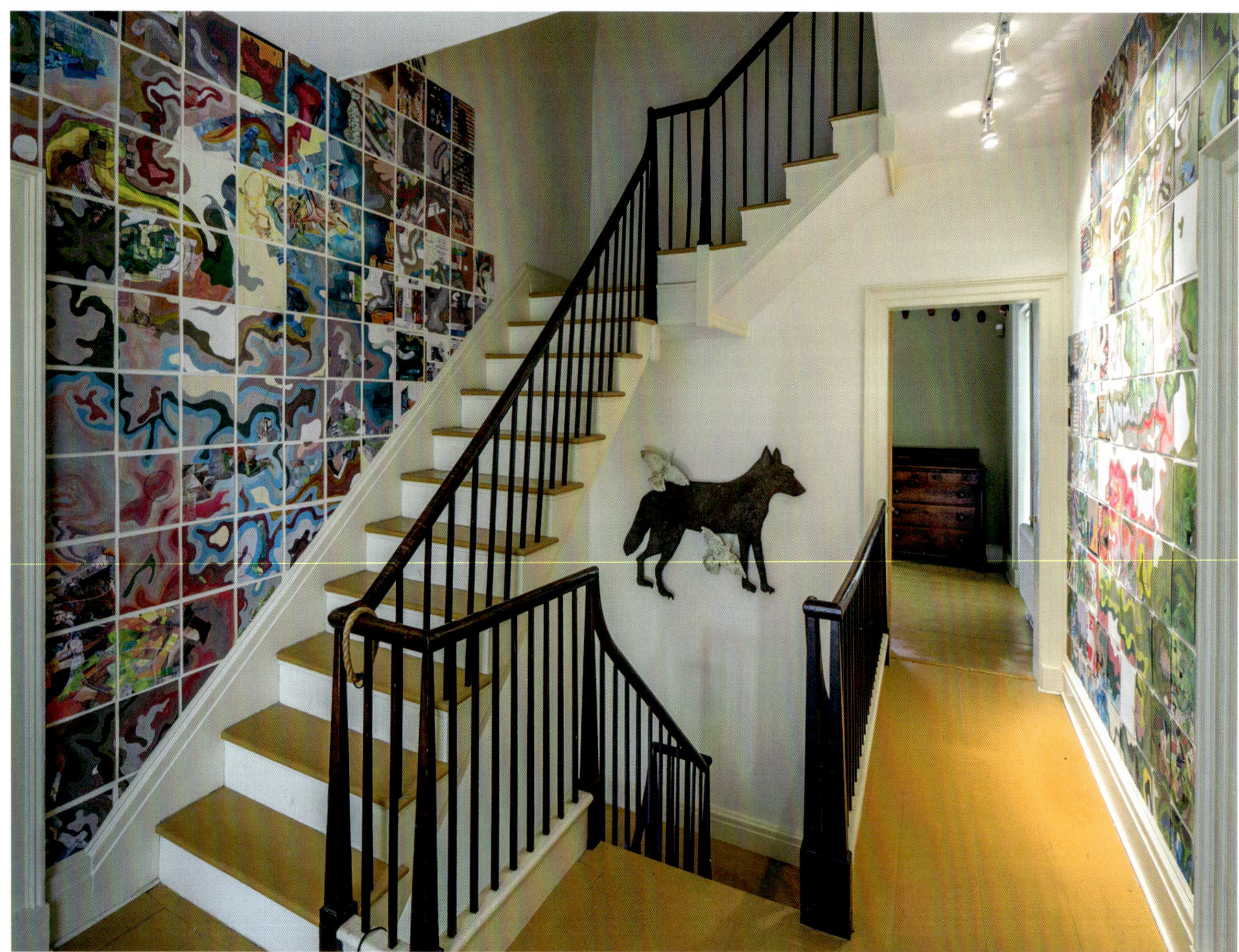

Kiki Smith, *Wolf with Birds III*, 2010 (plate 1) in the Staircase/Entry.

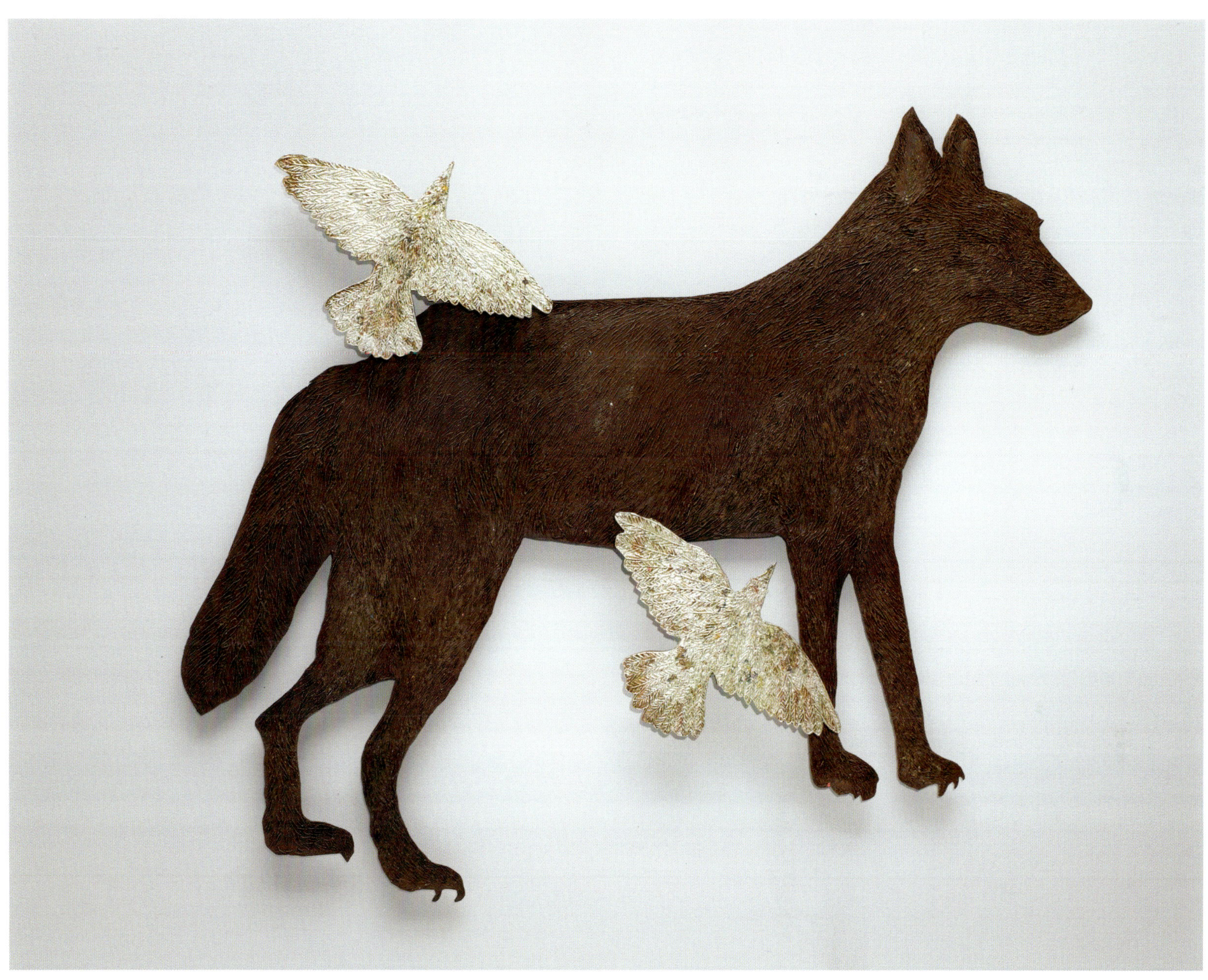

Wolf with Birds III, 2010. Bronze with gold leaf,
44½ x 54 x 2½ in. (113 x 137.2 x 6.4 cm), unique.
Collection of Maria and Conrad Janis. © Kiki Smith,
courtesy Pace Gallery. Photograph: Kerry Ryan
McFate, courtesy Pace Gallery.

JOEL **STERNFELD** (b. 1944)

A native New Yorker, Sternfeld has worked for five decades in the medium of color photography and with his preferred subjects of people and landscapes. His important series of works in and around New York, *Hart Island* (1998) and *The High Line* (2000–2001), continue his projects of illuminating little-known realms of the metropolis. In the genre of pure landscape, the title of *April 20, 2007, The East Meadows, Northampton, Massachusetts* from *Oxbow Archive* (plate 2) provides explication and specificity in the form of date, site, and the name of the series in Sternfeld's oeuvre. It was shot from just beyond a bank on the other side of which spreads the Oxbow, the famed extreme bend of the Connecticut River that was the subject of Cole's grand painting of 1836 (fig. 1) and long a motif in Stephen Hannock's work (plate 15). Sternfeld's image includes a distant view of Mount Tom, a modest peak that also features in Stephen Petegorsky's *Clouds, Mountains, Mist*, also on view at Cedar Grove (plate 10). At more than 7 feet wide, Sternfeld works in a scale now common in the photography of the likes of Candida Höfer (b. 1944), Andreas Gursky (b. 1955), Thomas Struth (b. 1954), and Stan Douglas (b. 1960). This print is from his *Oxbow Archive*, published as a book in 2008, and featuring 77 such images produced starting in 2006. It is questionable whether such works fully deny the traditional categories of the sublime or the beautiful, for they are immersive in scale, commensurate with the engaged approach to the viewing body in Jerry Gretzinger's *Jerry's Map* (plate 13), and even Hannock's panoramas, and connect with viewers in a vivid manner. Sternfeld's photographs function very differently from, for example, Lynn Davis's more removed, distant, and traditionally picturesque black-and-white images of depopulated landscapes (plates 38 and 39). Sternfeld's blend of precise naturalism with a sweeping breadth of vision and complexities of light lie closer to the aesthetic of late-nineteenth century Symbolist landscape paintings by John Everett Millais (1829–1896) and Vilhelm Hammershøi (1864–1916). There is a remarkable sensitivity of light in this quietly awesome scene, along with multiple vanishing points, and the dramatic bulk of the Mount Tom range rises in the background beyond a scrim of golden-flecked trees, mountains that seemingly by magic are not reflected in the placid body of water in the middle ground.

April 20, 2007, The East Meadows, Northampton, Massachusetts, negative: 2007; print: 2008. Digital C-print, 72 x 88½ in. (182.88 x 224.79 cm). Collection of the artist. © Joel Sternfeld; courtesy of the artist and Luhring Augustine, New York.

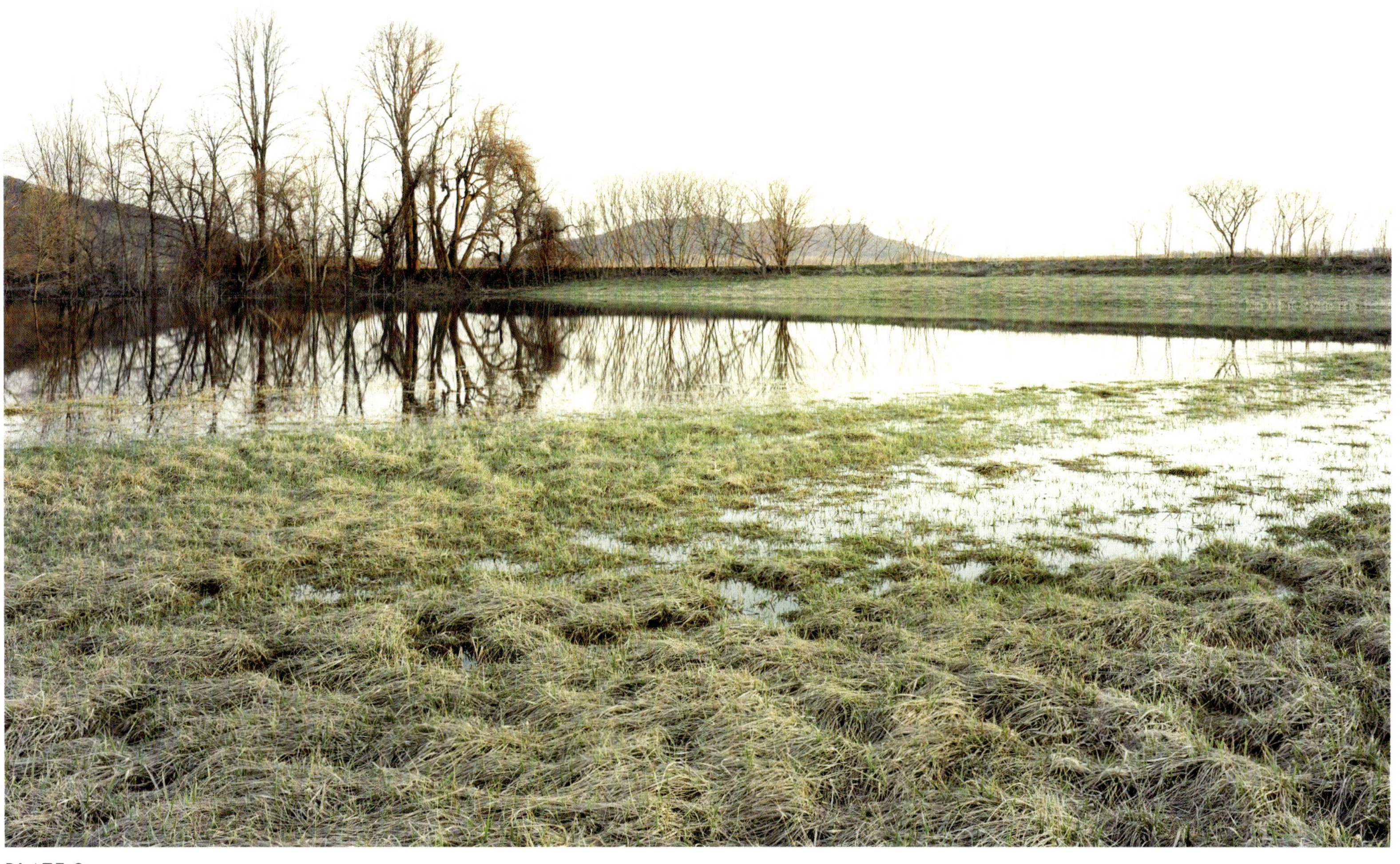

PLATE 2

THOMAS NOZKOWSKI (b. 1944)

A resident of the region since 1977, Nozkowski talks of "using memory as a kind of strainer," in the production of his remarkable, consistent, and continually unexpected paintings.[1] His five works are displayed in the Sitting Room at Cedar Grove, wherein Cole is presented as a Renaissance man, with his architecture desk, musical instruments, scientific materials, and publications. With the exception of a few works on a larger scale, 30 by 40 inches, he has worked in the same two low and wide sizes for 40 years. Two works in the show are 16 by 20 inches (plates 3 and 4), a size he does not work in anymore, in preference to the 22-by-28-inch medium format that he now prefers (plates 5 and 7). Although abstract, each of his paintings is based on his walks through the landscape, as discussed in "*River Crossings:* 'An unbounded capacity for improvement by art'" in this volume (pp. 12–21). The imagery is derived from what he sees, sometimes quite directly, although it is translated to canvas in such a way that the inspiration is subsumed into variable abstracted forms. Paintings such as the top-heavy *Untitled (8-129)* (plate 7), which hangs above Cole's desk and diagonally from the view out the window west to the Catskills, develop without a final goal, but are formed in a process of pictorial and coloristic discovery in the studio, where he can be found working on up to a dozen paintings at a time. *Untitled (7-61)* (plate 3) was featured in a catalogue and exhibition titled *An Autobiography* and accompanied by Judy Linn's photograph of the portico of a Greek Revival Church in New-

burgh, New York, and a map of the town.[2] Although the interior parallelogram bears an architectonic quality, the scrim of fluid paint seemingly draining from the top edge, and the craquelure at right where a bright under-painting breaks through, constitute equal elements of interest. The tonality and hues call to mind Umberto Boccioni's (1882–1916) exploration of color and sentiment in his series, *States of Mind* (1911) at MoMA. Nozkowski has said that he wants "to be surprised at the end of the piece," and that joy in painterly discovery—and the uncertainty that follows—is part of the complexity of his art and the satisfactions it supplies.[3] The decorative intensity of the artist's work, in the sense that Henri Matisse (1869–1954) pursued the term as lines, colors, and shapes taking precedence over subject matter, is the key to its strength. The variety of color and shape that Nozkowski employs is fully on display in the five works in the Sitting Room, and they well reveal the engaging new realities he constructs from his immersive experiences in the region.

---

1. Conversation with the artist, July 14, 2014.

2. *Thomas Nozkowski: An Autobiography* (High Falls, NY: Cedar Hills Press, 1995), XV.

3. The artist in conversation with Robert Storr and James Siena, Pace Gallery, New York, April 10, 2015.

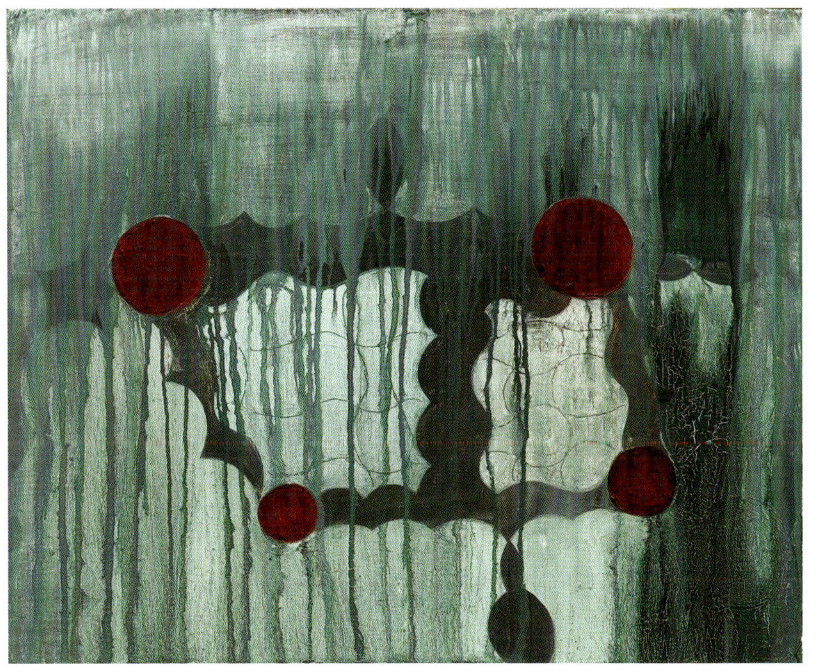

PLATE 3

Untitled (7-61), 1995. Oil on linen on panel, 16 x 20 in.
(40.6 x 50.8 cm). Collection of the artist. © Thomas
Nozkowski, courtesy Pace Gallery. Photograph: Kerry
Ryan McFate, courtesy Pace Gallery.

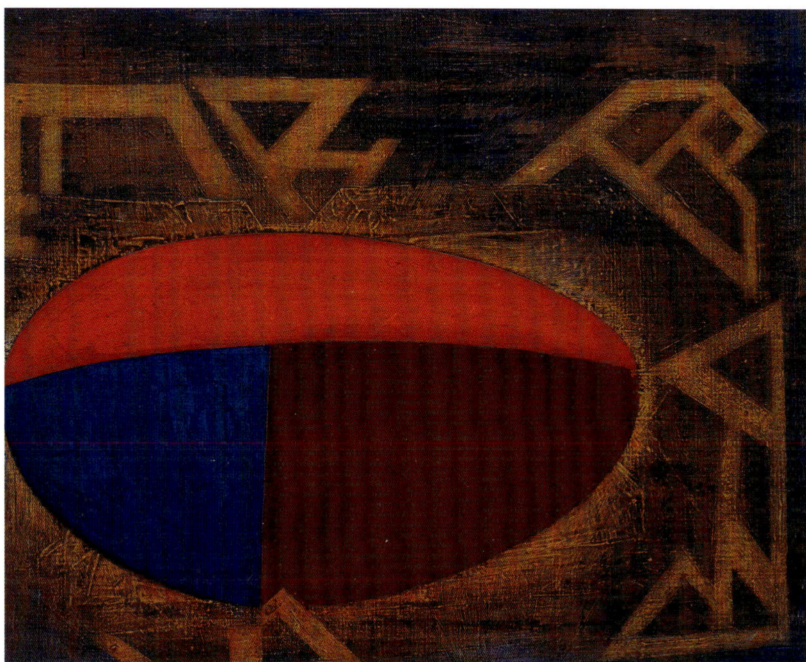

PLATE 4

Untitled (7-66), 1995. Oil on linen on panel, 16 x 20 in.
(40.6 x 50.8 cm). Collection of the artist. © Thomas
Nozkowski, courtesy Pace Gallery. Photograph: Kerry
Ryan McFate, courtesy Pace Gallery.

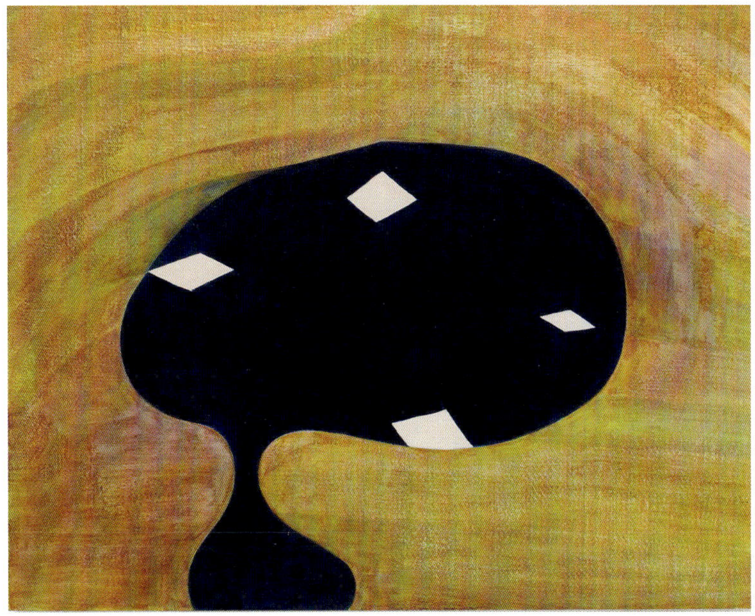

PLATE 5

Untitled (9-3), 2011. Oil on linen on panel, 22 x 28 in.
(55.9 x 71.1 cm). Collection of the artist. © Thomas
Nozkowski, courtesy Pace Gallery. Photograph: Kerry
Ryan McFate, courtesy Pace Gallery.

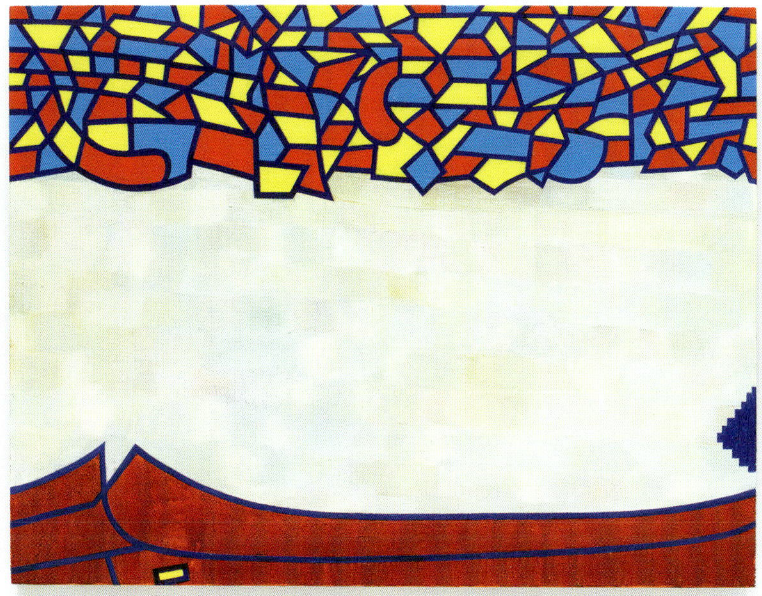

PLATE 6

Untitled (9-25) (Sam's Point), 2012. Oil on linen on
panel, 30 x 40 in. (76.2 x 101.6 cm). Collection of the
artist. © Thomas Nozkowski, courtesy Pace Gallery.
Photograph: Kerry Ryan McFate, courtesy Pace
Gallery.

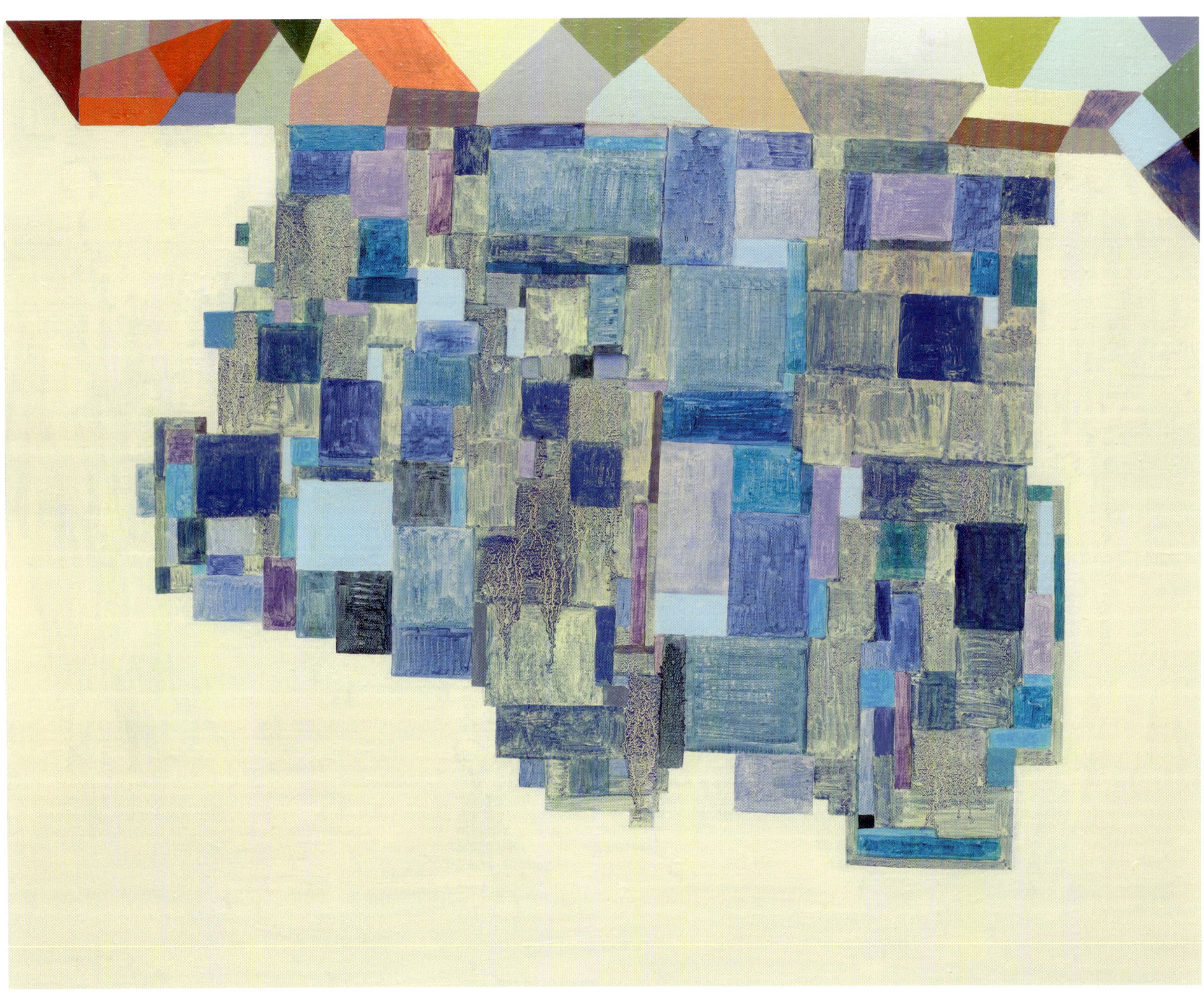

PLATE 7

Untitled (8-129), 2010. Oil on linen on panel,
22⅛ x 28⅛ in. (56.2 x 71.4 cm). Collection of the
artist. © Thomas Nozkowski, courtesy Pace Gallery.
Photograph: Kerry Ryan McFate, courtesy Pace
Gallery.

Thomas Nozkowski, *Untitled (8-129)*, 2010 (plate 7) in the Sitting Room.

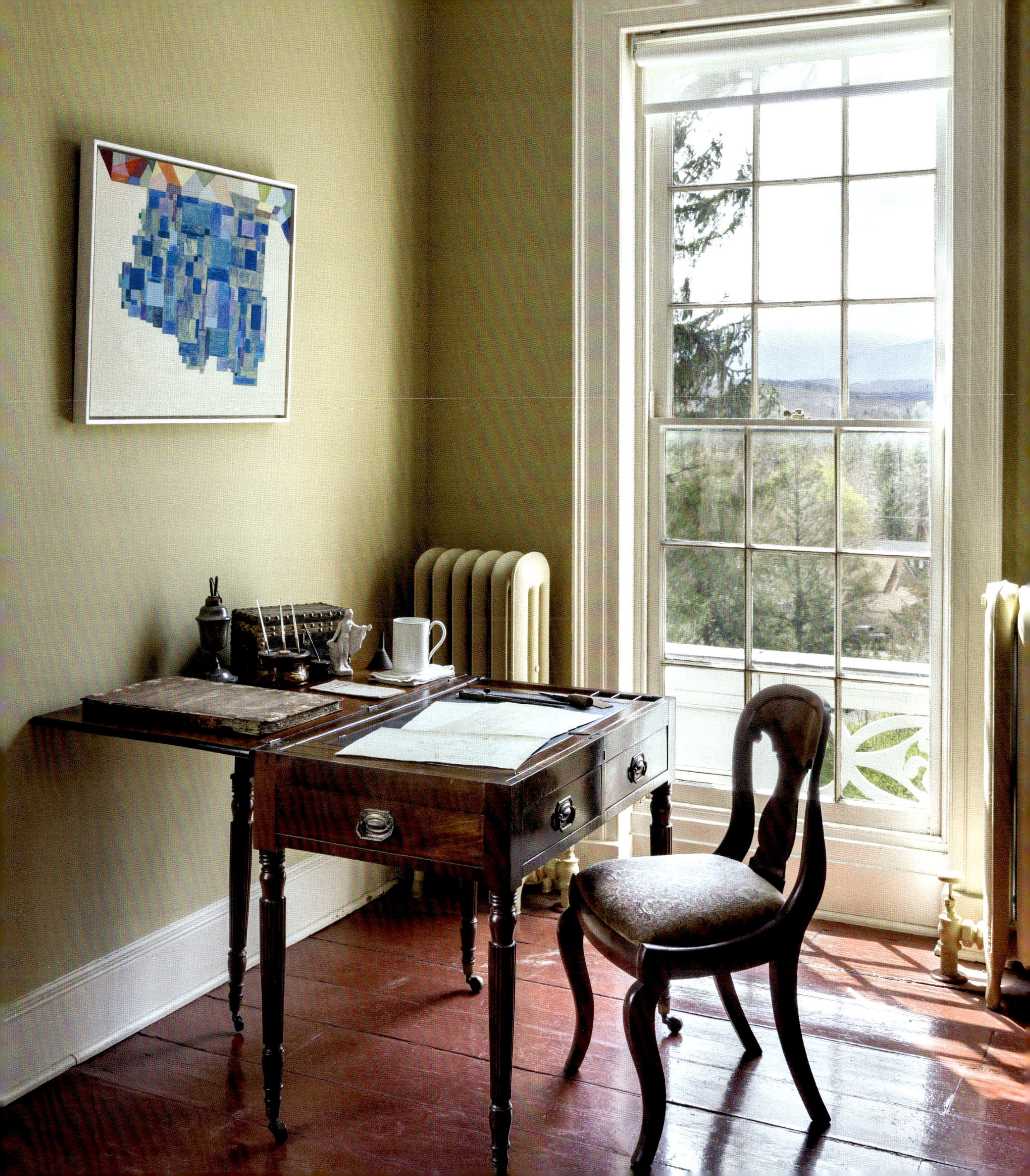

STEPHEN **PETEGORSKY** (b. 1954)

A quartet of Stephen Petegorsky's black-and-white photographs in the second-floor gallery at Cedar Grove represent a presiding concern in his art—the documentation of his decades of rambles around the Meadows region near the Oxbow, in the Connecticut River Valley. Usually, the artist takes the broader view of Cole and Church, with wide-frame images of landscapes and the distant forms of the encircling mountain ranges. Sometimes the ground at his feet garners his attention, as in *Dead Fox* (plate 11), wherein the desiccated and picked-over form of the mammal achieves a level of poignancy, and the texture of aerated pumice, like the casts of bodies of innocents burnt at Pompeii. Other works in this vein, such as *Dead Crow with Frost,* achieve a delicacy of detail worthy of Albrecht Dürer's (1471–1528) watercolors and prints. *Clouds, Mountains, Mist* (plate 10) achieves a high-skied simplicity akin to that of Caspar David Friedrich's (1774–1840) Romantic-era views of the German highlands, and in the far distance is Mount Tom, also visible in Joel Sternfeld's view of the nearby East Meadows (plate 2). The one-point perspective of *Plowed Field and Fog* (plate 9) with the just-turned furrows serving as orthogonals organizes the view but leads nowhere, into a bank of impenetrable and atmospheric mist.

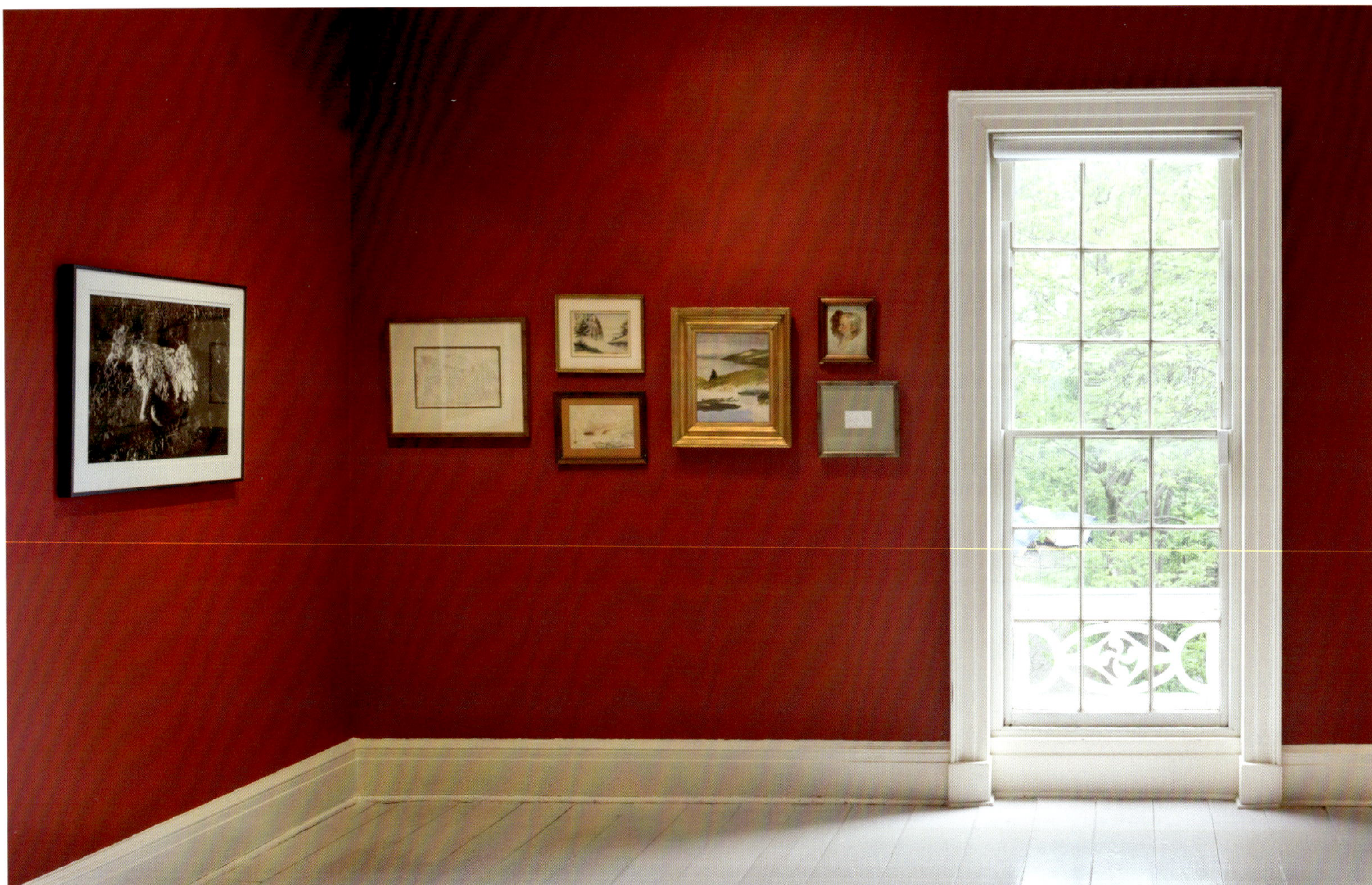

Stephen Petegorsky, *Dead Fox, The Meadows*, 2009 (plate 11) in the Second-Floor Gallery.

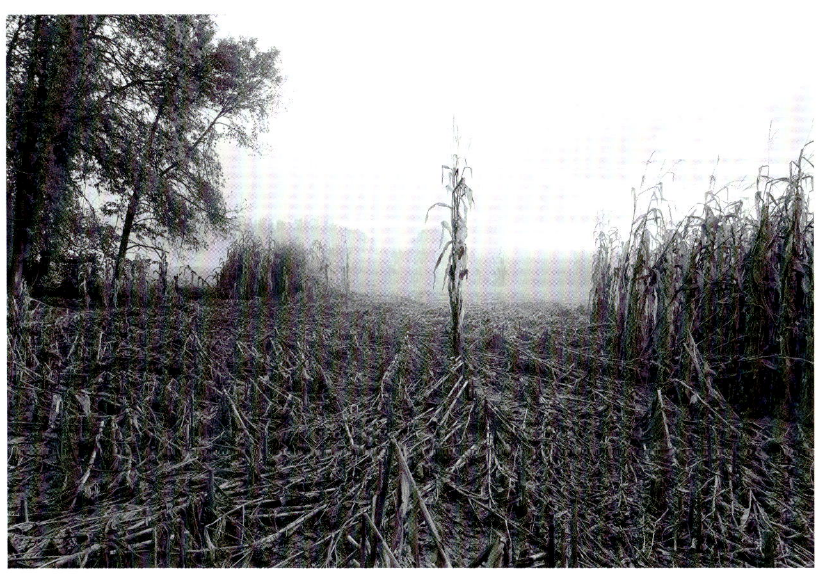

PLATE 8

October Corn, Early Morning, 2011; printed 2013. Archival ink-jet print, 24 x 33 in. (61 x 83.8 cm). Collection of the artist. Courtesy of the artist.

PLATE 9

Plowed Field and Fog, 2009; printed 2013. Archival ink-jet print, 24 x 33 in. (61 x 83.8 cm). Collection of the artist. Courtesy of the artist.

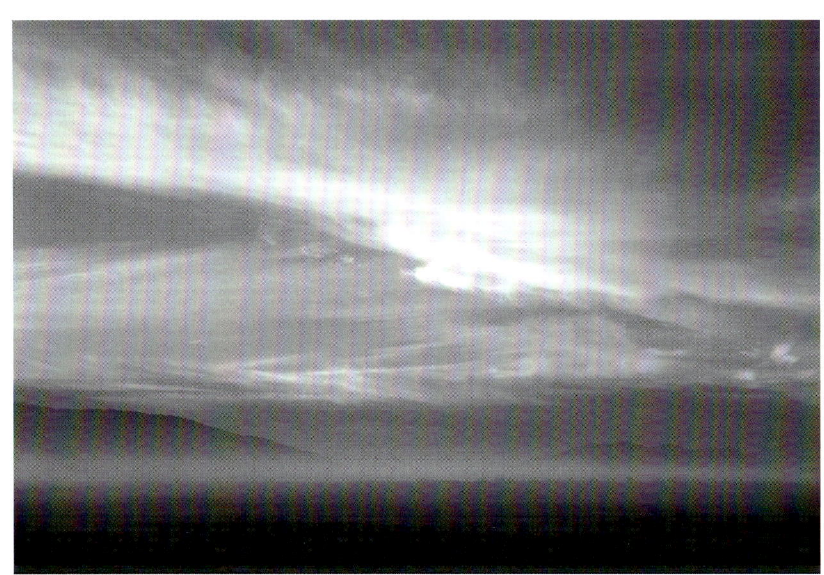

PLATE 10

Clouds, Mountains, Mist, 2011; printed 2013. Archival ink-jet print, 24 x 33 in. (61 x 83.8 cm). Collection of the artist. Courtesy of the artist.

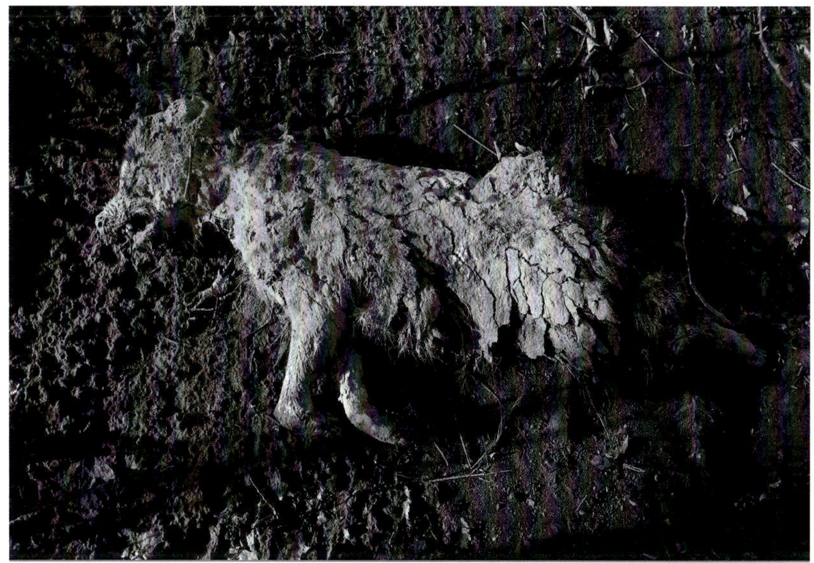

PLATE 11

Dead Fox, 2009; printed 2013. Archival ink-jet print, 24 x 33 in. (61 x 83.8 cm). Collection of the artist. Courtesy of the artist.

GREGORY **CREWDSON** (b. 1962)

Brooklyn-born Crewdson is a photographer who specializes in tab-leaux of painstakingly arranged and lit scenes that serve as settings for stories. Cindy Sherman (plates 17–20), in her early series *Untitled Film Stills* (1977–1980), produced single images that bear elements implying a prior narrative and one yet to come, a narrative never to be explored beyond the single image provided. Crewdson's work expands the concept in terms of picture scale and scope of story and characters, removes the personal that is so central to Sherman's probing aesthetic, and trends toward the surreal, under the gloss of a hyperreality. Filmic in their influences, the pictures become set and scene in one, exquisitely designed and shaded. In this work (plate 12), from a series titled *Sanctuary*, Crewdson moved from the employment of actual American places as setting for his works, to the artificial environs of Cinecittà, the famed film studio in suburban Rome. It is installed in the second-floor gallery at Cedar Grove next to Cole's painting *Tower by Moonlight*, circa 1838 (see below). Crewdson's black-and-white image forms a modern *verduta*, a detailed urban view popularized in European images of Italian cities in the Baroque era, to Cole's *capriccio*, an imaginary topographical scene wherein motifs are combined in a seamlessly collaged manner to present a comprehensive view that appears to be real, but is not of any one identifiable location. In producing such a work, the product of his travels to Italy, Cole trod in the footsteps of the Venetian Francesco Guardi (1712–1793) and the Welshman Richard Wilson (1713/14–1782). Crewdson follows in the stead of Italian Modernist postwar filmmakers Federico Fellini and Michelangelo Antonioni, as well as Stanley Kubrick and Francis Ford Coppola. With their seductive and velvety surfaces, yet tawdry state of the depicted settings, his depopulated and still images—depleted of sentiment and action—represent the lure of Italy and a nostalgic idea of the Old World that has been a presiding element of American artistic culture for two hundred years.

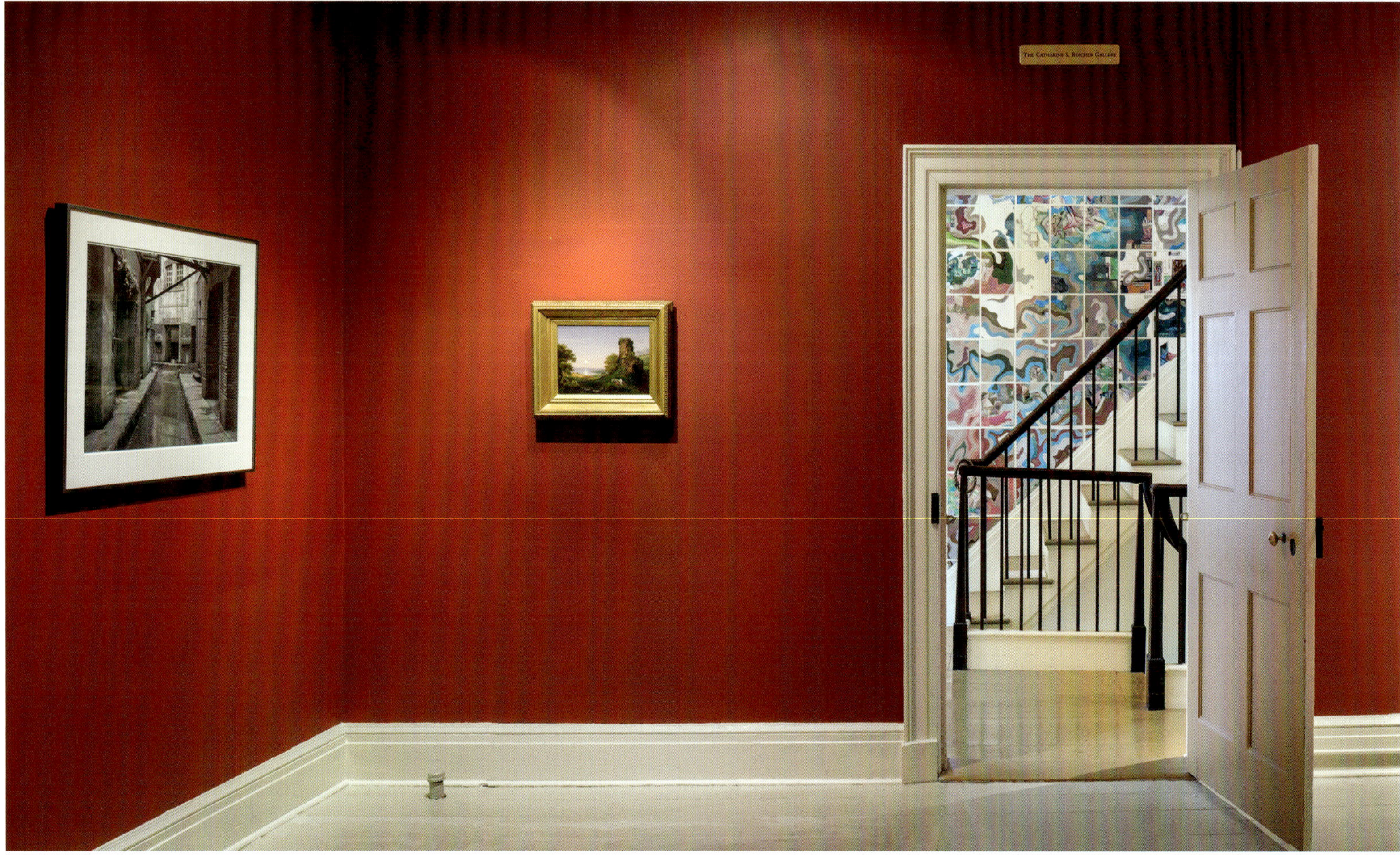

Gregory Crewdson, *Untitled (21)*, 2009 (plate 12) in the Second-Floor Gallery and Jerry Gretzinger, *Jerry's Map*, 1963 to present (plate 13) in the Second-Floor Hallway.

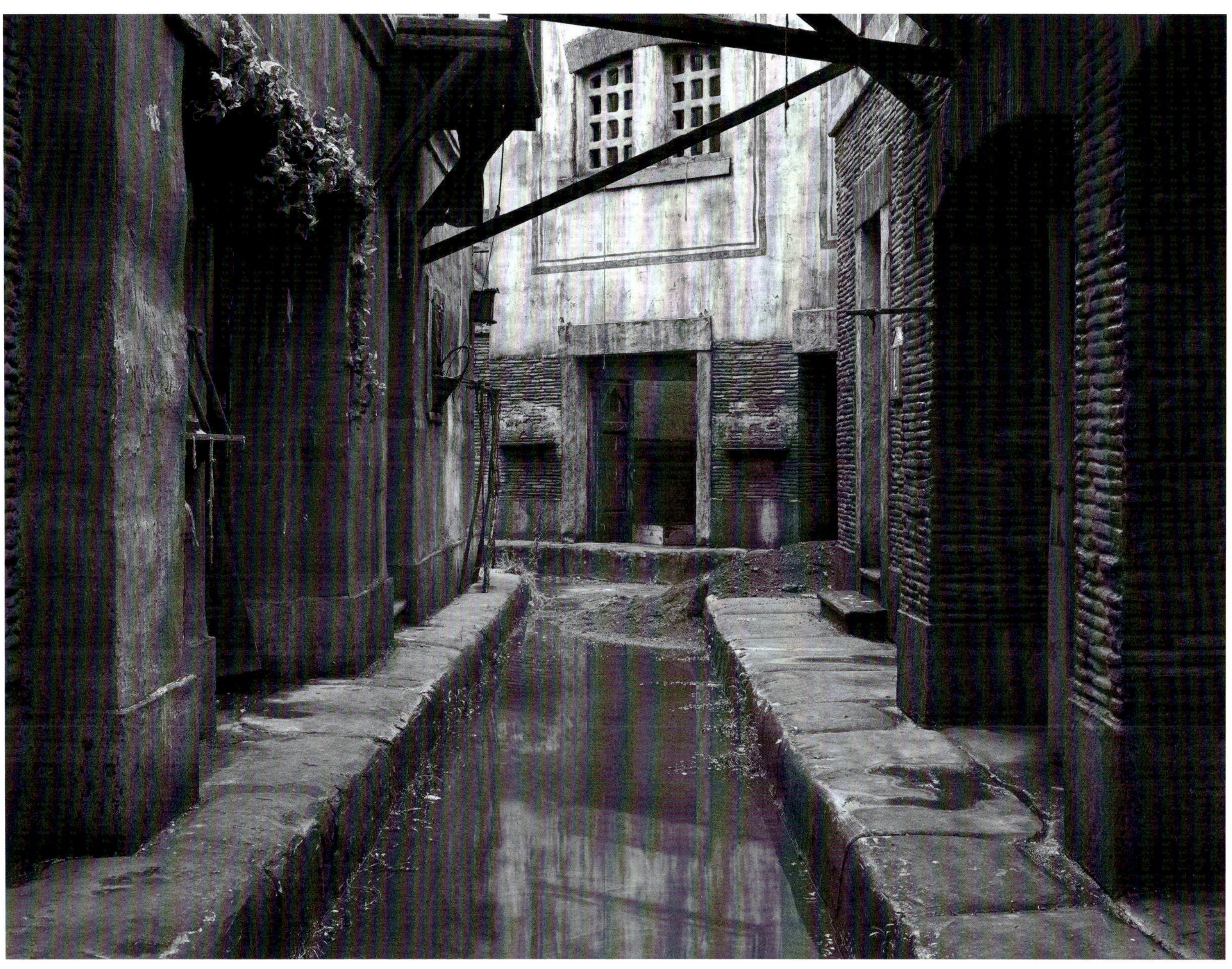

PLATE 12

Untitled (21), 2009. Pigmented ink-jet print, 28½ x 35½ in. (72.4 x 89.5 cm). Collection of the artist. © Gregory Crewdson. Courtesy Gagosian Gallery.

JERRY **GRETZINGER** (b. 1934)

Gretzinger lived in Manhattan from 1973 to 1990, before moving to Wappinger and then Cold Spring in the Hudson Valley. Since 2012 he has been based in Maple City, Michigan. He began work on his *Jerry's Map* (plate 13) project in 1963 while working in North Africa in the Peace Corps, after having studied to be an architect at the University of Michigan and UC Berkeley.[1] It started as scribbled drawings of an invented world in lead pencil and ballpoint pen on typing paper and has since expanded to its present extent, at more than 1,800 square feet and consisting of more than 3,200 10-by-8-inch panels. There are currently three complete sets of the *Map*: one master in the studio in Michigan; a full second version recently displayed at MASS MoCA in North Adams, Massachusetts, and now at the Palais de Tokyo, Paris;[2] and a third set, a portion of which is in *River Crossings*. The back of each panel has its exhibition history, called its "pedigree," and the map continues to expand, although the quadrants into which it now moves are determined by chance, using a modified deck of 114 playing cards with crafted instructions, in a nod to Dada and early experiments with chance in Western art in the last century. Surfaces can be covered with heavy, dense collage and then paint. Recent iterations of the map have included what the artist calls an invasive "Void"—regions of white that have been moving over the imagined landscape, blanking out areas. These are evident in some of the panels on display at Cedar Grove. Across the surfaces there are invented names for waterways, streets, parks, cities, etc., such as "Yagoria" or "Dedalus Park." As in Stephen Hannock's paintings with text (plate 15), Gretzinger incorporates people he knows, artists, and locations into the personal nomenclature that he has developed in the *Map*, and as in J.R.R. Tolkien's writings, has dreamt up new languages specific to each of what he terms "parishes," the conclaves of human activity that coalesce in sections of the scheme. There is a fine sense of fantasy, and humor, in this practice. And the variety of the quadrants is evident in the distinction between the dense urban fabric of "Ukrainia," the largest city in the entire scheme, visible on the east wall of the second-floor staircase landing, and the more amorphous, abstract, and painterly panels leading up the staircase and on the wall by Cole's bedroom that represent the extremities of the *Map*. Some of these newer panels incorporate fragments of Snyder's pretzels bags, some include works by other "guest" artists, in a kind of collaboration. Entrancing and immersive, Gretzinger's half-a-century-old, open-ended project rivals similarly scaled cartographical installations such as the lobby of the Daily News Building on East 42nd Street (1929–1930), or the Queens Museum of Art's *Panorama of the City of New York* from the World's Fair of 1964, as a source of both grandeur and wonder, and something that encourages reconsideration of one's place on the planet.[3]

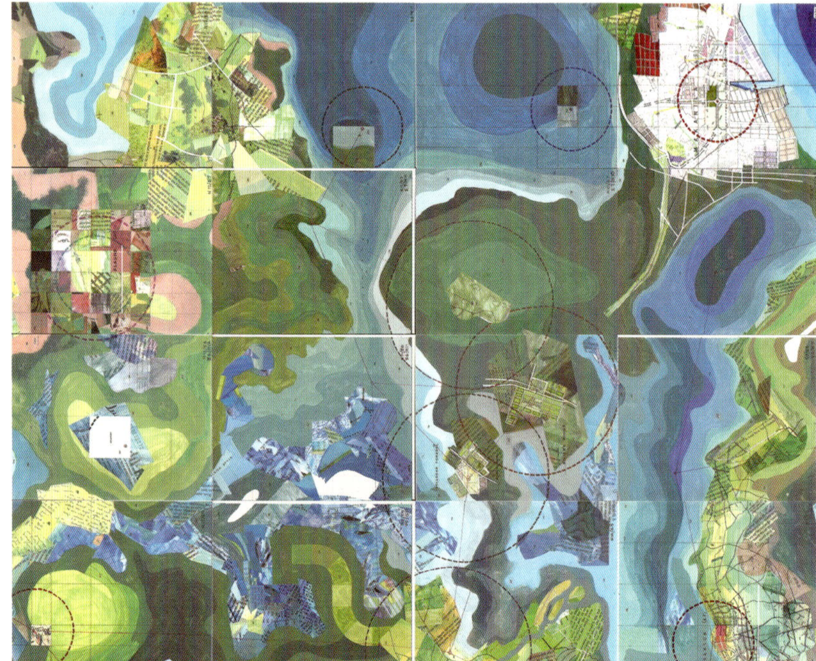

Detail of Jerry's Map.

1. Conversation with the artist, April 23, 2015. Gretzinger's website is an invaluable source of information about the project: http://jerrysmap.blogspot.com.

2. http://www.massmoca.org/event_details.php?id=760.

http://www.palaisdetokyo.com/en/exhibition/jerry-gretzinger.

See also Philippe Rekacewicz, " Jerry Gretzinger's Magic Maps," in *Magazine Palais* 21 (2015), 72–87.

3. http://www.queensmuseum.org/2013/10/panorama-of-the-city-of-new-york.

Jerry's Map, 1963 to present, site-specific installation. Ink, pencil, acrylic, and paper collage on heavy paper, dimensions variable. Courtesy of the artist.

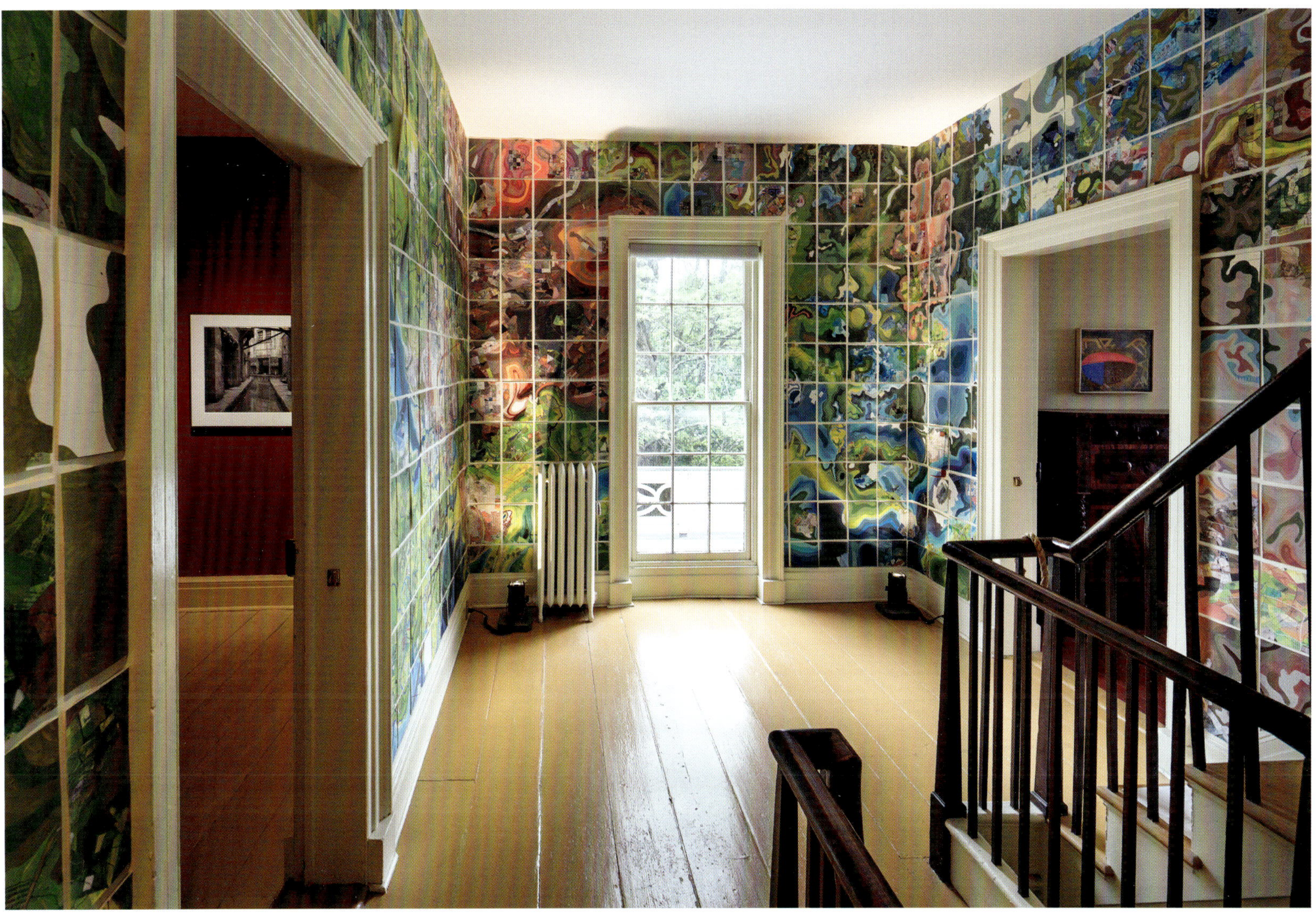

PLATE 13

In *Untitled (After Golden Delicious) II*, of 1972, the Chicago-born
Murray conveyed a physical sense of paint in a low and wide picture
that was part of a series of works marked by painted borders and
inner elements—here an arc—that seem determined by the edges
of the canvases. Such works reveal her interest in Paul Cézanne
(1839–1906), Cubism, Surrealism, postwar American abstraction, and
then-all-pervasive Minimalism, but her active surfaces, emphatically
hand-drawn lines, and energetic colors were bold for abstract painting in the period. Educated at The Art Institute of Chicago and Mills
College in Oakland, California, Murray taught at Rosary Hill College
in Buffalo from 1965 to 1967, and then moved to Manhattan to paint
and work at the Dwight School, during which time she painted this
work. From 1974 to 1977, she taught at Bard College in Annandale-on-
Hudson, and then again in 1999. The title of the picture alludes both to
the variety of apple, long a staple of New York State cultivators, and
the Golden Section, related to the mathematics of Euclid and Renaissance and Baroque aesthetic and architectural theory. Murray recalled
that to produce her surfaces she would "let things sit for a few days
so they'd get dry enough to smush them down and carve into them. I
couldn't use as much paint as I wanted to because I couldn't afford it."[1]
Such exercises in formal rigor, with their inexact cherry-red borders
and pulsing internal arcs, would soon expand to break free from traditional rectangular supports into the playful shapes and forms built
of similarly strident colors—with irregularly shaped edges floating in
space—of her mature style from the later 1970s until her death in 2007
in Washington County, New York, where she had resided since 1982.

---

1. Robert Storr, *Elizabeth Murray* (New York: The Museum of Modern Art, 2005), 175.

Untitled (After Golden Delicious) II, 1972. Oil on
canvas, 14¼ x 54 in. (36.2 x 137.2 cm). No. 45921
Alt # PTNG1972.7, Pace Gallery. © 2015 The Murray-
Holman Family Trust / Artists Rights Society (ARS),
New York.

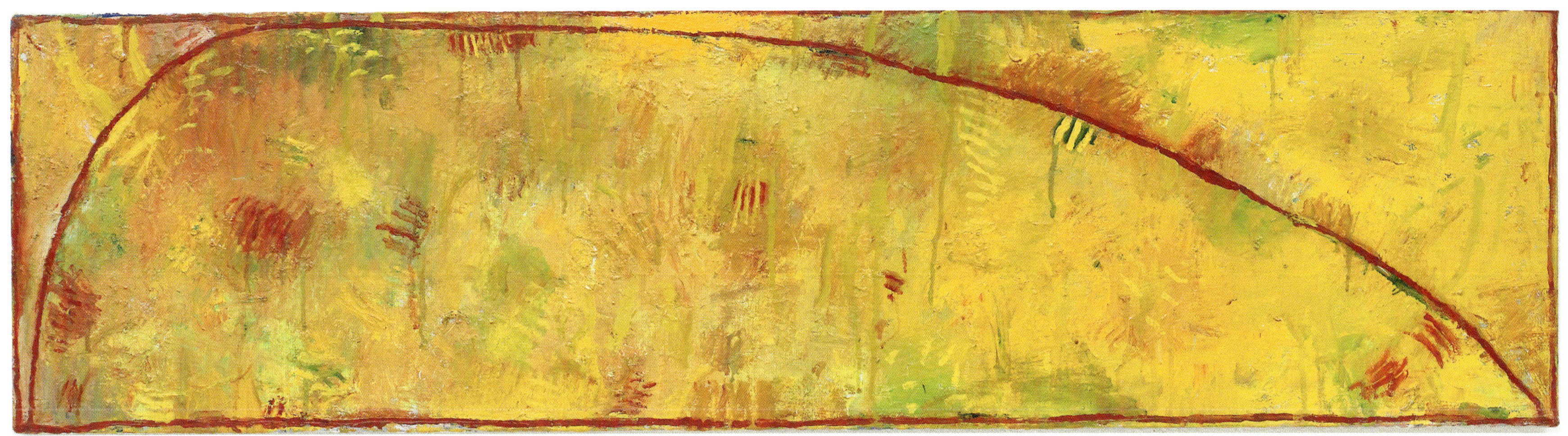

PLATE 14

Hannock's painting practice is a sophisticated channeling of the subject matter and scope of Cole and Church, and in his large works it is overlaid with pasted materials redolent of his own experience and inscribed across sections of the surface with block-print text that serves a similar function. No mere topographical transcriptions, Hannock's personalized landscapes serve as panoramic and cinematic templates for the artist's stories, presented as stream of consciousness, nostalgic musings, or the recitation of autobiographical history. Born in Albany, New York, Hannock went to college in the Connecticut River Valley, where he first began to use the Oxbow as a subject. He later lived in Manhattan and now has a studio in North Adams, Massachusetts, and considers MASS MoCA his home institution. In 2013, Hannock became the first artist to receive the Frederic E. Church Award from The Olana Partnership.

As Church did, Hannock rides the rails between Albany/Hudson and New York City, and was inspired on one such journey by the dusk effects on the river looking west from Garrison to paint *Homage to the River Keeper* (plate 16), the larger version of which, with written text, is in the Albany Institute of History & Art. In it, the hills of Highland Falls on the river's right bank, dotted with will-o'-the-wisp-like lights, merge with the fog-enshrouded Hudson below. As in nearly all of Hannock's paintings, there is no foreground; instead, vision is led directly into distance. Despite the moniker given to Cole and Church of being members of the "Hudson River School," these artists rarely focused on the river itself as subject. Its impressive breadth defeated them. Often it lies, narrowed and diminutive, in the paralleled middle ground of their landscapes, but the river is too wide and normally too rigidly linear to provide the kind of circuitous incident that the Connecticut does, in the marvel of the Oxbow. Hannock's *The Oxbow, Flooded, for Frank Moore and Dan Hodermarsky (MASS MoCA #196)* (plate 15) is the latest iteration of his trademark depiction of this location, one that has been his subject for more than 20 years. In his transformation of Cole's image from The Metropolitan Museum of Art (fig. 1), Hannock has flooded the omega-shape bend of the Connecticut River in this view from Skinner Park on Mount Holyoke and added railway embankments and highways, while expanding the mountain range to the west. Close viewing of the work will reveal the pasted papers and scrawled text lying under layers of acrylic and oil glazes, polished using power sanders in the artist's original and luminescent style. It is dedicated to Dan Hodermarsky, who first stirred a passion for art in Hannock while teaching him in high school at Deerfield Academy, and Hodermarsky's nephew Frank Moore, whose works are featured in *River Crossings* in the Kitchen Alcove at Cedar Grove (plates 30 and 31). Hannock's *Oxbow* hangs on the east wall of the West Parlor in Cole's house, its back to the Hudson that streams past the property less than 2,500 feet to the east. But as noted above, the Hudson was more conduit than subject for these artists. And, as Church brilliantly realized at Olana, it could be corralled into performing as a picturesque motif through distance, being viewed from a height and being dwarfed to a degree by the majesty of the Catskills range beyond. This is what Hannock has done to the Connecticut River in his stirring and winged views of the Oxbow.

The Oxbow, Flooded, for Frank Moore and Dan Hodermarsky (Mass MoCA #196), 2013. Polished mixed media on canvas over panel, 48 x 72 x 1 in. (121.9 x 182.9 x 2.54 cm). Collection of Yale University Art Gallery, gift of Tiger and Caroline Williams, Class of '84. Photograph: David Lachman.

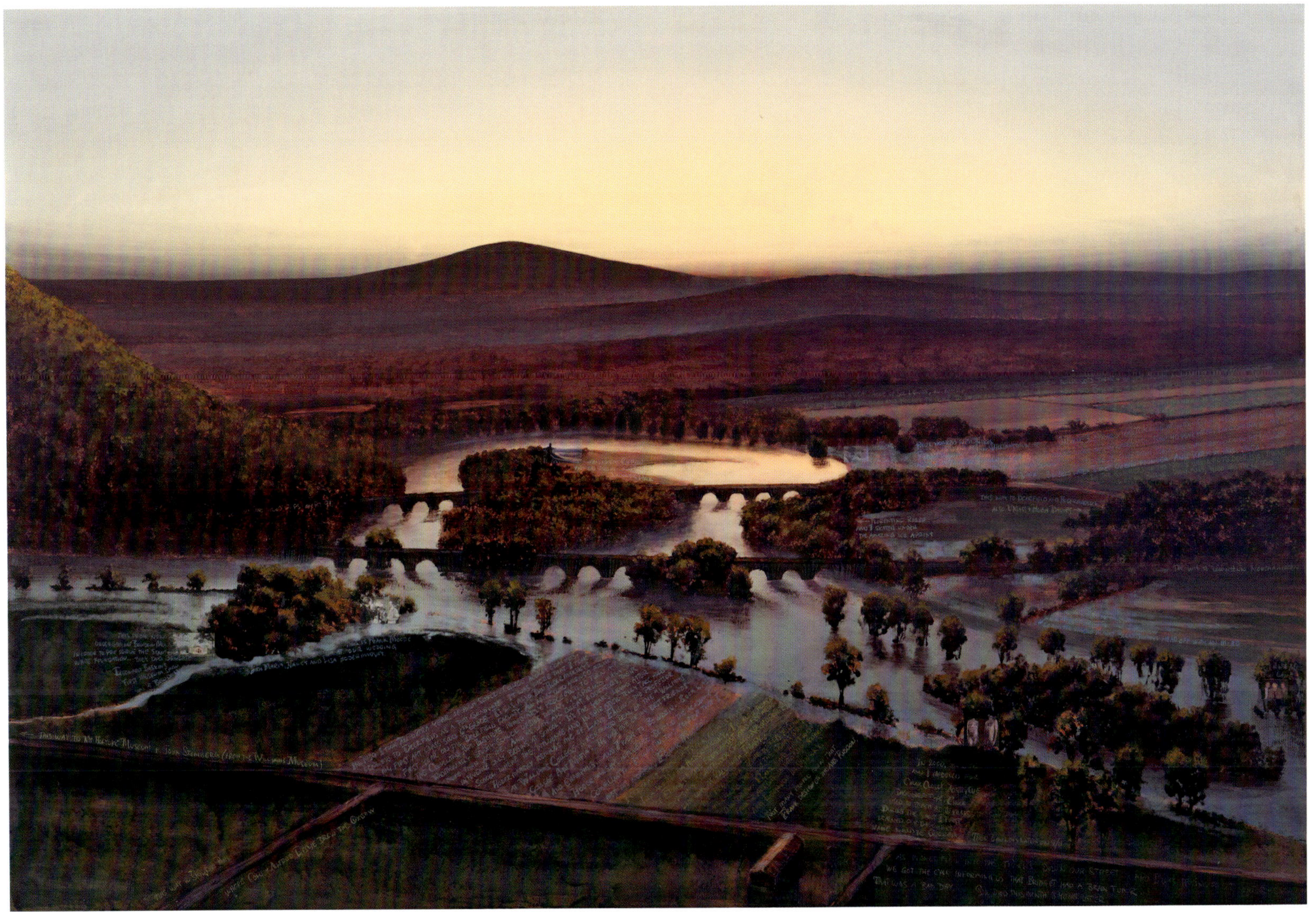

PLATE 15

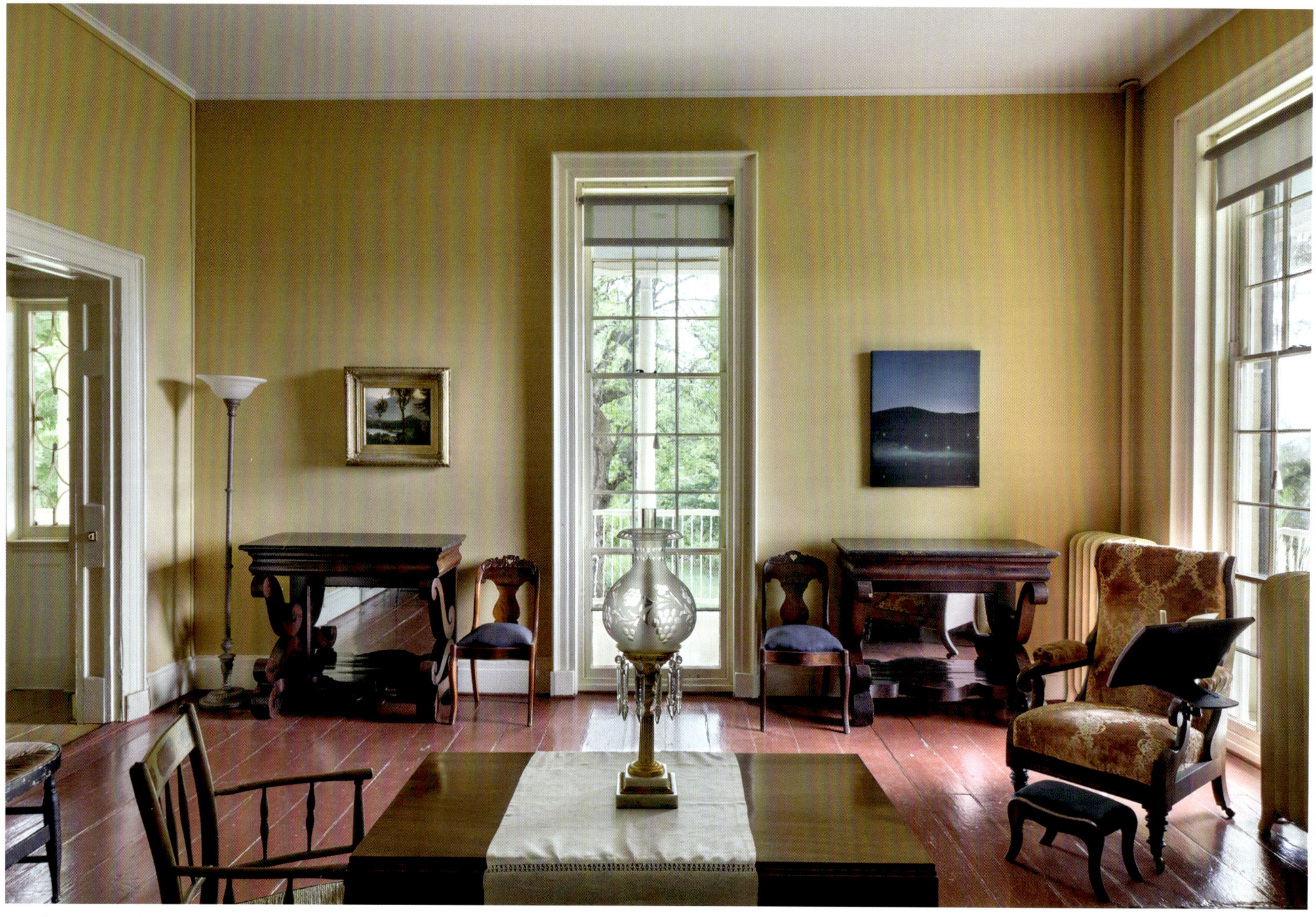

Stephen Hannock, *Homage to the River Keeper*, 1993 (plate 16) in the West Parlor.

Homage to the River Keeper, 1993. Polished oil on canvas, 30 x 24⅛ in. (76.2 x 61.3 cm). Bowdoin College Museum of Art, Brunswick, Maine; gift of the artist. Photograph courtesy of Bowdoin College Museum of Art.

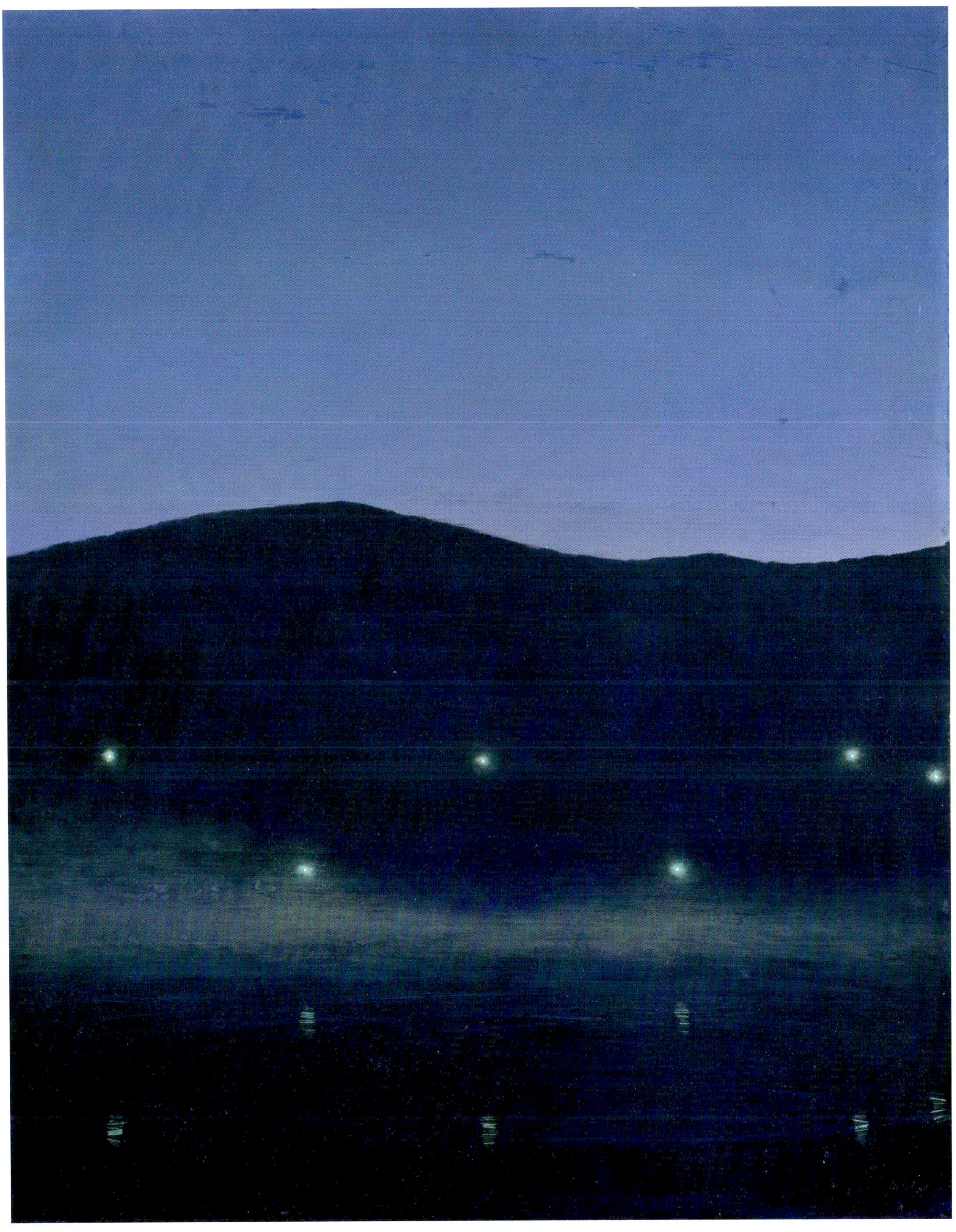

PLATE 16

CINDY **SHERMAN** (b. 1954)

Along with the work of Chuck Close (plate 35) and the recently deceased On Kawara (1932–2014), Sherman's exploration of cultural identity and art history in her photographic self-portraiture, or perhaps better described as her photographs in which she uses herself as model, represents the most compelling and conceptually consistent body of work in contemporary art today. Raised on Long Island in Huntington Beach, New York, Sherman studied fine arts at SUNY Buffalo State College, which is where she began her career.[1] The present series of 12 prints made in 2011 derive from the last work she made before moving to Manhattan from Buffalo in July 1977, a set of 35 cutout images of herself as various characters linked with hands touching titled *Line-up for Linda from Robert* (fig. 2).[2] Four images are included in this exhibition. The original cut-outs showed her transformation from posed standing in a long white dress to wearing a long black dress, with interstitial images resulting in her seeming to be an aviator or jockey, a toreador, then donning a mask and satin jump pants,

and evolving into a type of dominatrix figure or carnival-clad reveler. Such transitional identities, treated almost like the stop-motion nineteenth-century photographs of Eadweard Muybridge (1830–1904), and joined in a grouping like paper dolls, were transformed in the present prints into full-sheet works that reveal the environs of her Buffalo studio, with visible outlet and plugs, a seam in the wall board, her shadow on the left, and the calculatedly positioned cropped edge of a stool. This privileges the process, technique, and fiction over the emphasis on transformation and tradability in the original *Line-up* of 1977.

---

1. For this period, see Gabriele Schor, *Cindy Sherman: The Early Works 1975–1977* (Ostfildern, Germany: Hatje Cantz Verlag, 2012).

2. Ibid., 78–80.

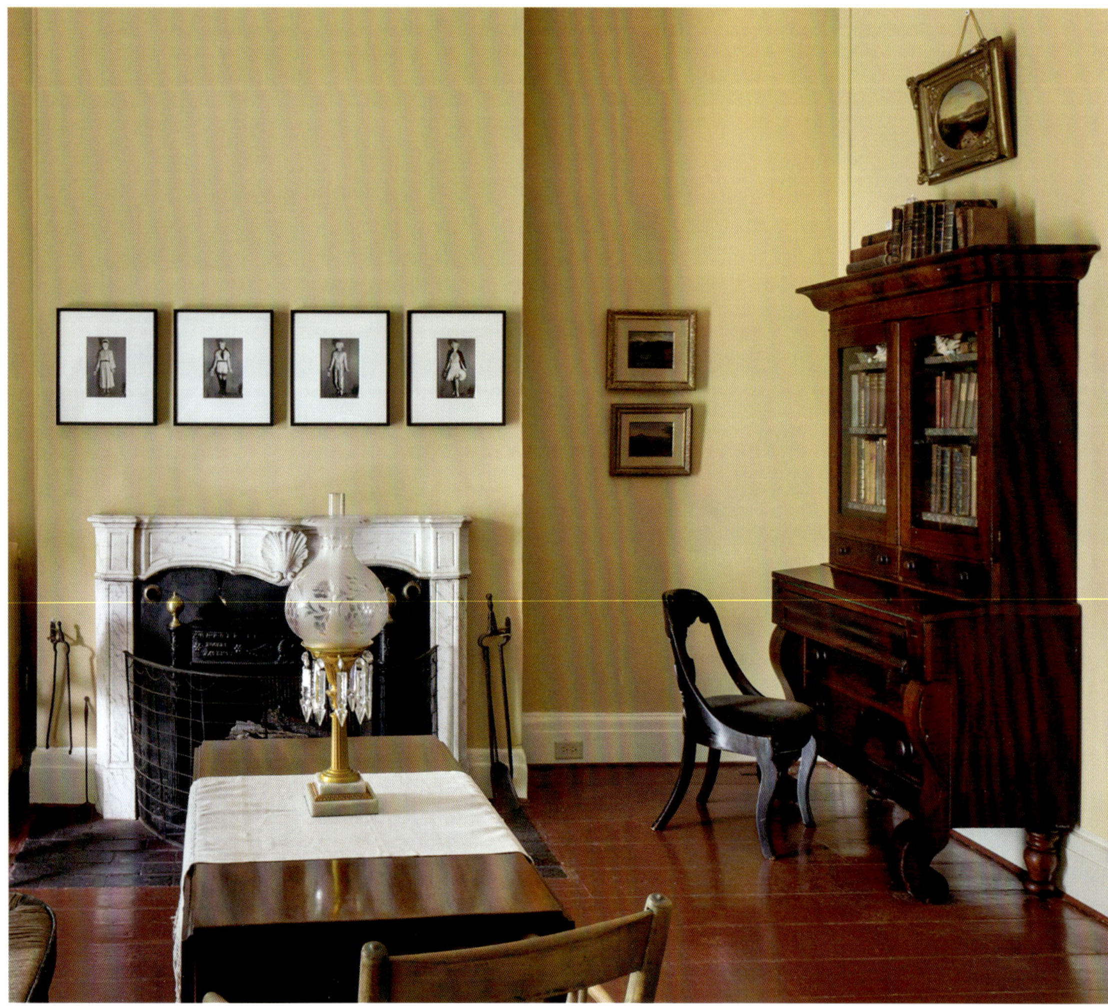

Cindy Sherman, *Untitled #507*, 1977/2011; *Untitled #502*, 1977/2011; *Untitled #505*, 1977/2011; and *Untitled #501*, 1977/2011 (plates 17–20) in the West Parlor.

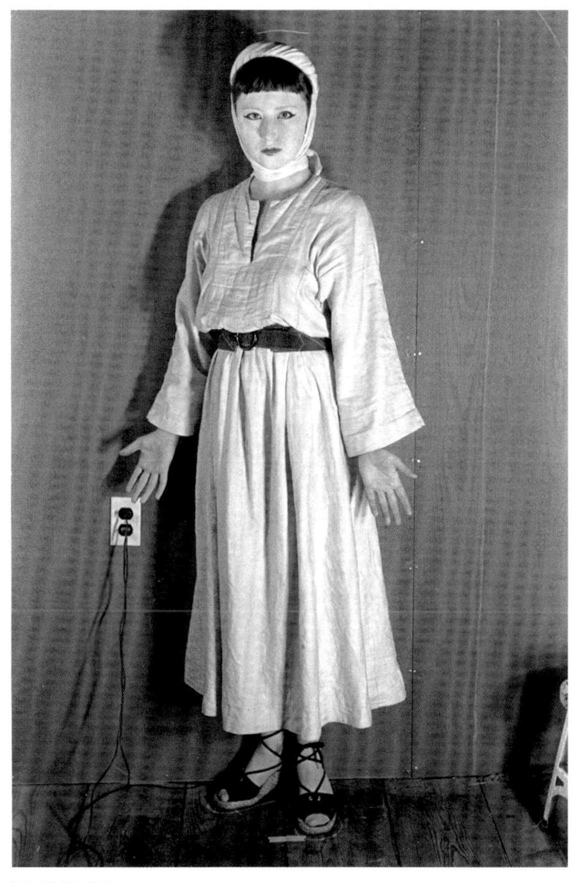

PLATE 17

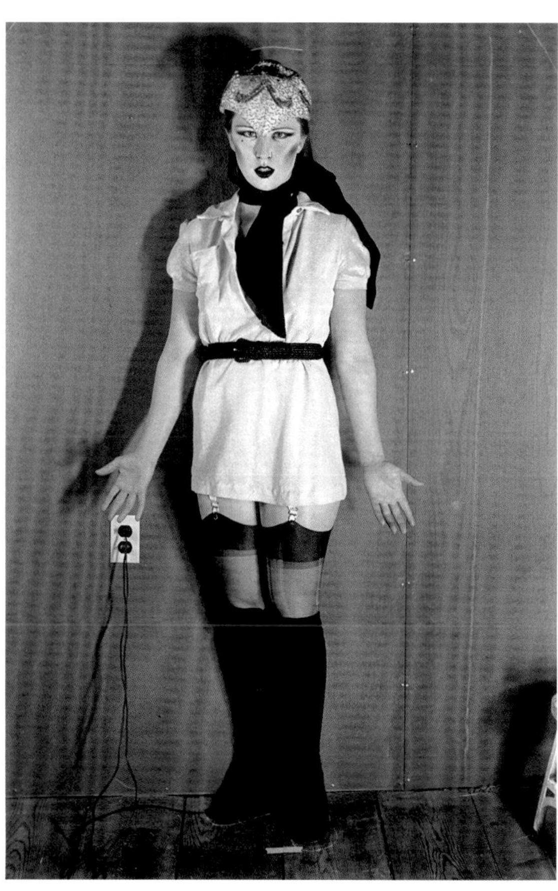

PLATE 18

LEFT TO RIGHT, TOP TO BOTTOM

Untitled #507, Untitled #502, Untitled #505, Untitled #501, 1977/2011. Gelatin silver prints, images: 8¾ x 6⅞ in. (22.2 x 17.5 cm); frames: 17 x 15 in. (43.2 x 38.1 cm). Collection of the artist. Courtesy of the artist and Metro Pictures, New York, NY.

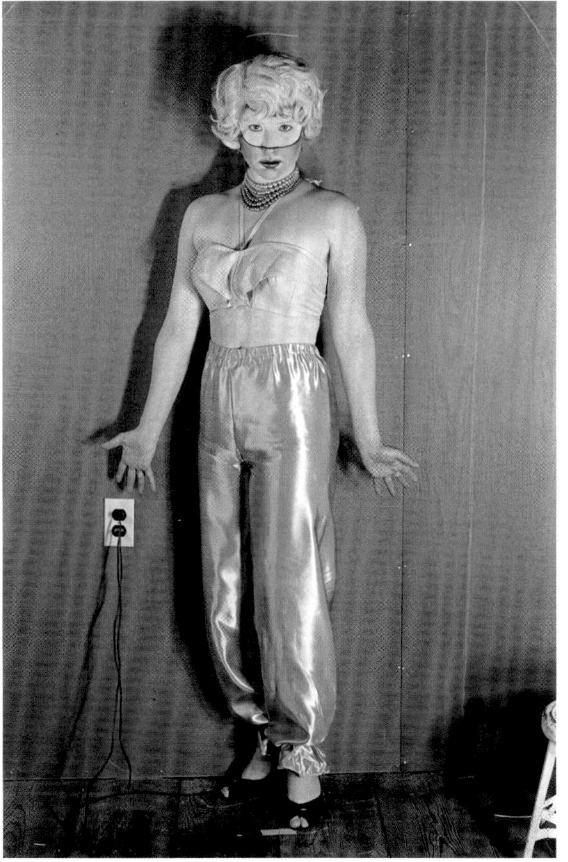

PLATE 19

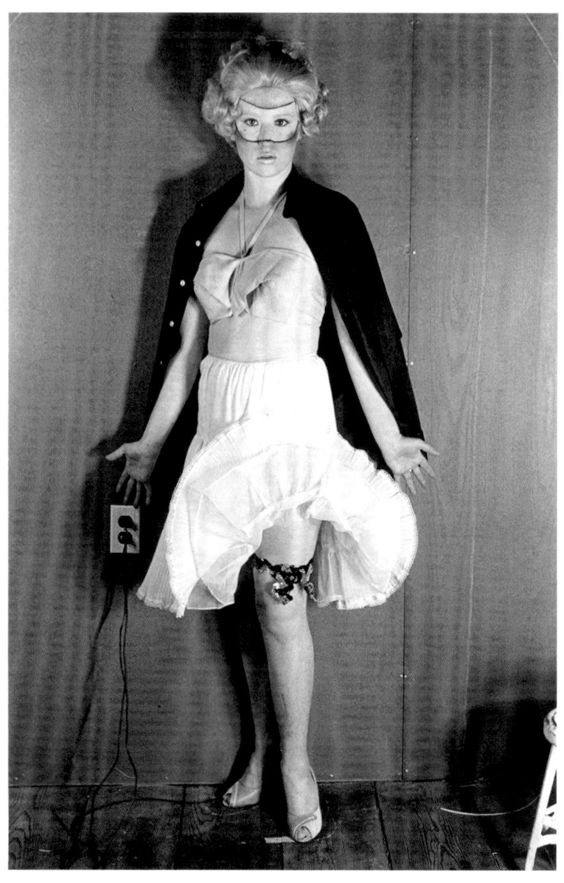

PLATE 20

ANGIE **KEEFER** (b. 1977)

Artist, writer, editor, and co-founder with David Reinfurt (b. 1971) and Stuart Bailey (b. 1973) of *The Serving Library*,[1] Angie Keefer was born in Huntsville, Alabama, and she lives and works in Hudson and Catskill. Her highly responsive artistic practice is resolutely inclusive, often favoring collaboration over individual exertions, sometimes through direct orchestration or enablement of other artists' initiatives. This is most evident in the works she created with Kara Hamilton and Kianja Strobert (plates 23 and 24) for *River Crossings*. But there are two other installations at Cedar Grove that represent her own endeavors, and both metaphorically and literally deal with economic issues. In *Area Variance* (plate 21), Keefer painted the front facades of two connected houses on Columbia Street in Hudson with a tawny-gold, auto-body pigment. After the local council blocked a plan to tear down the houses and build new apartments, the owners unsuccessfully continued to seek an "area variance" in order to replace the dilapidated properties before inviting Keefer to use them as a canvas. The valuation of the work—consisting of a large-format photograph printed on Duraflex iridescent paper, mounted in a gilded frame, and lit by a sharply focused theater spotlight—is the most recent sale price of the property in Hudson. The rear-projected *Fountain* (plate 22) is controlled by live stock market data delivered via web server. Previously installed in the Whitney Biennial of 2014 and in landscape format, where it featured footage of a man-made waterfall in Zurich blended with stock imagery, this portrait-format iteration includes multiple views that Keefer shot of water coursing over Niagara Falls projected onto a transparent screen. As with *Area Variance*, the valuation of the piece is fluid, in this case symbolically equivalent in dollars to the total points of the Dow Industrial Average at the time of sale. The projection emulates abstract painting in glowing pixels, with Niagara's flowing water running forward or backward, depending on whether commodities futures indexes are rising or falling. An essay titled "Futures," which is rewritten and republished each time the work is exhibited, accompanies *Fountain*.[2] The title *Fountain* is a loaded one in terms of the history of art, calling to mind Marcel Duchamp's (1887–1968) reconfigured readymade urinal of 1917. It also is linked metaphorically with the dual roles of fountains in cities and gardens since ancient times— the propagandistic largesse of the powerful in supplying potable water to large populations in cities, as in Rome—and displays of aqueous aesthetics and dialogues of control at private residences such as Chatsworth in England and Versailles in France. The selection of Niagara as source for the imagery in Keefer's *Fountain* is one that also celebrates American distinctiveness and was a prime subject in both Cole's and Church's art, and their own economic successes as artists.[3]

1. http://www.servinglibrary.org.

2. Angie Keefer, "Futures." http://www.servinglibrary.org/read.html?id=150085.

3. See John F. Sears, *Sacred Places: American Tourist Attractions in the Nineteenth Century* (Amherst: University of Massachusetts Press, 1998).

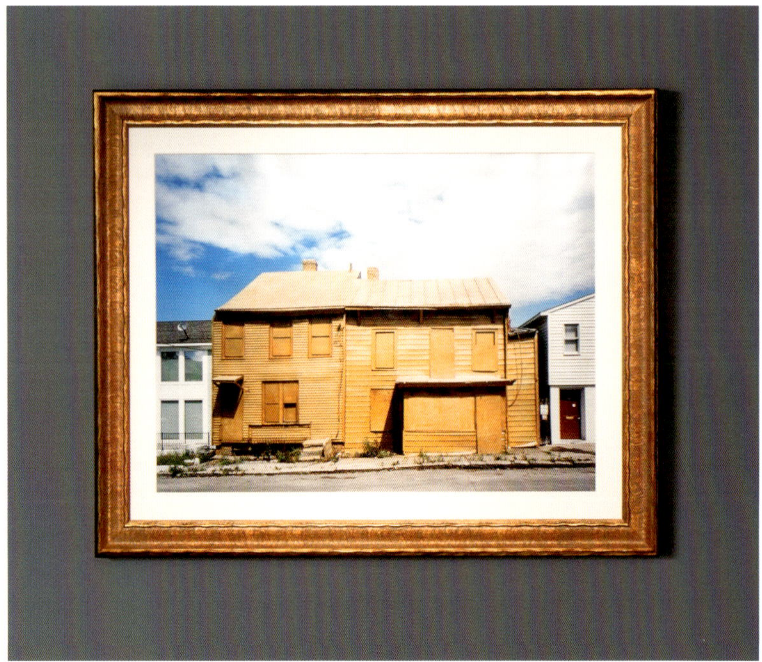

PLATE 21

Area Variance, 2014. Duraflex print, gilded frame, and attenuated spotlight , 30 x 40 in. (76.2 x 101.6 cm). Artist's proof. Collection of the artist. Site-specific installation.

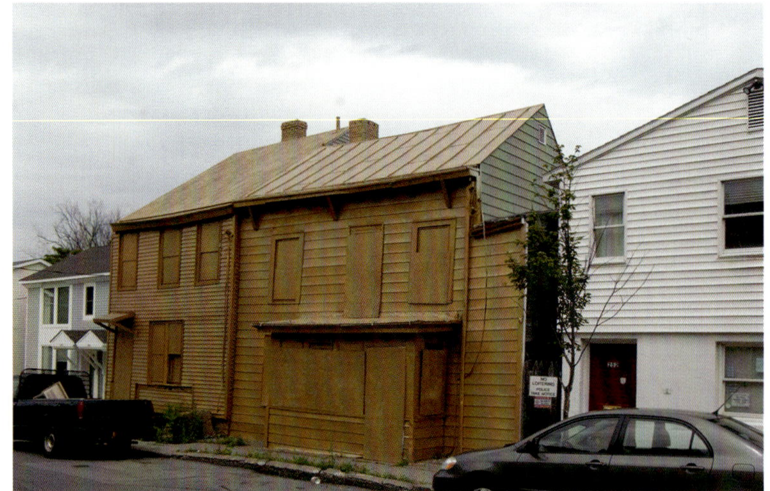

Conjoined houses, Hudson, New York, 2014. Photograph courtesy of the author.

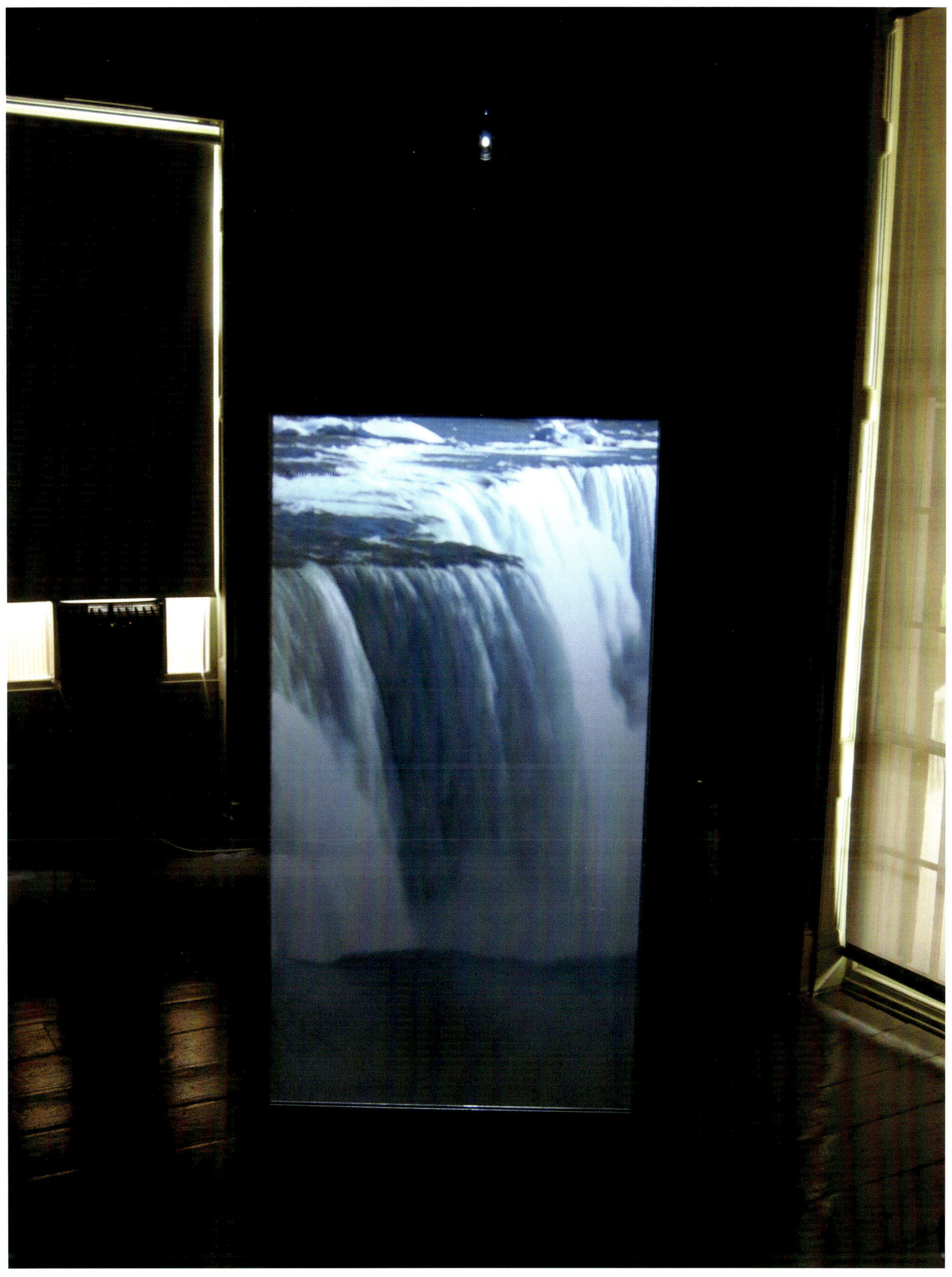

PLATE 22

Fountain, 2014. Projector, transparent rear projection screen, computer, and commodities futures indexes data; dimensions variable. Courtesy of the artist. Site-specific installation. Photograph courtesy of the author.

ANGIE **KEEFER** (b. 1977) and KARA **HAMILTON** (b. 1967)

Keefer met Hamilton at Yale University, where the latter was a teaching assistant for one of her classes. Hamilton lived for many years in Ulster County and has recently returned to her native Toronto. A short while ago, the two collaborated with David Reinfurt on a publication of Hamilton's jewelry presented as an auction catalogue and titled *Old Gold*. Hamilton's work forms a combination of jewelry making and sculpture, and for this installation she fabricated a floor lamp, the lens of which is made of cast glass embedded with Herkimer diamonds (plate 23). The low light levels are to accommodate safe viewing of a large daguerreotype, devised in 1839 as the earliest form of permanently fixed photography. This particular image is one of two known portraits of Thomas Cole. Unlike a photographic print made from a negative, the daguerreotype, with its exquisitely detailed image emerging from a mirrored silver background, is the negative itself; thus this object was in the presence of the painter and retains a startling power, amplified by the sense of unity with subject that arises when the viewer sees her or his own face reflected in its surface. Below the plate is a standing case full of labeled rocks and architectural fragments that Cole collected in his travels. The geological fascination encourages a return to Hamilton's lens, with its Herkimer diamonds that she surface mined herself—these are half-a-billion-year-old quartz crystals that are faceted on two ends and found in Herkimer County in the central part of the state; their popularity dates to the late-eighteenth century. A kind of fool's gold, the diamonds have been fashioned into a standing lamp, and the artists cite Edgar Allan Poe's 1840 essay, "The Philosophy of Furniture," as a reference in its musings on the value of glass and its use in domestic illumination.[1] This installation, along with *Fountain* (plate 22) and *Empire State* (plate 24) in the same room, represents a trio of works that envelope the economics of the local landscape and a kind of artistic resurgence, embodied in this exhibition.

---

1. Edgar Allan Poe, "The Philosophy of Furniture," *Burton's Gentleman's Magazine* (May 1840), pp. 243–245; http://www.eapoe.org/works/essays/philfurn.htm

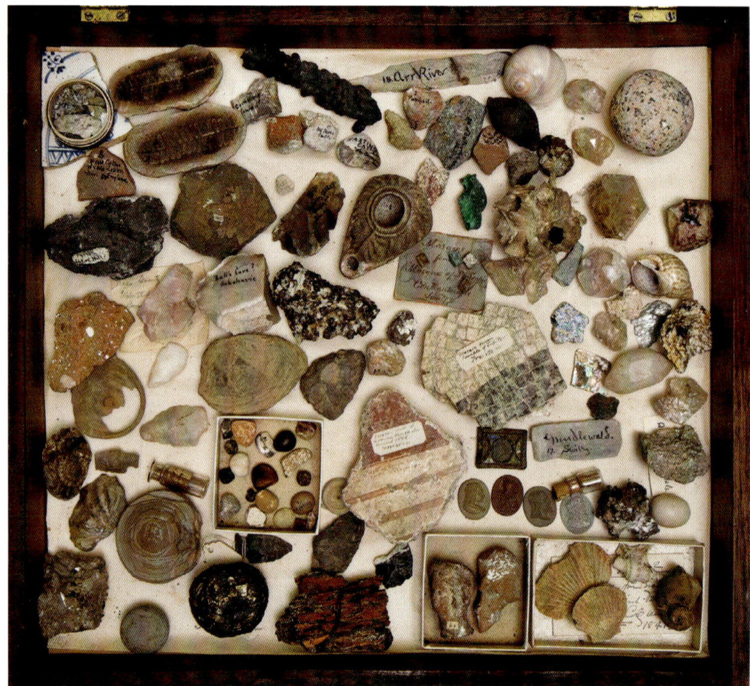

Detail of Thomas Cole's Box of Minerals, c. 1830–1848.

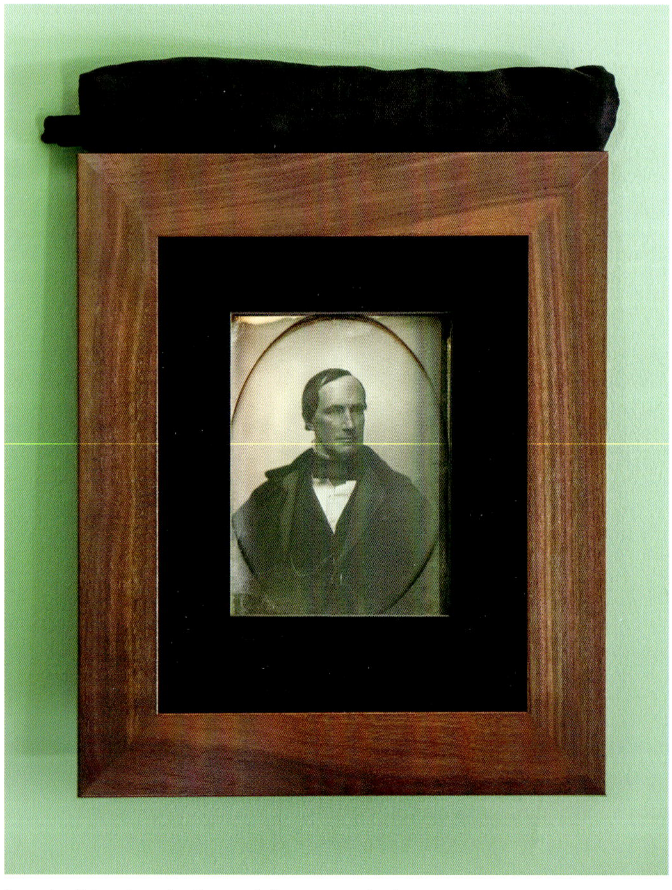

Detail of *Unidentified Man* (*Thomas Cole?*), c. 1843–1848.

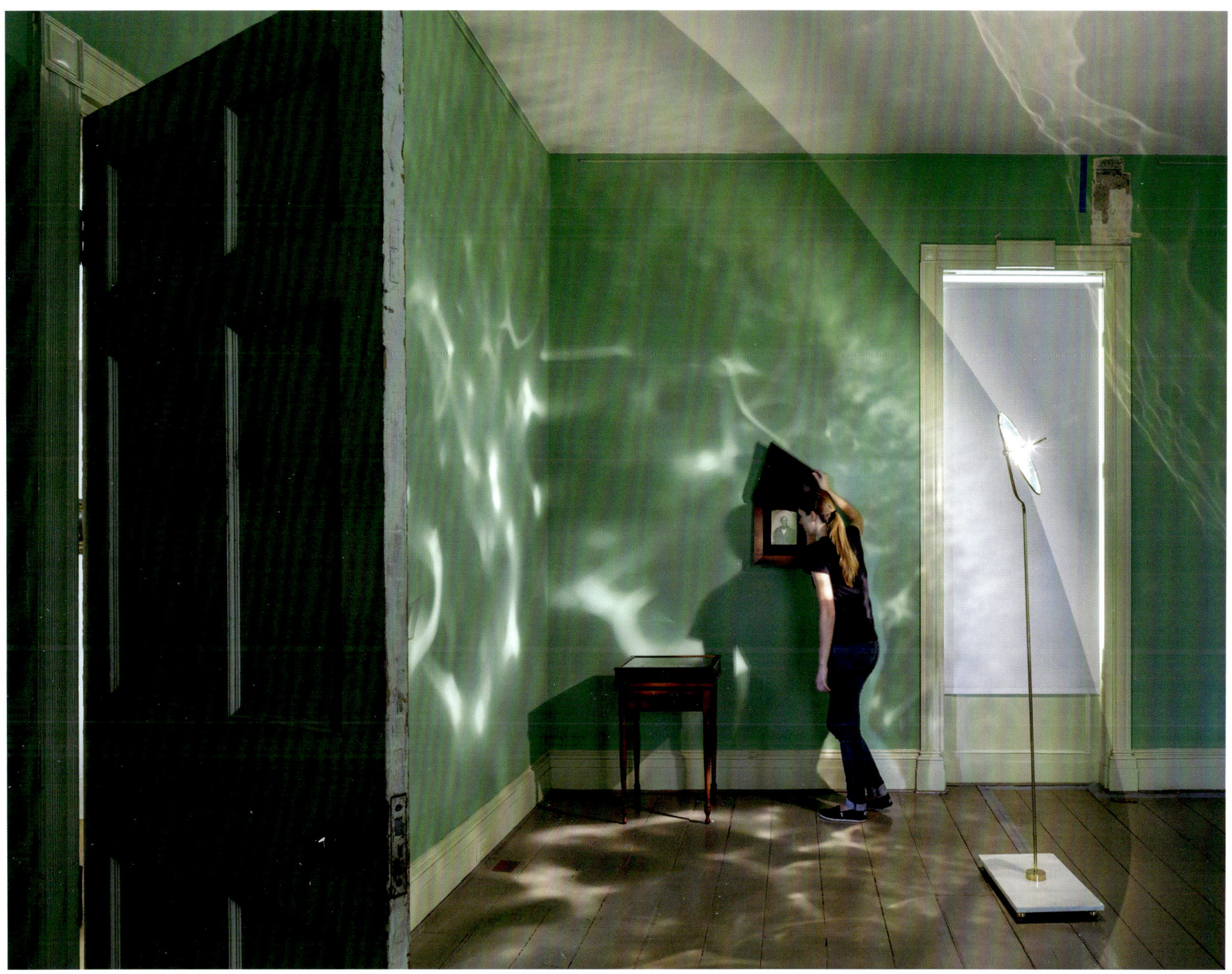

Heavy Fixture, 2014. Installation of gold, silver, stainless steel, Herkimer diamonds, and light, with Albert Sands Southworth (1811–1894) and Josiah Johnson Hawes (1808–1901), *Unidentified Man (Thomas Cole?)*, c. 1843–1848, whole plate daguerreotype, 8½ x 6½ in. (21.6 x 16.5 cm), George Eastman House, International Museum of Photography and Film, gift of Alden Scott, 1974:0193:0084; and Thomas Cole's *Box of Minerals*, c. 1830–1848. Collection of rocks, minerals, shells, and fossils, 3 x 19¾ x 18 in. (7.6 x 50.2 x 45.7 cm). Thomas Cole National Historic Site, gift of Edith Cole Silberstein and the Greene County Historical Society. Photograph: Michael Fredericks. Site-specific installation, dimensions variable. Courtesy of the artists, George Eastman House, and Thomas Cole National Historic Site.

The twin screens showing *Empire State* (plate 24) are animate post-cards that hover above the mantelpiece in the Coles' Dining Room, in a spot normally reserved in such a house for an impressive peer glass or disapproving-faced portraits. Here, at head height, are two slightly more than four-minute films that play in a loop and present, unaffect-edly, stable views of the environs and art collection of the much-un-loved Empire State Plaza in Albany, a place of High Modernism equally unfriendly to humans and artworks alike. Brightly painted geometric abstractions by lesser luminaries like Jack Youngerman's (b. 1926) *Eastward* (1967) hang in low bunker-like surroundings with their identifying plaques carelessly placed in front of them, and in any viewers' field of vision. If there were viewers, for the windswept plaza where Harrison and Abramovitz's iconic *Egg* (1966–1978) theater sits, the main goal of

people who are forced to traverse these spaces is to get, as quickly as possible and in the straightest of lines, from point A to point B. Keefer and Strobert's tribute to soulless international Modernism, and the faceless government that it seems to house, ultimately asks how we think of, experience, and treat fine art and the possibly misguided application of a presumed largesse. The collection, like Seymour Lipton's (1903–1986) metal sculpture *The Empty Room* (1964), displayed at the end of an elevator bank, off its podium, and next to a red warning sign seems lifeless and forlorn, desperate for some kind of human contact, which the artists, in a surprising and haptic act of willful dis-obedience—and empathy—provide, in caressing its unflinching and unresponsive bronze hide.

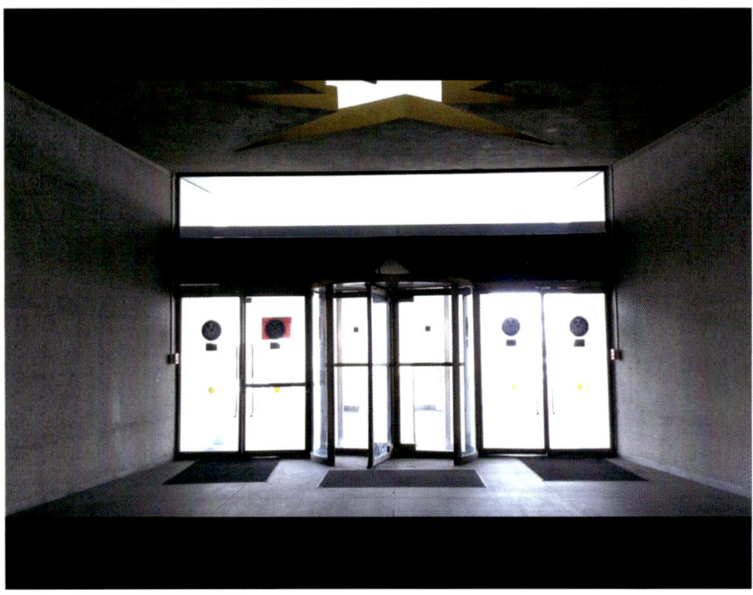

Video still, plate 24

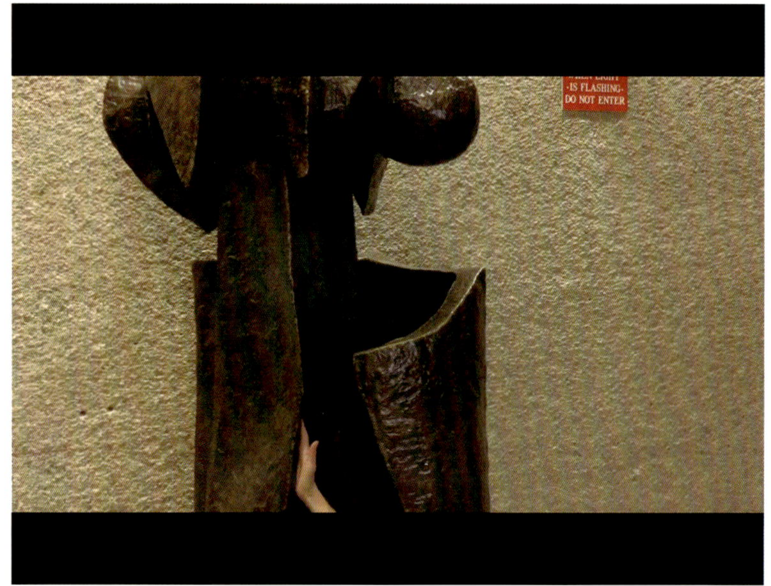

Video still, plate 24

Empire State, 2014. HD color video and two LED monitors, dimensions variable. Courtesy of the artists. Site-specific installation at Thomas Cole National Historic Site.

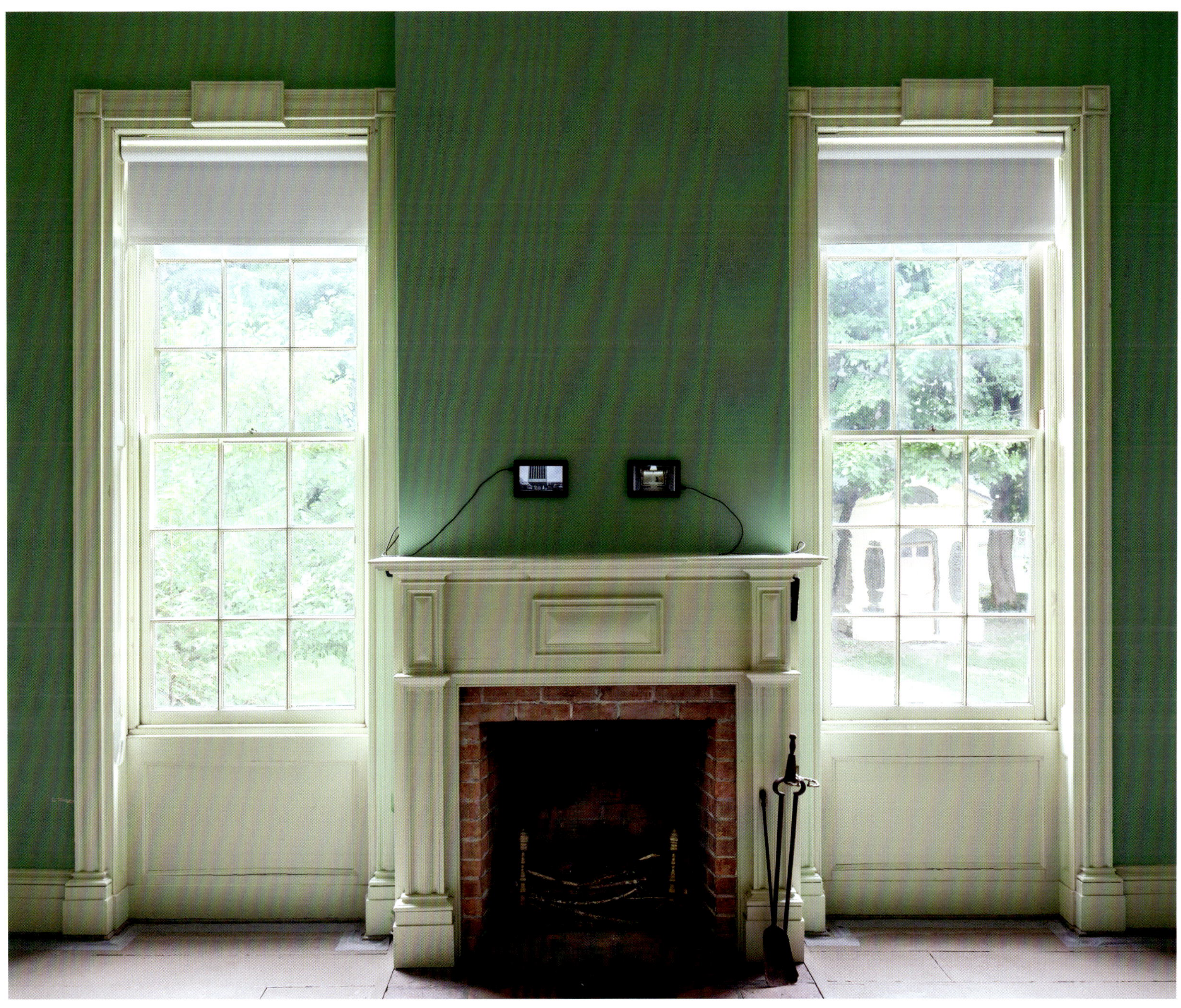

PLATE 24

KIANJA **STROBERT** (b. 1980)

Brooklyn native Kianja Strobert studied at Cooper Union in New York, The Art Institute of Chicago, and earned an MFA from Yale University. She lives and works in Hudson and recently was featured in a remarkable solo exhibition, *Of This Day in Time*, at The Studio Museum of Harlem.[1] Although noted as a studio-based artist, her film collaboration with Angie Keefer, *Empire State* (plate 24), takes her outside the creative confines and into the world. But her refined paintings on paper create whole worlds of their own, marked by dynamic conceptions of space and depth, and very fine color. Writers on Strobert's work cite prior artists such as Barnett Newman (1905–1970), Mark Rothko (1903–1970), and Sam Gilliam (b. 1933),[2] as influences and that may be so, but the clotted abstractions in Philip Guston's (1913–1980) early work, the coiled energy and complications of Lee Krasner's (1908–1984) late painted collages, and the alternatively penetrative and convex dynamics of Lee Bontecou's (b. 1931) sculptural reliefs seem more aligned to Strobert's aesthetic. *Untitled* (plate 25) is a particularly delicate example of her recent paintings, framed yet unglazed, comprised of floated pieces of paper that are covered with graphite, pumice, and enamel.

No less concerned with imagined nature, Strobert's spelunking paintings explore caverns of coloration, rewarding close looking into and about their shimmering surfaces, in a continuation of a dialogue with form, surface, and materials seen in Elizabeth Murray's work of the 1970s (plate 14). The intimately scaled *Untitled*, with its golden tonality, resembles a Byzantine icon without its Holy Family, or Andy Warhol's (1928–1987) *Gold Marilyn* (1962, MoMA) without Ms. Monroe, or the subtle variations in monochromatic tone in Chinese scroll painting. However, Strobert's color abstractions elicit connections not to religiosity, celebrity, nor landscape, but stand as new and absorbing paintings bearing a rigorous search for an abstract language of intense human connection and spatial exploration.

---

1. http://www.studiomuseum.org/exhibition/kianja-strobert-day-in-time.

2. Christopher Y. Lew, "Kianja Strobert: Serial Energy," in *Fore* (New York: The Studio Museum of Harlem, 2012), 88–89.

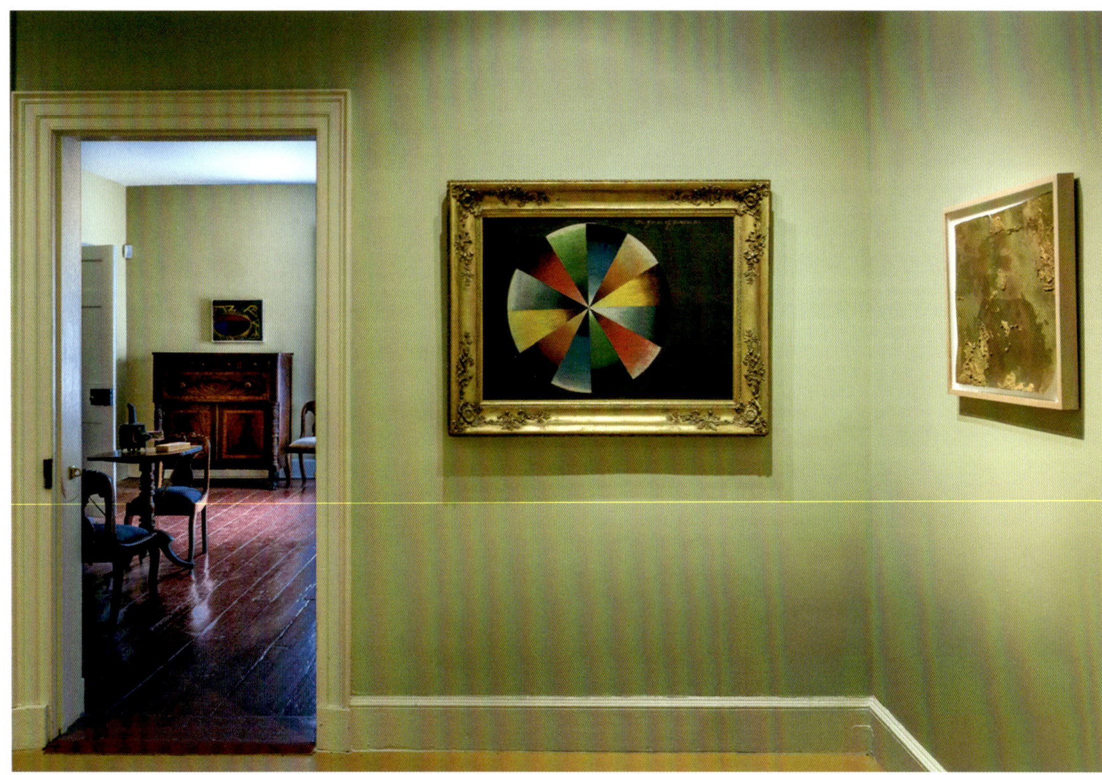

In the North Room, Kianja Strobert, *Untitled*, 2011 (plate 25) juxtaposed with Thomas Cole, *Diagram of Contrasts*, 1834, oil on panel, 23½ x 33 in. (59.7 x 83.8 cm). Collection of Richard Sharp.

Untitled, 2011. Graphite, pumice, enamel, and brush bristles on paper, 17¾ x 18½ in. (45.1 x 47 cm). Collection of Zach Feuer and Alison Fox. Photograph: Christopher Burke Studios.

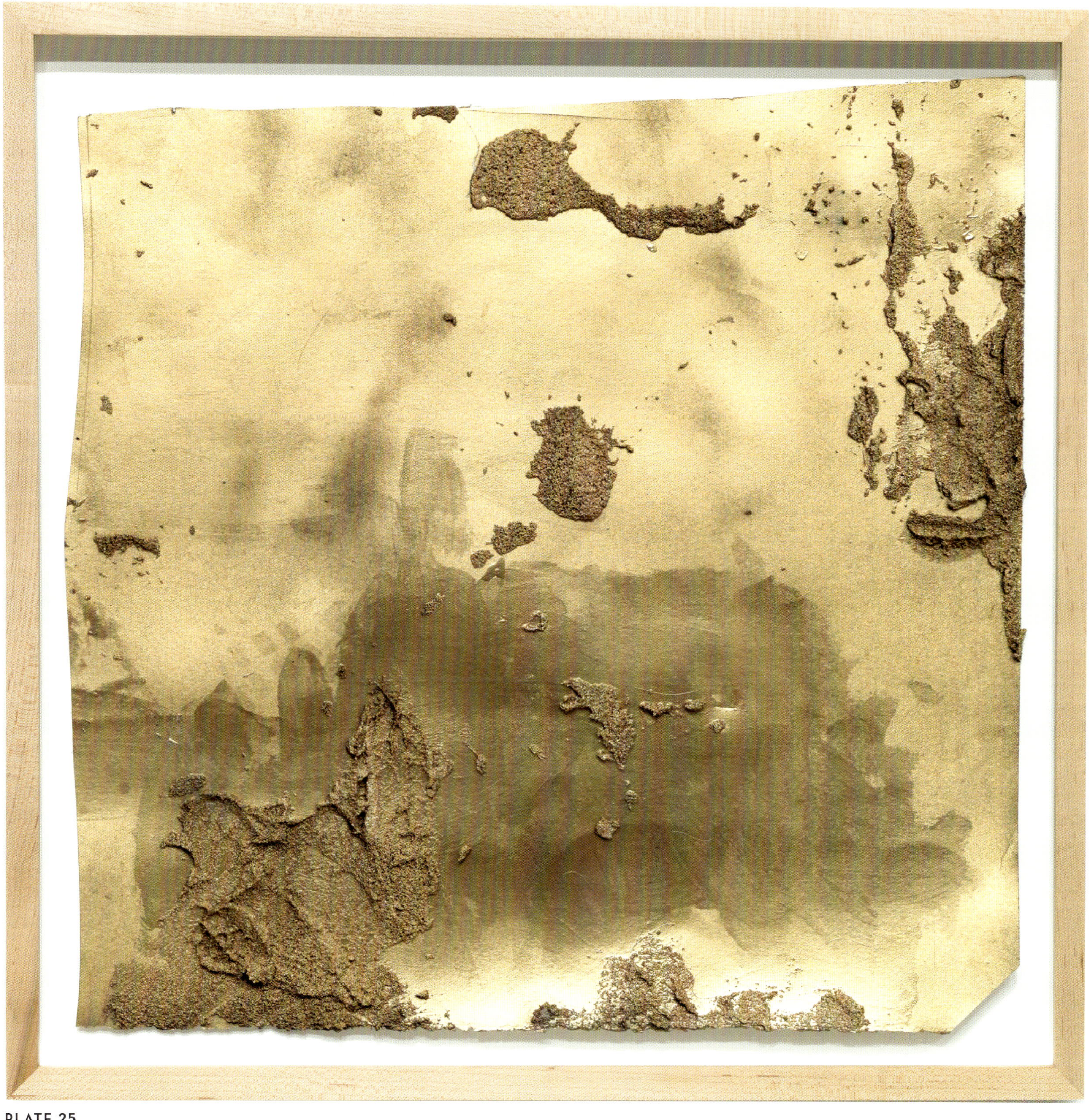

PLATE 25

Following an infancy spent in Charlotte, North Carolina, Bearden moved to New York City in 1914. He grew up there and also off and on in Pittsburgh, Pennsylvania, eventually graduating from New York University and beginning a career as a cartoonist. Establishing himself as a fine artist after wartime army service and studying in Paris, he lived on Canal Street from 1956 until his death. In 1968, he helped found the Studio Museum in Harlem. *Prelude to Farewell* (plate 26) was first exhibited at Cordier & Ekstrom Gallery in New York in 1981 as part of Bearden's autobiographical series of collages, *Profile/Part II: The Thirties*. It represents the continued evolution of a mode of art making that Bearden had pursued for more than two decades, in its use of collaged fabric, papers, foil, and paint.[1] Robert G. O'Meally has productively considered this work in terms of jazz elements in Bearden's art, revealing the status of Harlem as long the "cultural capital of black America," the personal history of the artist, and his investment in the community.[2] In *The Thirties*, Bearden presented the story of the migration of blacks from the south to the north, underpinned with echoes of autobiography. Transport is a common theme, and in *Prelude to Farewell* there is a train visible through a window or in a picture on the wall—a symbol of the idea of flight and escape to a new life, while its implied sounds add a musical aurality to the work. Other characteristic Bearden motifs include the emphasis on domestic chores and ritualistic bathing, in "works concerned with rites of ablution and purification, with confronting the disorder of the world. . ."[3] The writer Albert Murray's accompanying lines in the catalogue read: "She came to the depot in her best dress to see me off. As the train began to move she ran alongside blowing kisses," providing a sequel narrative to the represented image, with its perfectly measured composition featuring a burning stove, a totemic mother/conjur woman figure, and a modern Venus Anadyomene, these three main forms moving diagonally back in space to the right in a plunging perspectival cadence.[4]

---

1. Albert Murray, *Romare Bearden Collages, Profile/Part II: The Thirties* (New York: Cordier & Ekstrom, 1981).

2. Robert G. O'Meally, "'We Used to Say 'Stashed': Romare Bearden Paints the Blues," in Ruth Fine and Jacqueline Francis, eds., *Romare Bearden, American Modernist* (Washington, DC: National Gallery of Art, 2011), 64.

3. Ibid., 69.

4. Murray, *Romare Bearden Collages.*

Prelude to Farewell, 1981. Mixed-media collage, 49 x 37¼ in. (124.5 x 94.6 cm). The Studio Museum in Harlem; gift of Altria Group, Inc. 08.13.2. Photograph courtesy of The Studio Museum in Harlem.

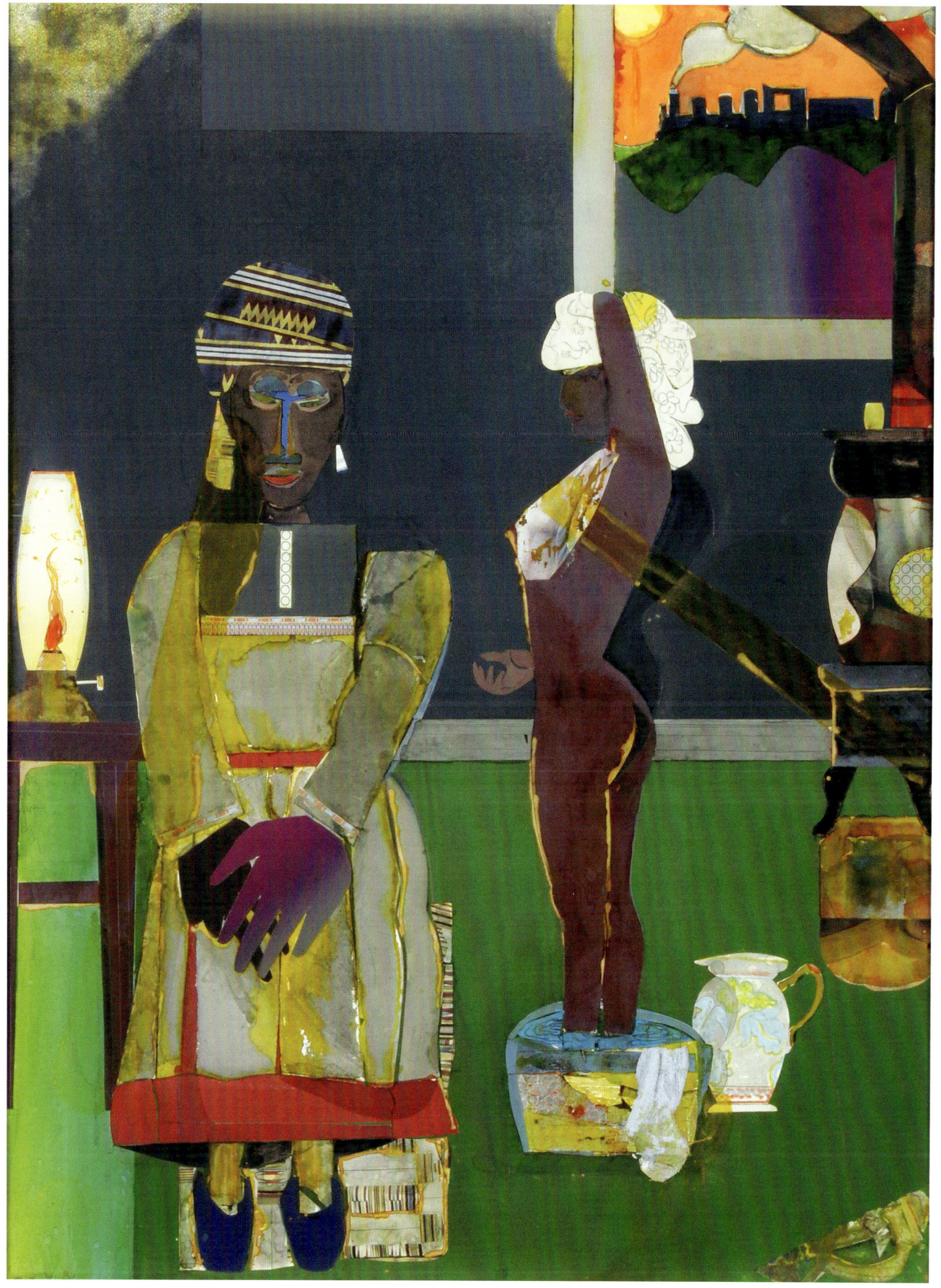

PLATE 26

SIENNA **SHIELDS** (b. 1976)

The Alaskan-born artist studied history at Lewis & Clark College in Portland, Oregon, and works in paint, collage, quilting, performance, and multiple media including video. She lives and works in New York City, and *Untitled* (plate 27) might appear to be a continued response to the geometries of urban life familiar since the scaffolded abstractions of Fernand Léger (1881–1955) and coloristic brilliance of Sonia Delaunay (1885–1979) in Paris, and especially in the New York work of Piet Mondrian (1872–1944) and Romare Bearden (plate 26). While at school she became interested in vintage fire-insurance maps wherein as buildings and lots were altered, new images of modified constructions and street schemes were layered on top of existing maps to save on costs for the municipality.[1] Along with the Modernist masters cited above, these archival collages seem to be the root of Shields's 6-foot-high, imposing works such as *Untitled*, with its shimmering collaged surface of painted paper using acrylics and oils. The technique involves glazing bits of paper with various types of pigments and treating them as *froissage* elements—crumpling them up and overlaying randomly splattered paint onto the wrinkled forms. Then the paper is ripped and cut into segments to be pasted into compositions.[2] Works such as *Untitled* may seem to "hint at an abstracted urban topography," as Tasha Parker has written, but they more closely resemble a satellite photograph of inhabited realms of the earth, with darker areas reading as forest or bodies of water, absent of civilization, blended with the patchwork nature of cultivated land seen from above—a bifurcated vision similar to that of Thomas Cole in his *Oxbow* (fig. 1), with its dichotomy between sublime darkened and storm-tossed unruly nature at left and vision of peaceful agrarian enterprise in a cultivated picturesque landscape at right. Shields's works contain a similarly ambivalent view of nature, but they do not seem so much maplike they do generalized notions of blocks of human incursions into the landscape, evidence of what the exploration of unsettled nature has begot, and in this sense linked to the photographic landscape work of Letha Wilson (plates 43 and 44).

---

1. Tasha Parker, "Sienna Shields: A Middle Landscape," in *Fore* (New York: The Studio Museum of Harlem, 2012), 86–87.

2. Joyce Lovelace, "Intuitive Mapping," *American Craft Magazine* (April/May 2013); http://craftcouncil.org/magazine/article/intuitive-mapping.

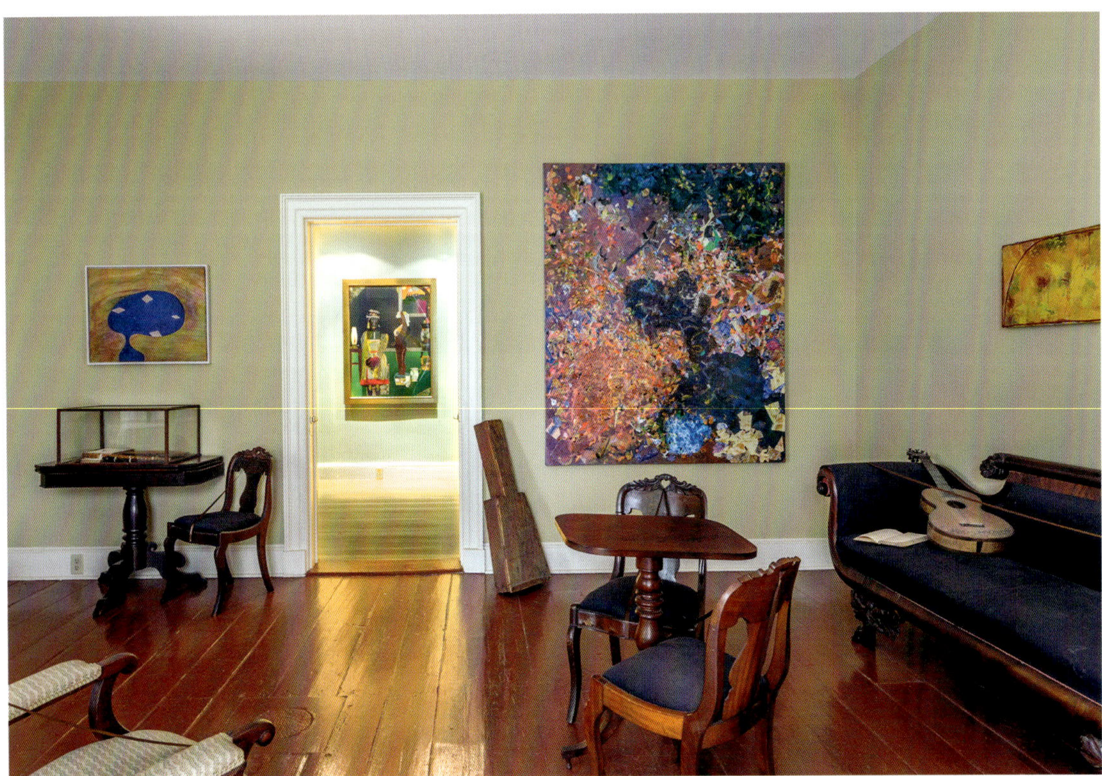

Romare Bearden, *Prelude to Farewell*, 1981 (plate 26) in the North Room; Thomas Nozkowski, *Untitled (9-3)*, 2011 (plate 5); Sienna Shields, *Untitled*, 2010 (plate 27); and Elizabeth Murray, *Untitled (After Golden Delicious) II*, 1972 (plate 14) in the Sitting Room.

Untitled, 2010. Acrylic paint and paper on canvas, 72 x 60 in. (182.9 x 152.4 cm). The Studio Museum in Harlem; Museum purchase made possible by gifts from Carol Sutton Lewis and Amelia Ogunlesi. Photograph: Sienna Shields.

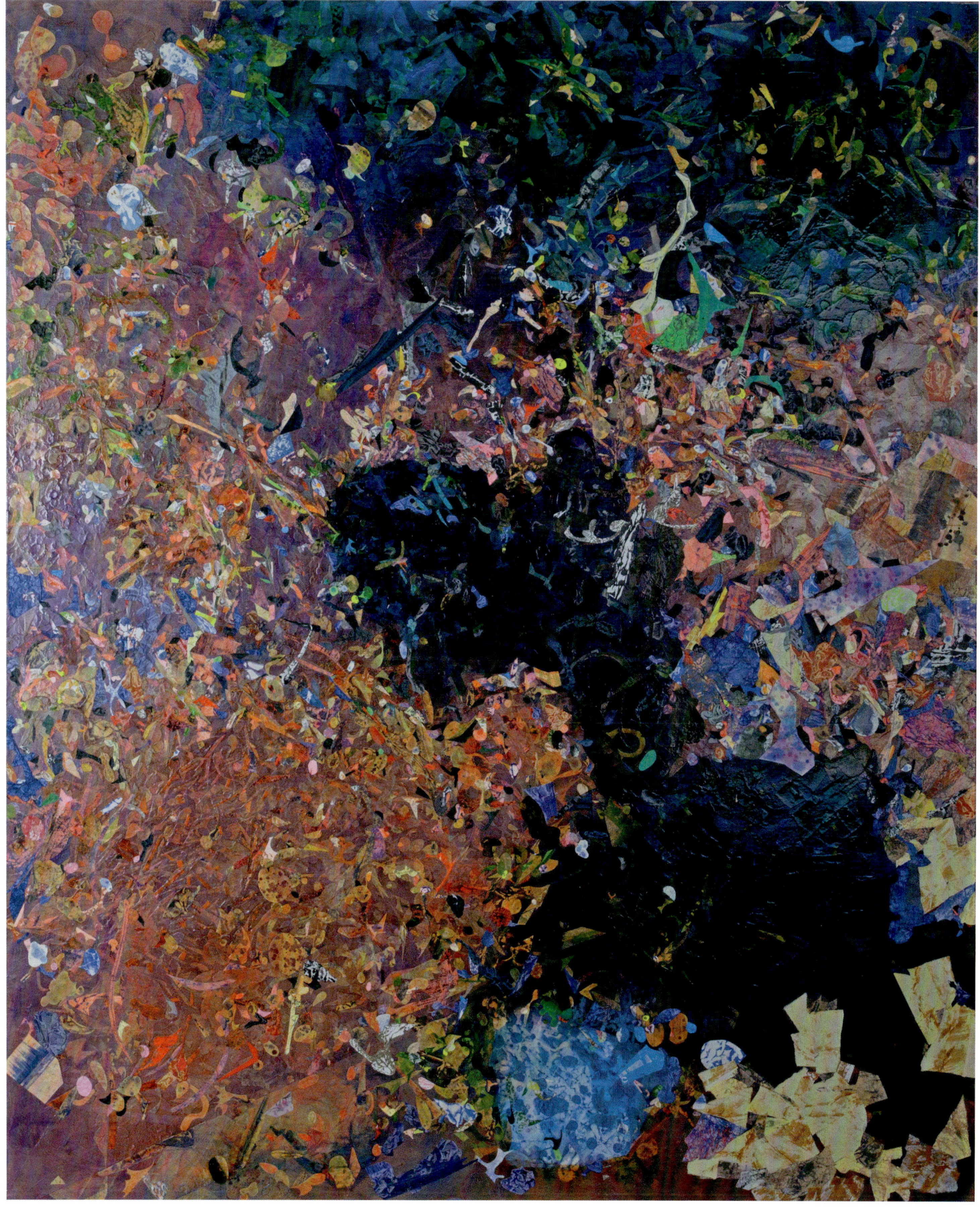

PLATE 27

CHARLES LeDRAY (b. 1960)

LeDray grew up in Seattle, Washington, and now lives and works in New York City and Hudson. He has installed *Village People* (plate 28) at Cedar Grove, in Thomas Cole's bedroom on the second floor, accompanied by Cole's own steamer trunk marked with his initials, in a harmonious dialogue in terms of wearable possessions. LeDray has been making hats at less than half scale since 1993. This present series of 73 caps forms a departure as they are largely based on real hats and subjects. They are all ball caps, with the exception of one brimless bicycle-racing cap labeled "Albany Calcium Light Co Inc.," referencing a now-defunct gas distributor from Loudonville. LeDray procures hats from thrift stores and flea markets, or from local businesses, looking for some connection to ancient rivers and place names, as in examples such as "Styx" and "Palatine Park Maintenance Germantown, NY," as discussed in "*River Crossings*: 'An unbounded capacity for improvement by art'" in this volume (pp. 12–21). He breaks down the component parts of the original hats and painstakingly remakes them on a small scale using hand-cut stencils to paint logos or meticulously embroider-

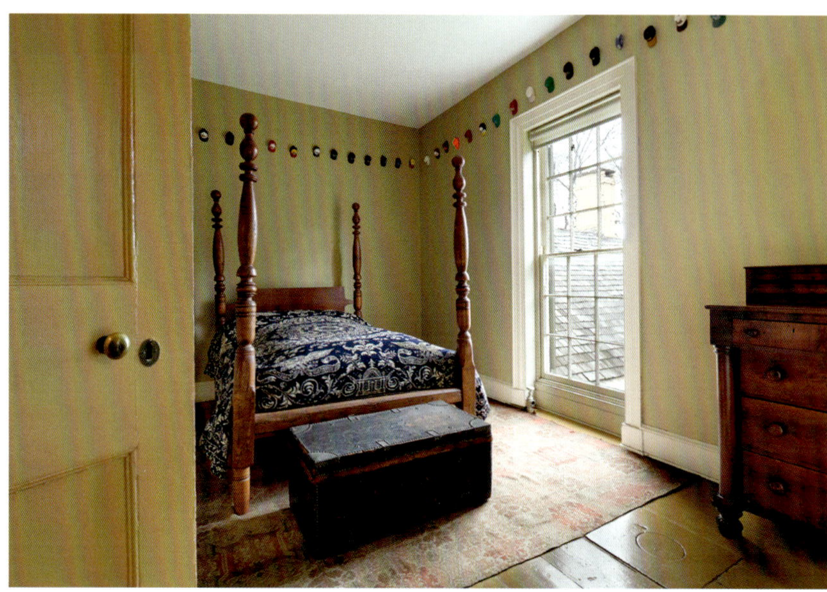

Charles LeDray, *Village People*, 2014–2015 (plate 28) in the Second-Floor Bedroom.

ing designs. Some of the hats, such as one for the CNN/FOX TV show "Lou Dobbs Tonight" positioned next to a punning one labeled "Pooh," seem integrated for pure variety, as well as a bit of humor. There is also a consistent transport theme, with numerous hats related to asphalt and roads and trucking and water. A few were designed by the artist using road signs for local businesses that caught his eye, such as "Sprinkles Soft Serve," a now-defunct creamery around the corner from Cole's house. Some hats have a political message, like "Shut 'em Down and Save," a hat protesting the railway freight company Conrail, which jives with Cole's own distaste for the effects of the freight lines that were being built all around him, and represents a steady seam of seriousness that underlies the mischievousness of LeDray's installation. There is a nod to this in the work's title, a reference to the American disco group from the 1970s and 1980s, for whom flamboyant costume, including of course hats, served as an everyman sheen for their incisive celebration of gay identity, and attendant musical and masculine message of community inclusivity.

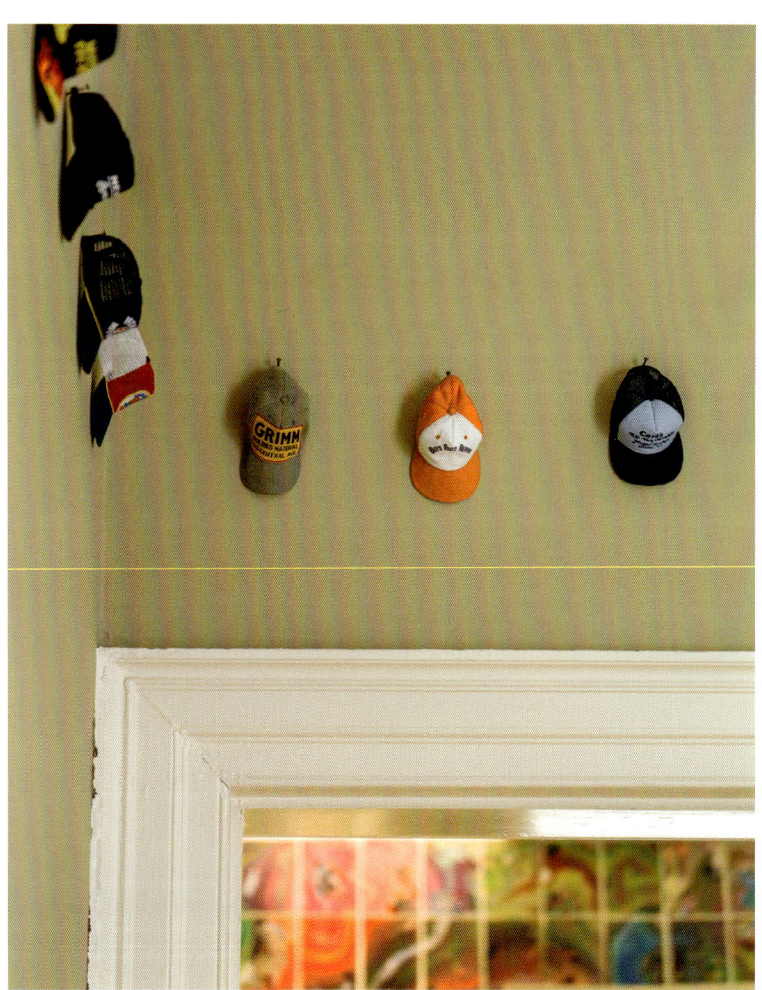

Detail of *Village People*.

Village People, 2014–2015. Fabric, thread, embroidery floss, and paint, dimensions variable, approx. 20 feet (6.1 m) in width. Site-specific installation. © Charles LeDray, 2015, courtesy of the artist and Sperone Westwater, New York, NY.

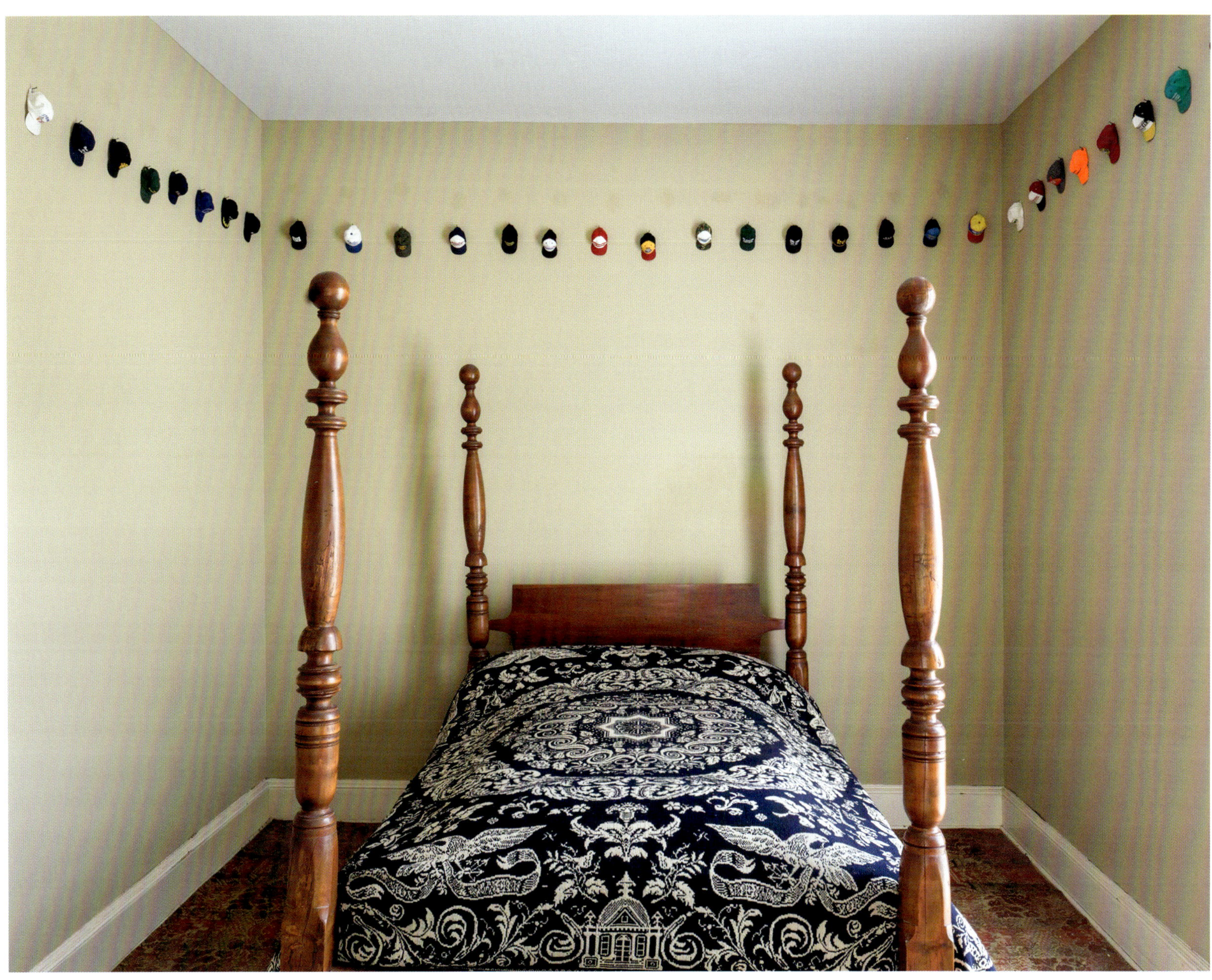

PLATE 28

DUNCAN **HANNAH** (b. 1952)

2013 Guggenheim fellow Duncan Hannah produces meticulously painted canvases that approach the world with an illustrative eye. Influenced by the pop visuals of pulp novel covers, cinema one sheets, and a simplified aesthetic associated with outsider art, his works have a quietude and bear a vaguely English nostalgic air that lend them a timeless resonance. They productively lie somewhere between painters Edward Hopper (1882–1967) and Glyn Philpot (1884–1937), and illustrators of *The Happy Hollisters* and *Nancy Drew* books in the 1950s and 1960s such as Helen Stroud Hamilton (1921–2014) or William S. Gillies (1911–2000). People in Hannah's paintings, even if recognizably based on the likes of Sean Connery or Monica Vitti, seem to be accessible, vulnerable, human. They do not seem to be acting. In *Little Swing* (plate 29), what appears to be a boy in shirt sleeves, cuffed khakis, and Oxford shoes leans back precipitously on the beginning of a down swing, gathering momentum as his legs kick out and the ropes bend under his forward motion. Framed against a lightly brushed blue sky, the boy seems impossibly elevated, with terra firma not in evidence. It is a deftly painted image of bodily release, at the moment when swinging one's body hovers between downfall and impending uplift, defying gravity. Hannah designed the original *Swing* image for the Robert Rosenblum–curated Art Against AIDS benefits in New York in 1987 for the American Foundation for AIDS Research.[1] The work was inspired by the African American spiritual "Swing Low, Sweet Chariot," and its image of Elijah ascending to heaven on the wings of angels. Hannah thus envisioned an adult in a child's swing ever ascending as a symbol of hope, at a time when a number of his friends were sick and dying in the early years of the epidemic.[2] This is one of a set of small, similar paintings that have expanded upon the original work, and it is displayed in *River Crossings* in the basement kitchen alcove at Cedar Grove, with two works by Frank Moore (plates 30 and 31), who died of complications from HIV/AIDS.

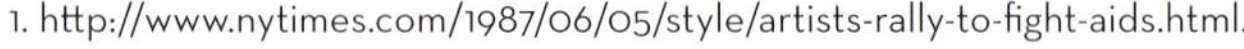

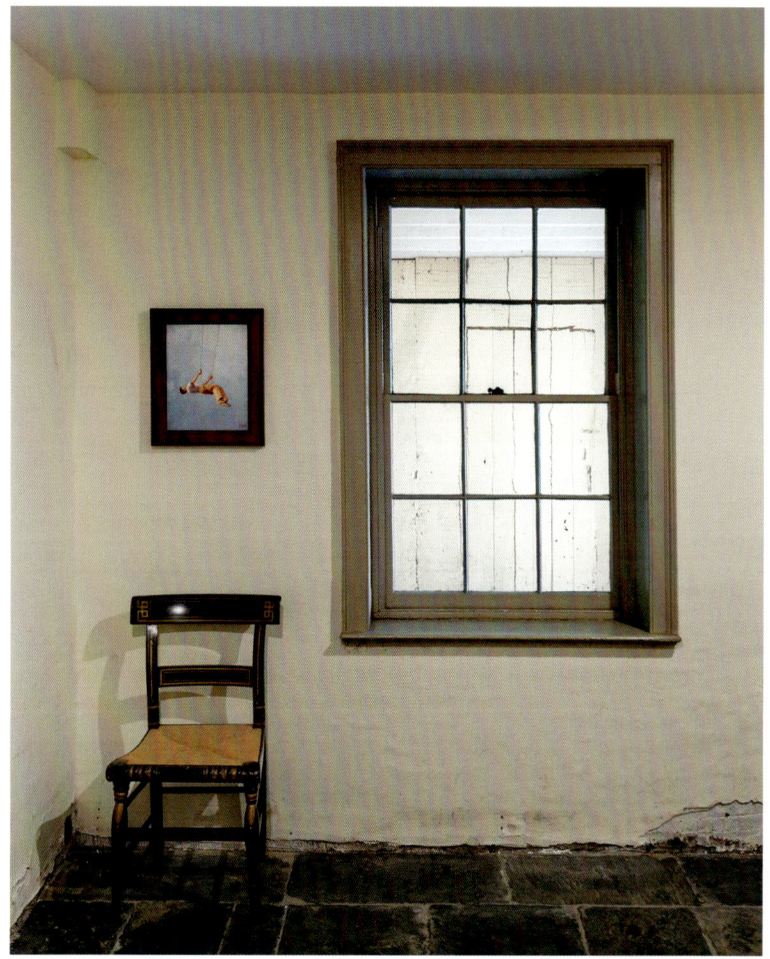

Duncan Hannah, *Little Swing*, 1999 (plate 29) in the Kitchen Alcove.

1. http://www.nytimes.com/1987/06/05/style/artists-rally-to-fight-aids.html.

2. Communication with Duncan Hannah, June 1, 2015.

Little Swing, 1999. Oil on canvas, 14 x 11 in. (35.6 x 27.9 cm); framed: 17 x 14¾ x 1¼ in. (43.2 x 37.5 x 4.4 cm). Private collection.

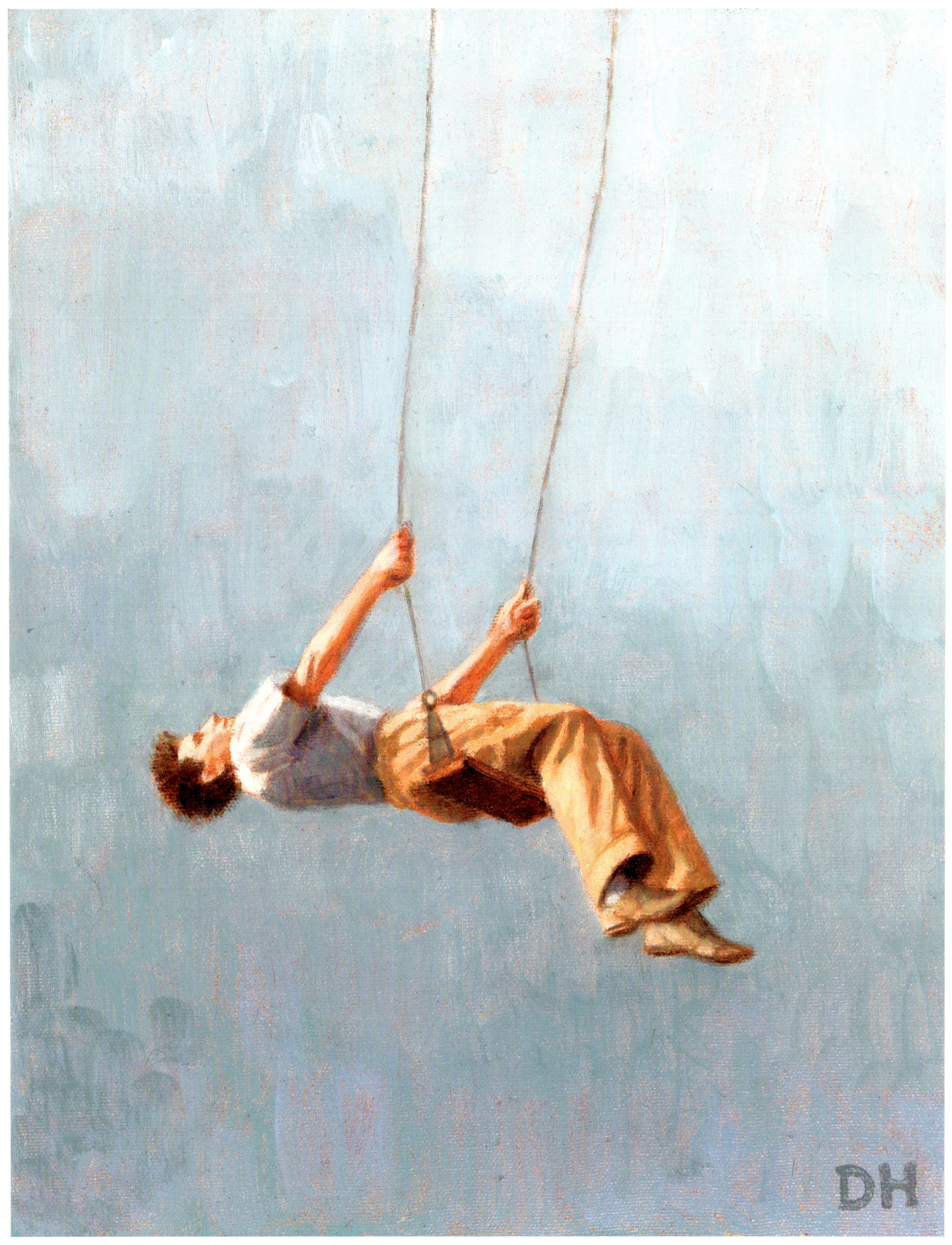

PLATE 29

Moore was born in Manhattan and grew up on Long Island with summers spent in the Adirondacks. He studied art and psychology at Yale University and began his career in New York in the mid-1970s. Moore tested HIV positive in 1987 and his art shifted to one as concerned with painterly traditions as a scientific analysis of his own condition. Moore designed the ACT UP red AIDS ribbon, and his strident art addressed his medical state in particularly suggestive and symbolic ways. In the woodcut print *Prairie* (plate 30), after his important picture *Lullaby* of 1997 (The Estate of Frank Moore), buffalo roam across a pristine white sheet on a hospital bed, with three pillows slightly tossed about. Tufts of grass poke out from the bedding. Snowflakes falling from the heavens accentuate the illusion of a wintry scene, in a surreal mode akin to the paranoiac-critical paintings of Salvador Dalí (1904–1989). But here, as in Hudson River School artist Albert Bierstadt's (1830–1902) late lament of a picture, *The Last of the Buffalo* (1888, National Gallery of Art),[1] wherein both the hunting Plains Indian and the hunted massive mammals are shown at the very moment of both species' near-extinction, Moore presented a tableau of a vanished American realm of peace and natural harmony, a symbol of the paradise lost through the onset of the AIDS epidemic.[2] This was one of a series of three landscapes Moore produced at The Grenfell Press in Manhattan. Joining *Prairie* in the basement kitchen alcove at Cedar Grove is Moore's small painting *Study for La Boccetta I* (plate 31), an image of an eruptive volcano in the mode of numerous works by Romantic artists such as Joseph Wright of Derby (1734–1797) or J.M.W. Turner (1775–1851), and later Frederic Edwin Church. It is a modern transformation of the sublime, that depiction of the frightful in nature and humankind's puny scale in the face of God's awesome wonders. But here, instead of the expected crimson pyroclastic flow, DNA double helixes and other scientific symbols for amino acids blast forth from the volcano's mouth and create a brilliant orange-and-yellow pool in the foreground. Characteristic of Moore's joint interests in the natural subjects of Romantic art and scientific analysis of the potent and toxic elements in the environment that both comprise and threaten human life, this was one of the final conceptions he was working on before he died of complications from HIV/AIDS on the 21st of April 2002.

---

1. http://www.nga.gov/content/ngaweb/Collection/art-object-page.124525.html.

2. Sue Scott, *Frank Moore: Green Thumb in a Dark Eden*, exh. cat. (Orlando Museum of Art, 2002); http://www.suescottgallery.com/programs/texts/Frank-Moore/.

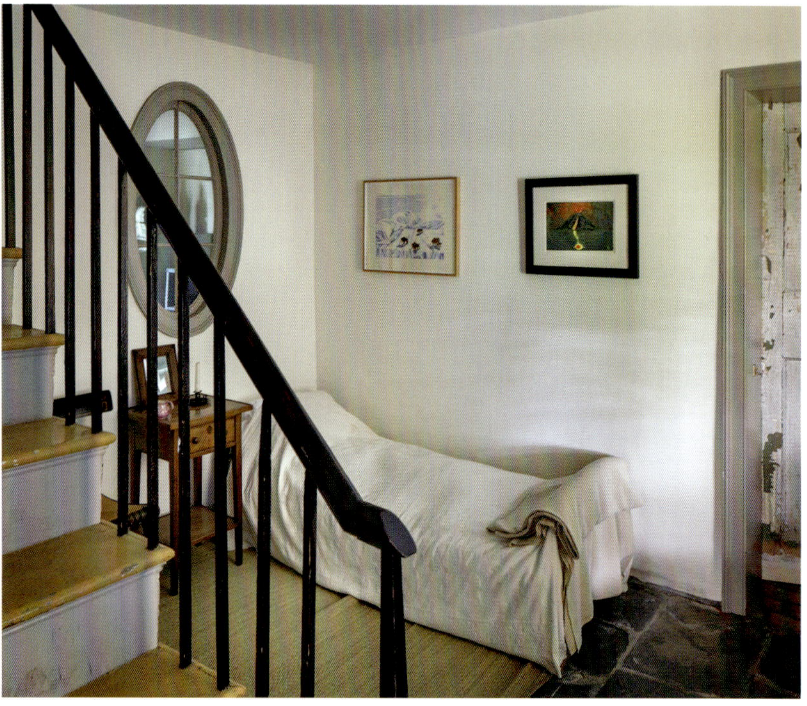

Frank Moore, *Prairie*, 1999 (plate 30) and Study for *La Boccetta I*, 2001 (plate 31) in in the Kitchen Alcove.

Prairie, 1999. Woodcut, 17½ x 22½ in. (44.5 x 57.2 cm). Courtesy of the estate of the artist and Elizabeth Moore and Sperone Westwater.

Study for *La Boccetta I*, 2001. Gouache, oil, and India ink on Arches paper, 8⁹⁄₁₆ x 12¹³⁄₁₆ in. (21.7 x 32.5 cm). Courtesy of the estate of the artist and Sperone Westwater.

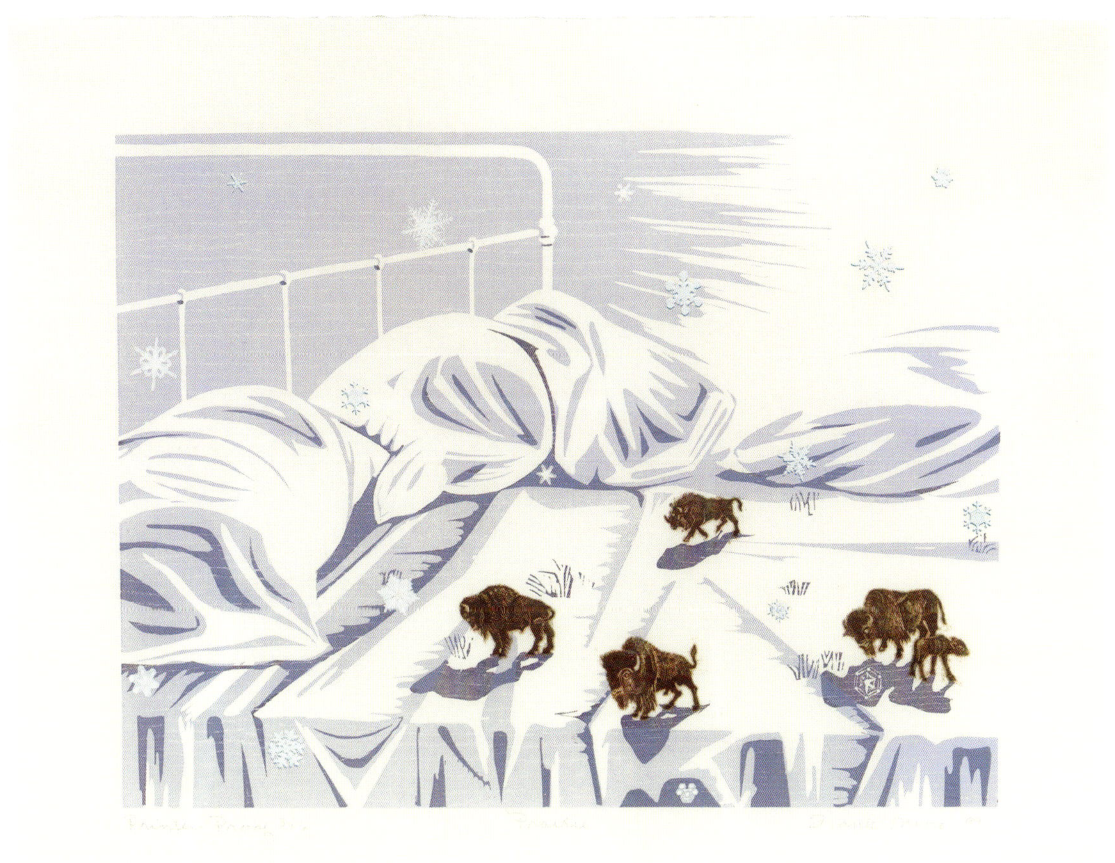

PLATE 30

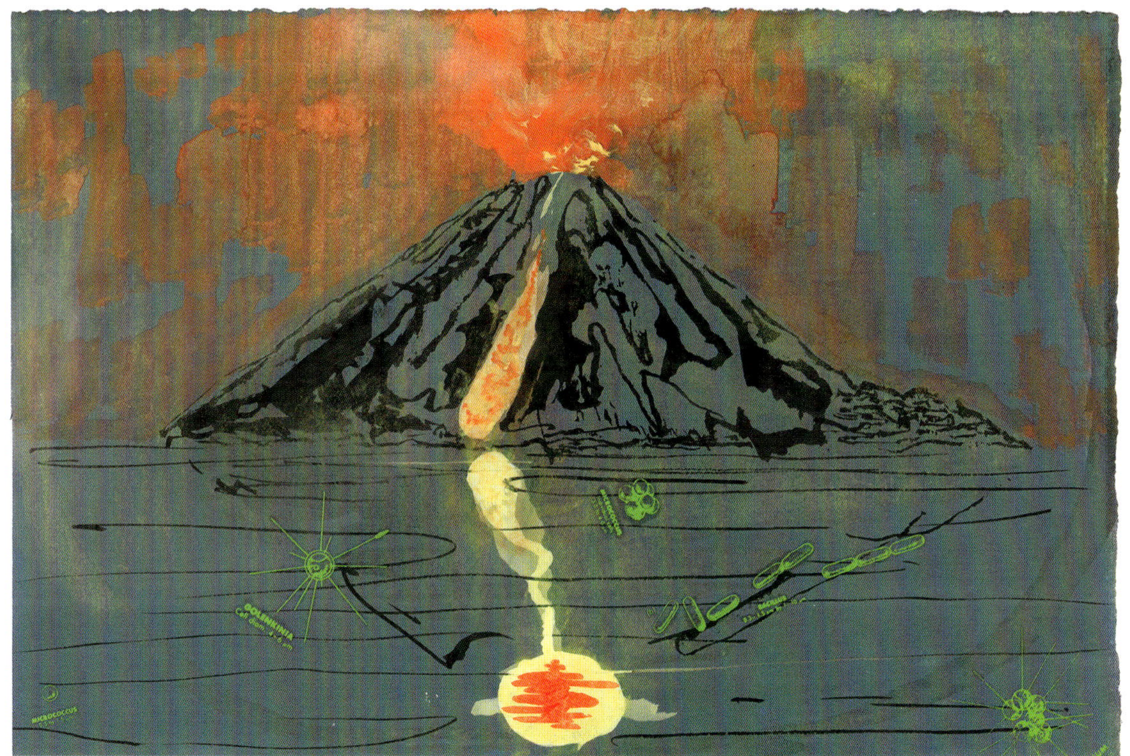

PLATE 31

Rashaad Newsome's *King of Queens* (plate 32) represents the continued evolution of his impressive and distinctive collage technique,
in a work that seems equally indebted to the innovations of Romare
Bearden (plate 26) as to the older traditions of Dada and Surrealism
in the work of Hannah Höch (1889–1978), Max Ernst (1891–1976), and
Salvador Dalí (1904–1989). Newsome's modern mash-ups of Baroque
arabesques and flourishes, gilded American frames, symbolic heraldry,
and Hip Hop associations form potent signs of the times. The regilded
frame of this work was actually procured from an antique shop in
Hudson, New York, and with its crowning eagle represents the rise of
republic era design appropriate to Cole's farmhouse and the types of
symbolic borders found around pictures, prints, or peer glass in the
early nineteenth century. Newsome added bamboo hoop earrings at
the top and crocodile skin around the border and as a background
field for the cartouche at top, on which floats a crown—associations
with the Hip Hop present. The idea of salvage in his work represents
a further continuity with aesthetic approaches to assemblage gleaned
in growing up in New Orleans and vivid in the ethos of Southern art,
especially in the sculpture of Martin Payton (b. 1948). Newsome works
in film, video art, and performance, and the papier collé inner elements of *King of Queens* serve in a way as stills for his work in other
media. Collaged printed materials from magazines and catalogues
are arranged in a painterly swarm, with locks of hair standing for
brushstrokes, and the inner image of male swagger and sexuality with
female appendages forming a spoked wheel mimics heraldic crests of
clenched fists and rampant animals, a kind of modern portraiture of
status, power, and opulence.

King of Queens, 2012. Mixed-media collage in
custom antique frame, 49 x 26 x 2¾ in. (124.5 x
66 x 7 cm). Collection of the artist. © Rashaad
Newsome, courtesy of the artist and Marlborough
Gallery, New York, NY.

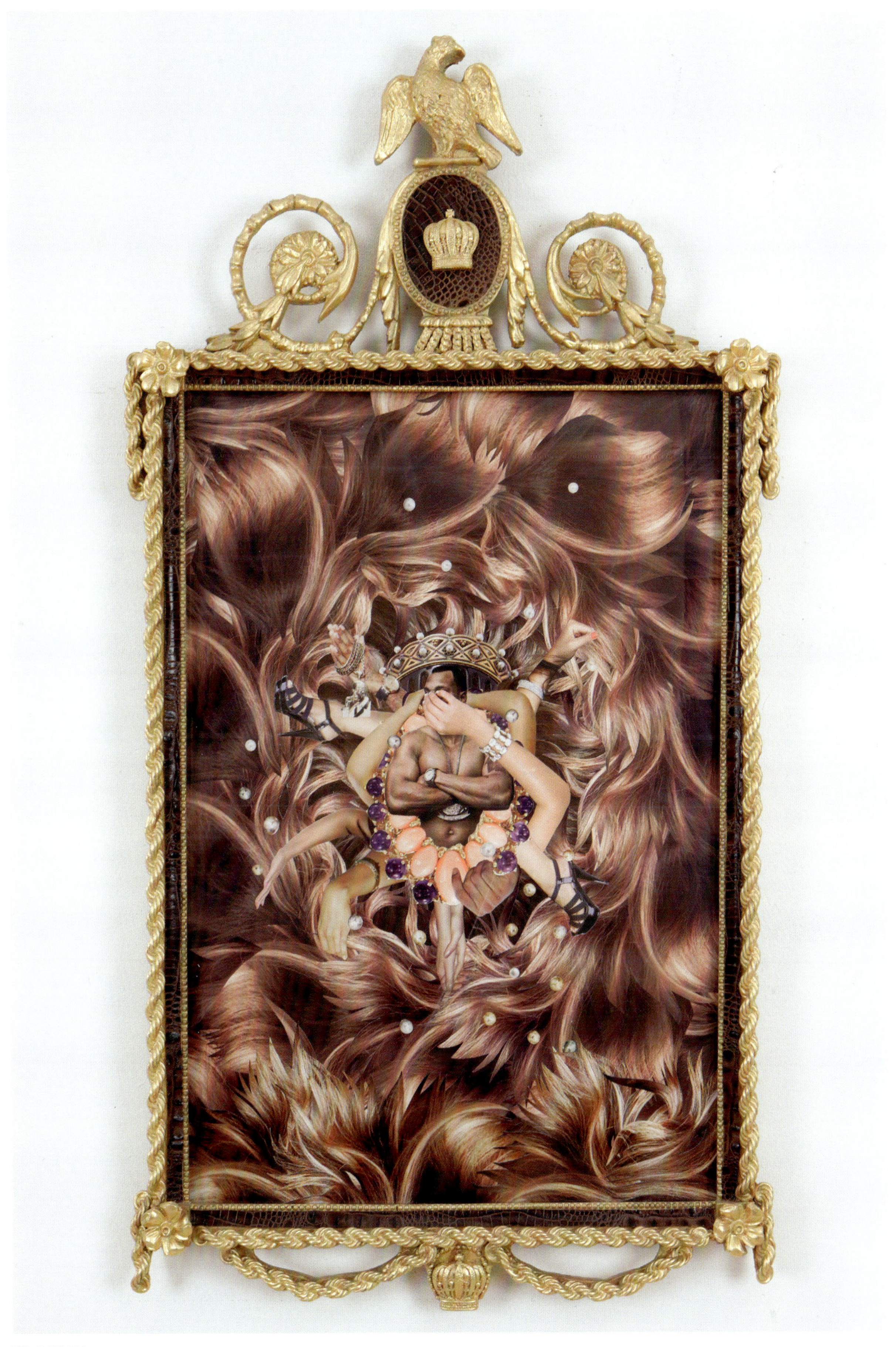

Born in Louisville, Kentucky, and raised in Indianapolis, Indiana, Gummer earned his BFA and MFA in sculpture at Yale University and now lives in Connecticut. He has been producing his imposing, complicated, but surprisingly light metal works for more than 40 years. The two tall sculptures at Cedar Grove establish a linear path directly between the main house and Thomas Cole's reconstructed studio to the south, nearing completion. They lead past the great honey locust tree on the front lawn and in a line to the northeast corner of the studio. The stately and Picassoid *Woman Reclining* (plate 33), on its reflective metal ground-plate, and *In the Fold* (plate 34), on its tapering concrete base, both elevate into the air, defying gravity as they build to latticed and undulating upper aluminum panels that seem to levitate as horizontal planes above the darker bronze funneling and spiraling forms below, high-mindedly recalling Atlas bearing his heavy load or, more humbly, a pizza maker tossing and rotating dough into upper space.

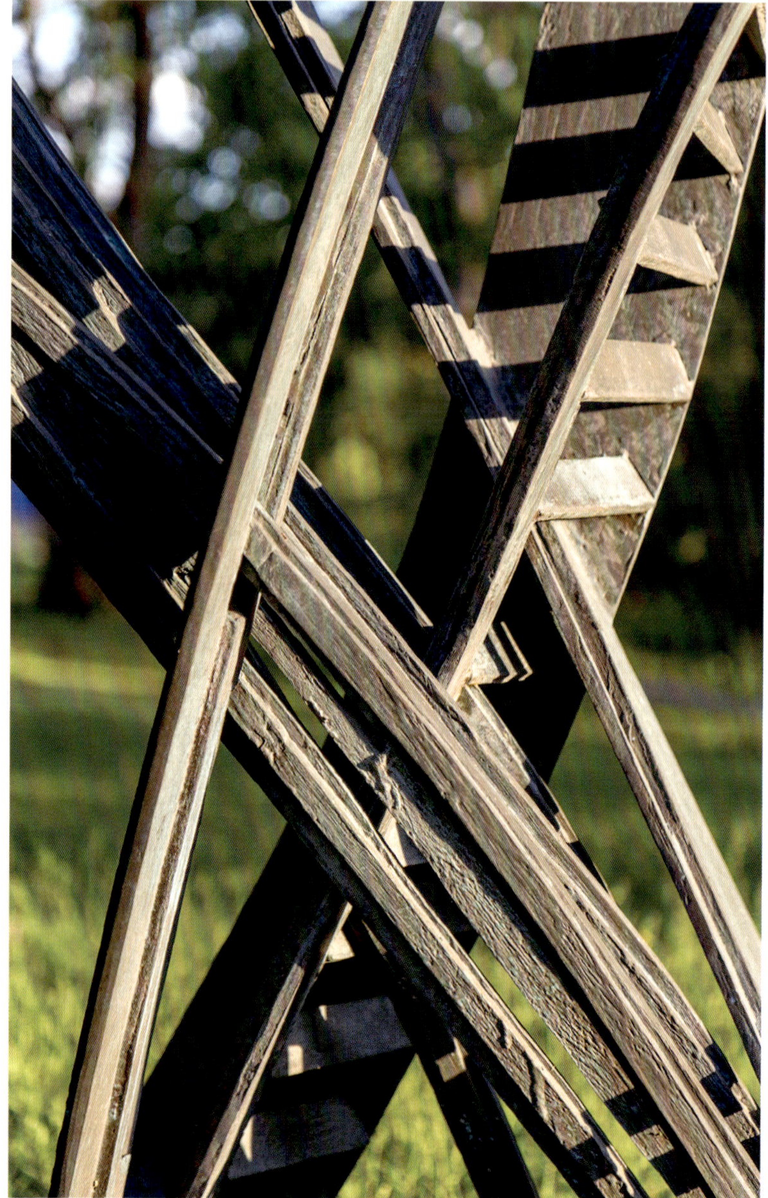

Detail of *Woman Reclining.*

Woman Reclining, 1993. Cast bronze and aluminum on concrete base, 95 x 86 x 42 in. (241.3 x 218.4 x 106.7 cm). Collection of the artist.

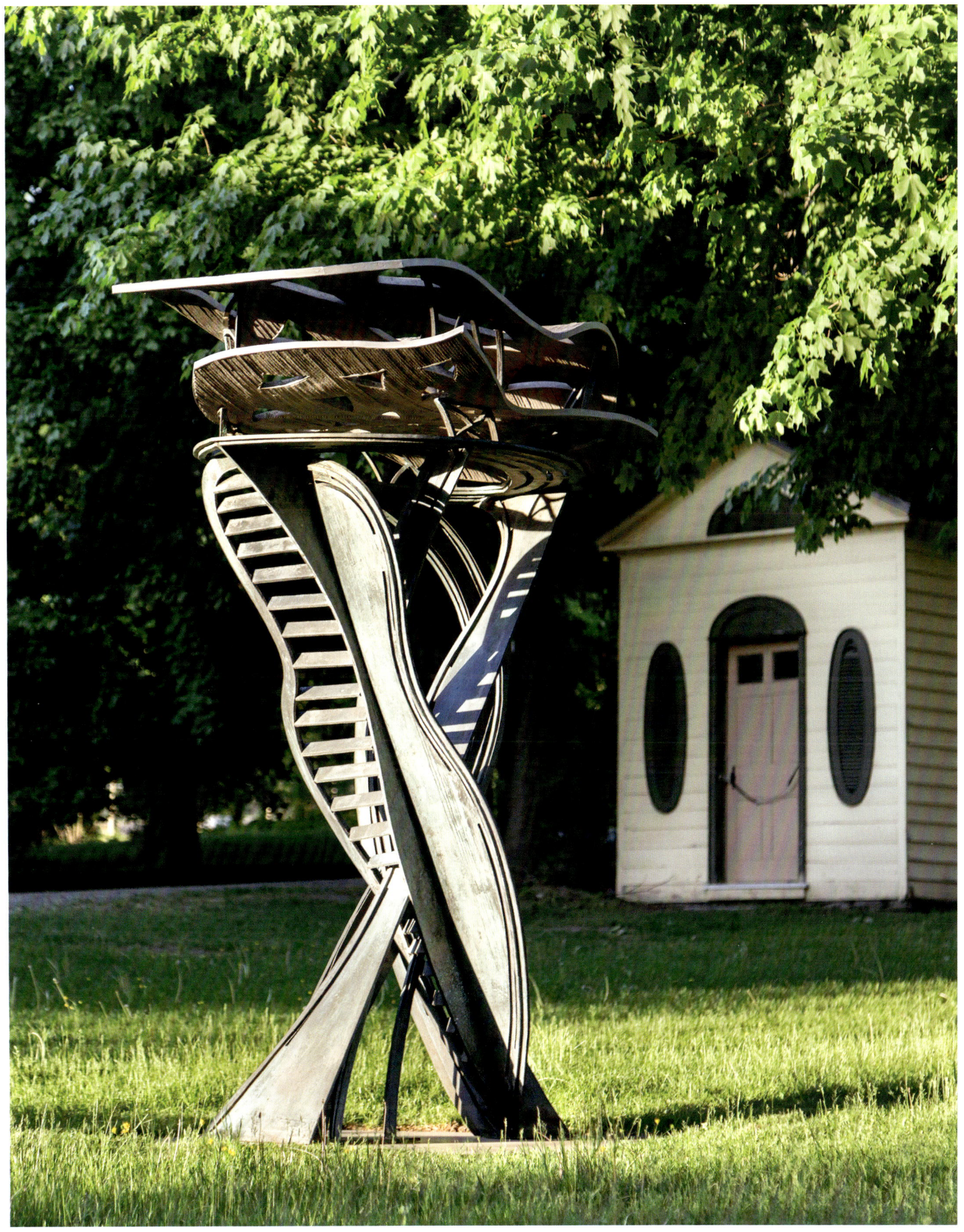

PLATE 33

79

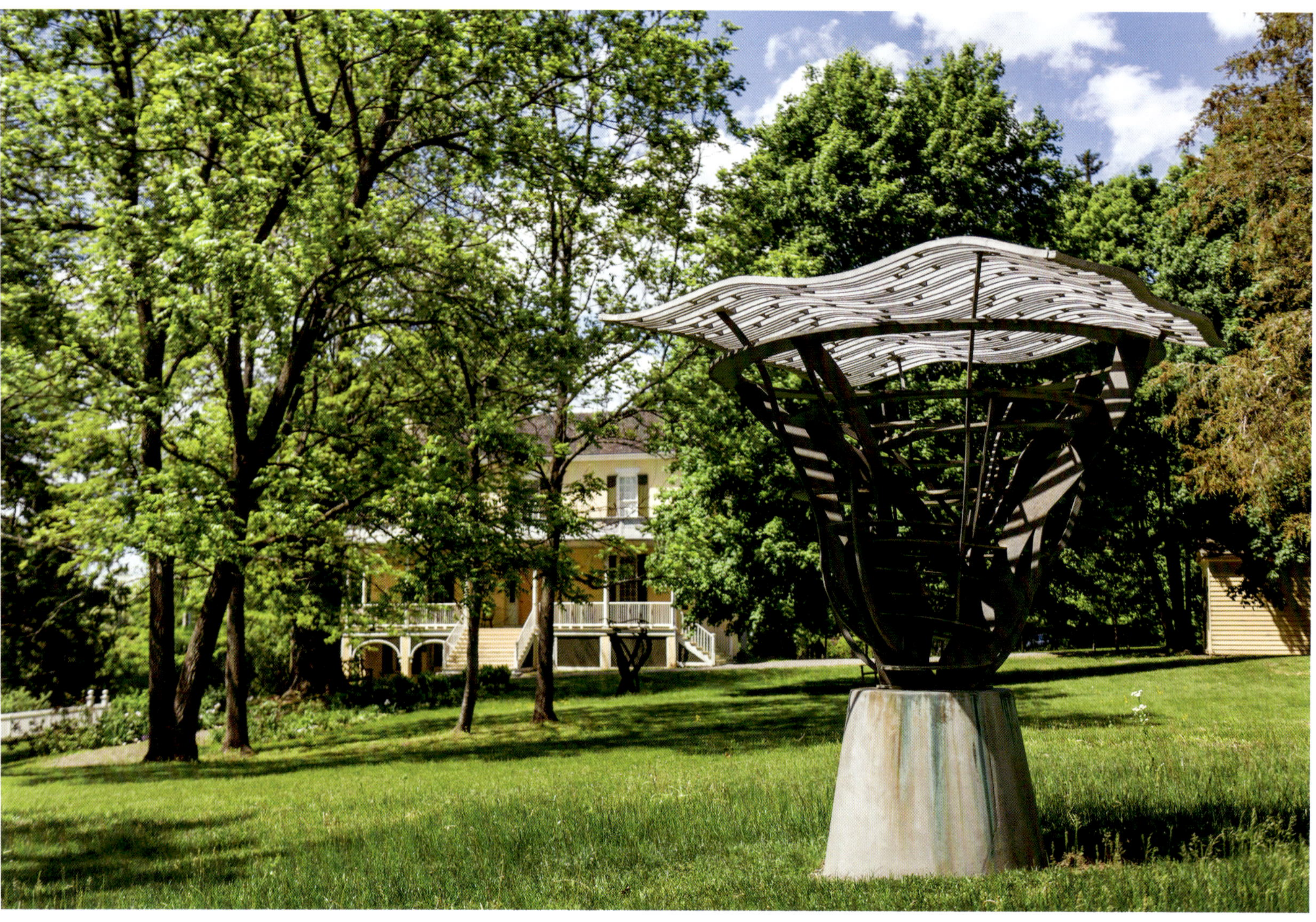

In the Fold, 1994. Cast bronze and aluminum on concrete base, 90 x 76 x 72 in. (228.6 x 193 x 182.9 cm). Collection of the artist.

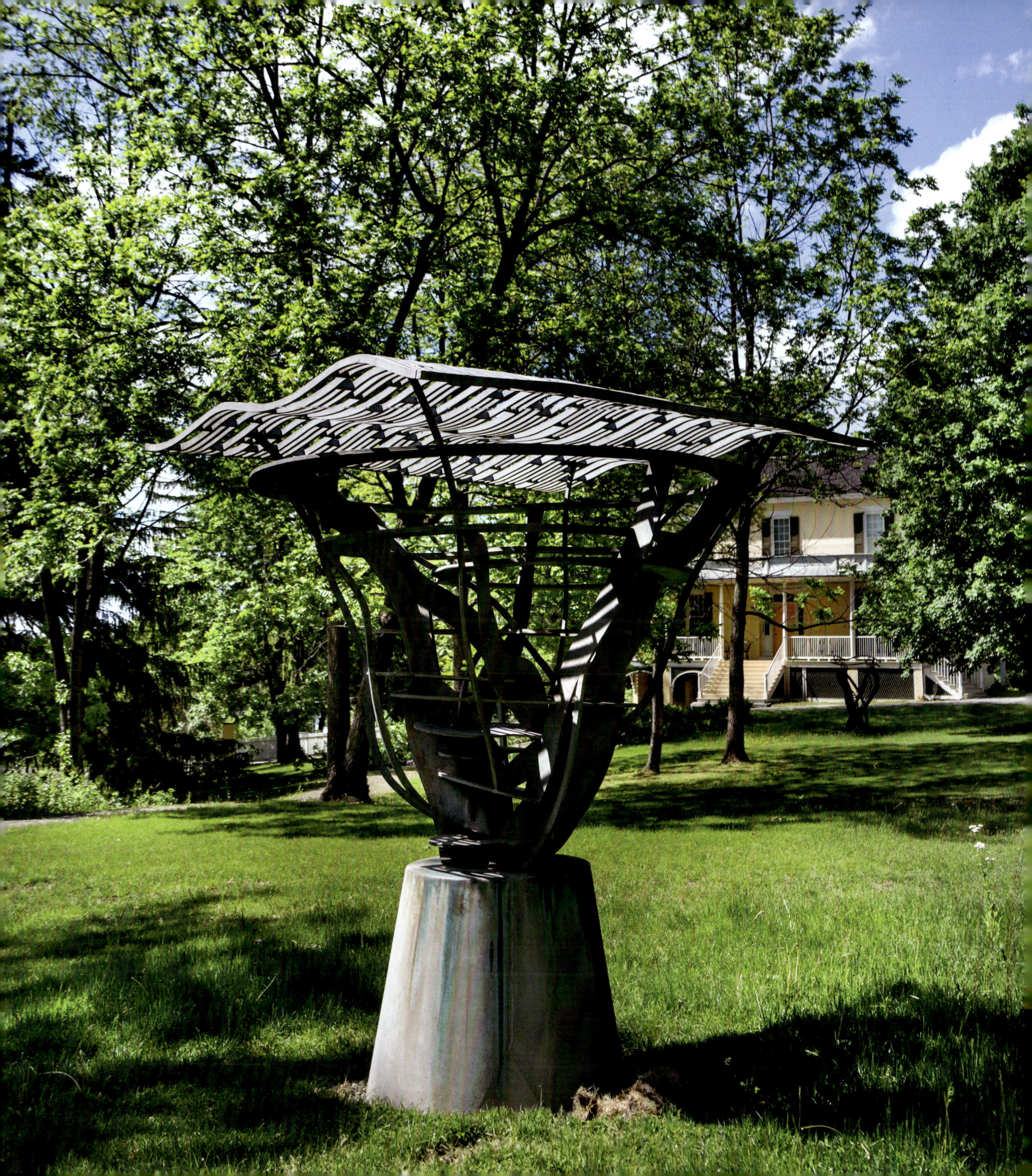

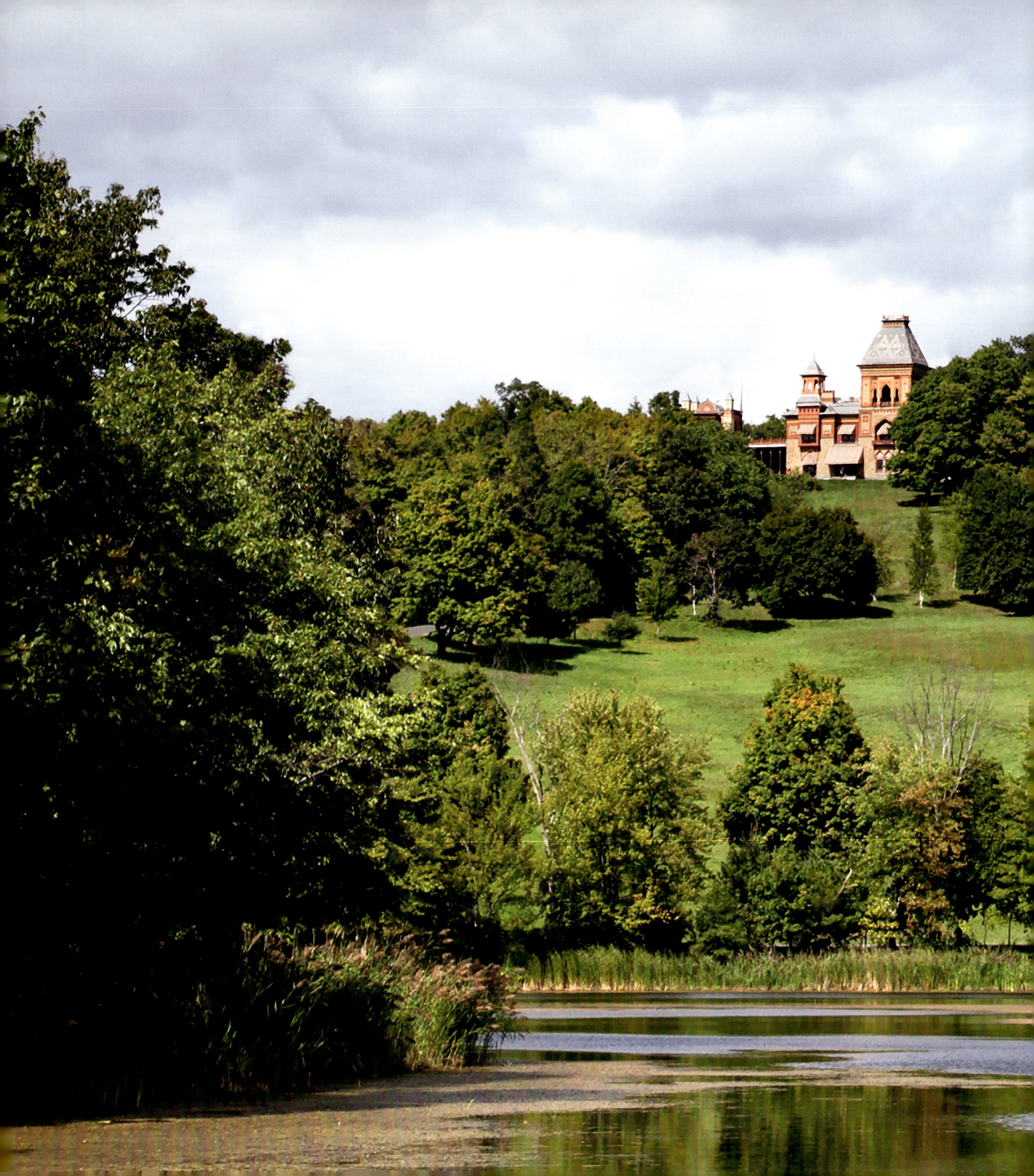

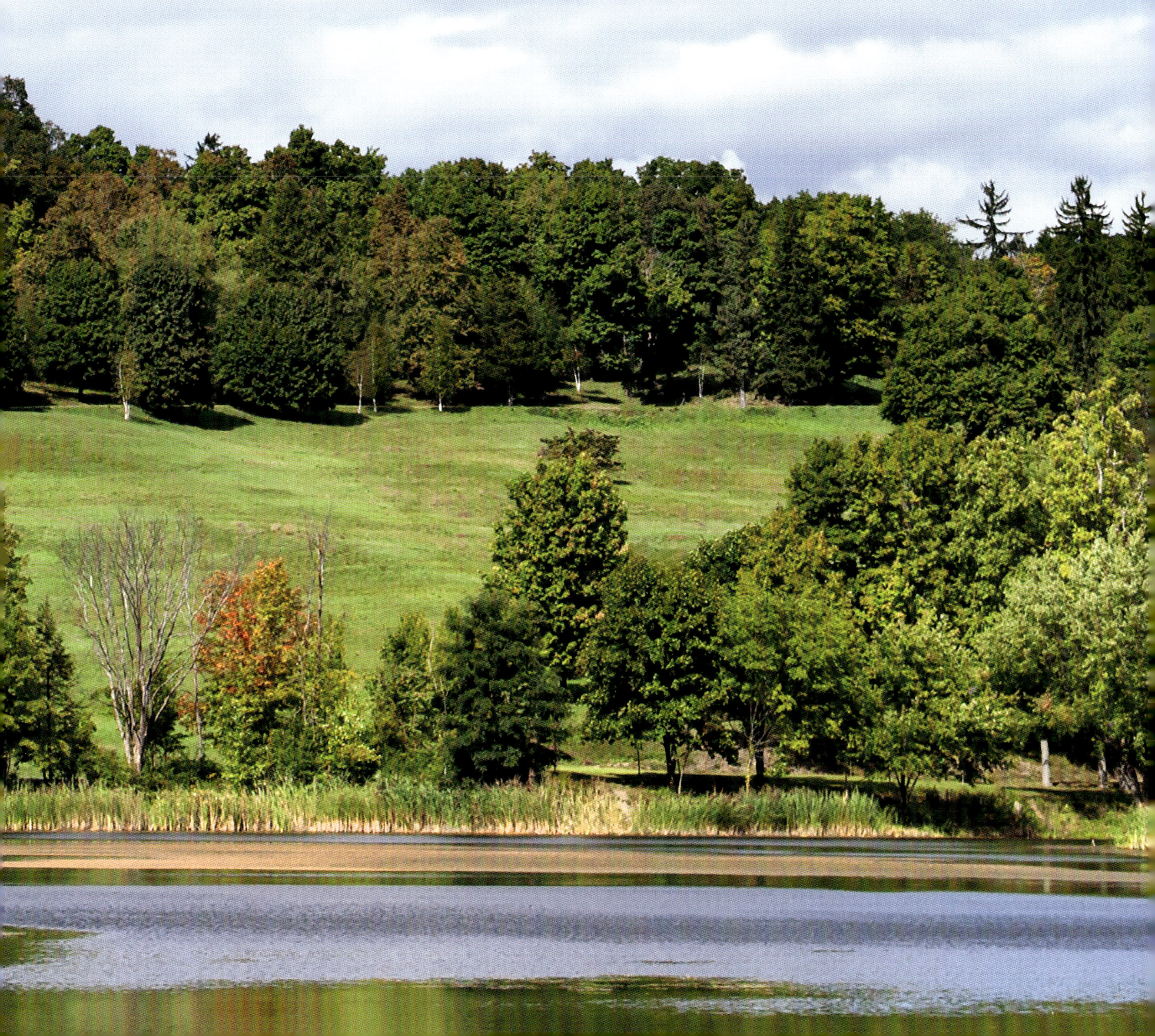

OLANA STATE HISTORIC SITE

"I have frequently heard of the beautiful and romantic scenery about Catskill . . . it would give me the greatest pleasure to accompany you in your rambles about the place, observing nature in all her various appearances."

—Frederic Edwin Church (age 18) to Thomas Cole (age 43), May 20, 1844

THUS BEGAN one of the great friendships in American art, as well as a great love affair between Frederic Edwin Church and the Hudson River Valley landscape. In 1845, under Thomas Cole's tutelage, Church created *Scene from Red Hill*, a graphite-and-chalk sketch, his earliest-known rendering from the property now known as Olana, showing the Hudson Valley and the town of Catskill, where Cole resided.[1] Cole probably directed his student to the scenic location, having himself sketched from the same place.

Over the next decade, Church tested his talent in far-flung locales (most famously, the Andes and Niagara Falls), but he had his eye on acquiring land in the Hudson Valley. After his marriage in 1860, Church bought land at the base of Red Hill, from which he had sketched fifteen years earlier. He and his wife lived with the Cole family while they built Cosy Cottage, their first home on the property. Ultimately he purchased the entire hillside, securing the hilltop and its sublime 360-degree views just before embarking for Europe and the Middle East in 1867. He built his Moorish fantasy near its pinnacle from 1870 to 1874, later adding a studio wing featuring a bird's-eye view over the property of his late teacher. Church spent the rest of his life designing, planting, and sculpting the landscape to resemble the paintings that had made the Hudson River region famous.

Church's relationship with the Coles lasted long beyond Thomas Cole's early death. Cole's son Theodore was the first property manager at Olana and worked directly with Church to implement his large-scale vision for the landscape, including a working and ornamental farm. As Theodore Cole wrote to Church in 1868, "It is a pleasure for me and no task to be of any service for you. I always feel almost as if I was doing something for my own Brother when I am doing anything for you."[2] The families spent a great deal of time together in ensuing decades, visiting each other across the Hudson River. Church had numerous Cole works at Olana and worked with Theodore Cole to assist in finding clients for the sale of his father's pieces to benefit the family, at times offering paintings from his own collection for sale to help assist in this effort. And in 1888, Church purchased Cole's large canvas *View of the Protestant Burying Ground, Rome* (c. 1833–1834, Olana) from a Boston gallery for display in his home, a definitive statement of the former pupil's steadfast and personal dedication to Cole's enduring legacy.

Besides Cole's work, Church hung paintings by other artist friends in his home, including Martin Johnson Heade, Jervis McEntee, Charles de Wolf Brownell, and Worthington Whittredge. These works can still be seen on the walls today. Many more artists partook of Church's frequent invitations to come paint the incredible views from and within Olana. So, when the acclaimed artist Stephen Hannock proposed the exhibition that has become *River Crossings* and brought in the art historian and curator Jason Rosenfeld as co-curator, notice had to be paid.

Dynamic dialogues and exchanges were an integral part of experiencing Olana during Church's lifetime. During the 1880s, Olana became a salon for the Churches' friends, including artists, writers, musicians, and scientists, to meet and share their ideas and experiences. While the British painter Marianne North showed her sketches of plants and flowers from Brazil to Japan there, local artist Benjamin Bellow Grant Stone asked for Church's sage advice. Many artists just wandered the magnificent landscape for inspiration. The main house at Olana is itself a prime example of an artistic collaboration between Church and the famed architect Calvert Vaux. The artists in *River Crossings* continue that broad conversation, exploring their creative process, artistic muse, and the role of art in defining the American spirit.

At Olana, Martin Puryear's *Question* (plate 37) mirrors the arches of the Court Hall and frames the view out to the Hudson River through the Ombra. Across from the Ombra, in the historic location of Church's Japanese scroll of the death of Buddha, hangs Chuck Close's *Self-Portrait (Yellow Rain Coat)* (plate 35). Close explores faces as if they are landscapes, subject to myriad interpretations. Church was as much an explorer as an artist, pushing the geographic borders of the Hudson River School into South America, and Lynn Davis shares Church's love of adventure: her photographs of exotic locales such as the Arctic and the American natural wonder Niagara Falls speak directly to Church's sketches displayed above them (plates 38 and 39).

Olana can be seen as a 250-acre naturalistic earthwork with an exceptional sense of place; Church created an experience for his guests and fellow artists. Within his three-dimensional naturalistic composition, he designed more than five miles of carriage roads to guide movement through native woodlands, past open meadows, around an artificial lake, above orchard fields—all in conversation with the atmospheric effects and sublime views of the Hudson River Valley. In *River Crossings*, the work of Don Gummer (plates 47–50) will highlight and continue that conversation for a new audience in new ways.

Significantly, it is a sign of the evolution within America's perception of its own culture and art that this exhibition has specifically "come home" to Thomas Cole and Frederic Church. Against all odds and against all fashion, the Church family kept Olana intact well into the twentieth century. In a visionary leap of faith in the 1960s, art historian David Huntington rallied forces to save Olana from destruction. Since that time, under a strong public/private partnership, Olana has continued to thrive as a historic site, a museum, an artist-designed landscape and park, a studio, and a source of inspiration for countless visitors from near and far. It is the legacy of Cole and Church that has fueled this combination of preservation and transformation, and has brought us to this exhibition.

Evelyn Trebilcock, Mark Prezorski, and Rena Zurofsky
Hudson, New York
April 2015

---

1. Olana Collection, dated May 1845, OL1980.1333A.

2. Theodore Cole to Frederic Edwin Church, November 29, 1868, Collection of Olana State Historic Site, OL.1998.1.176.

ON EXHIBIT AT OLANA

CHUCK CLOSE

VALERIE HEGARTY

MARTIN PURYEAR

LYNN DAVIS

MAYA LIN

ELIJAH BURGHER

LETHA WILSON

WILL COTTON

CHARLES LeDRAY

DON GUMMER

ELYN ZIMMERMAN

CHUCK **CLOSE** (b. 1940)

Raised and educated in Washington State, Close came east in 1961 having earned a scholarship to the Yale Summer School of Art and Music in Norfolk, Connecticut. It was on a road trip that summer that he first visited Olana; seeking water, and finding himself stuck inland in northwestern Connecticut, he gravitated toward rivers like the Hudson.[1] He subsequently moved to the Connecticut River Valley, teaching at the University of Massachusetts, Amherst, from 1965 to 1967, where he first started working with photography. Close adapted his characteristic large-scale, full-face portraiture technique to tapestries in 2005. Woven in an edition of 10 on a Jacquard Dornier loom in Belgium that has been programmed to accept a scanned image, they are comprised of nearly 18,000 Italian dyed-cotton warp threads in 8 colors and weft threads in 10 varieties. These combine optically to produce more than one hundred colors.[2] The source image is a 24-by-20-inch Polaroid that is then transformed into a digital "weave file" at Magnolia Editions in Oakland, California, so it can be understood by the loom programming.[3] Close has also produced this composition across other media: as a more than six-foot-tall watercolor pigment print and in small-scale multiples using felt stamps and oil paints. With its shimmering, exquisite, light-responsive surface, the tapestry combines the medieval with the digital and is evidence of Close's constant seeking out of new materials, methods, and effects. The artist's remarkable project of unsparing self-revelation is now in its 48th year, eclipsing Rembrandt van Rijn's (1606–1669) similar enterprise by seven years. Its modern introspective majesty matches the achievement of the Dutch painter, as Close continues similarly to document and share the transformations of a life.

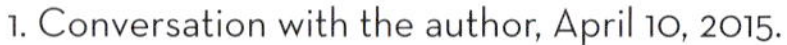

1. Conversation with the author, April 10, 2015.

2. Lilly Wei, "Face Time," in *Chuck Close: Selected Paintings and Tapestries 2005–2009* (New York: PaceWildenstein, 2009), 8.

3. Nick Stone, *Self-Portrait (Yellow Raincoat)* (Oakland, CA: Magnolia Editions, 2013), http://www.magnoliaeditions.com/artworks/self-portrait-yellow-raincoat-2/. See also Stone, "Tapestries at Magnolia Editions" (2014), http://www.magnolia editions.com/wp-content/uploads/2014/12/About_Magnolia_Tapestries2.pdf.

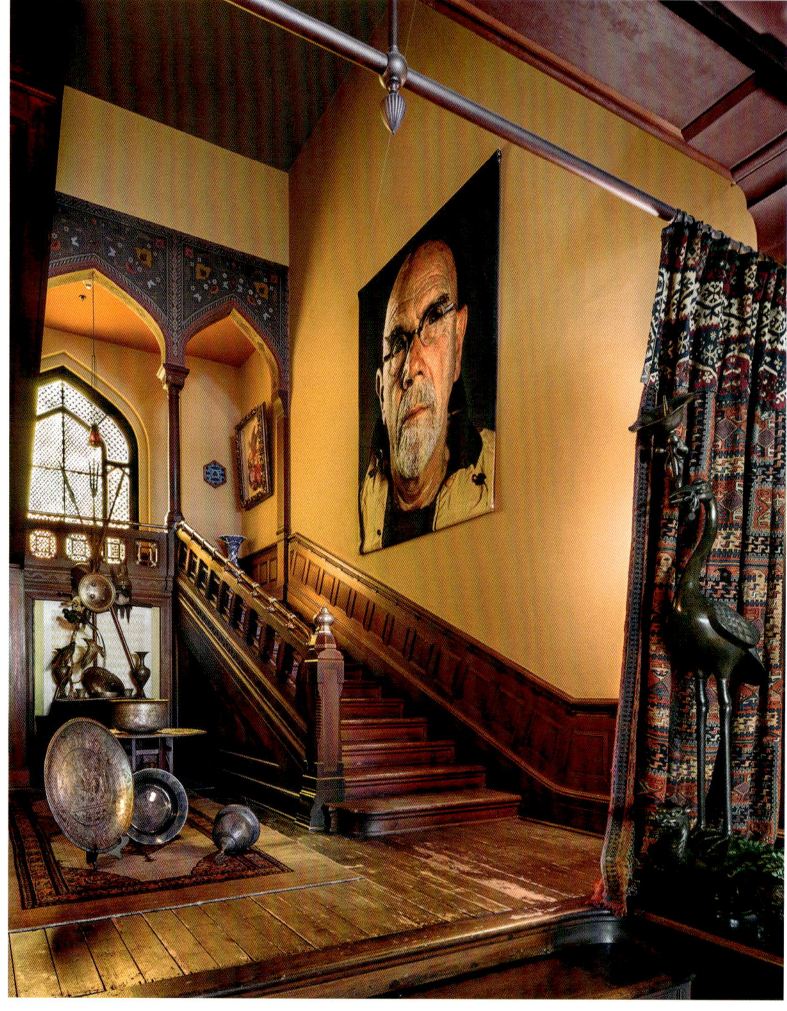

Chuck Close, *Self-Portrait (Yellow Raincoat)*, 2013 (plate 35) on the Stair Hall wall.

Self-Portrait (Yellow Raincoat), 2013. Jacquard tapestry, 93 x 76 in. (236.2 x 193 cm). Private collection. © Chuck Close in association with Magnolia Editions, Oakland. Photograph courtesy of the artist and Pace Gallery.

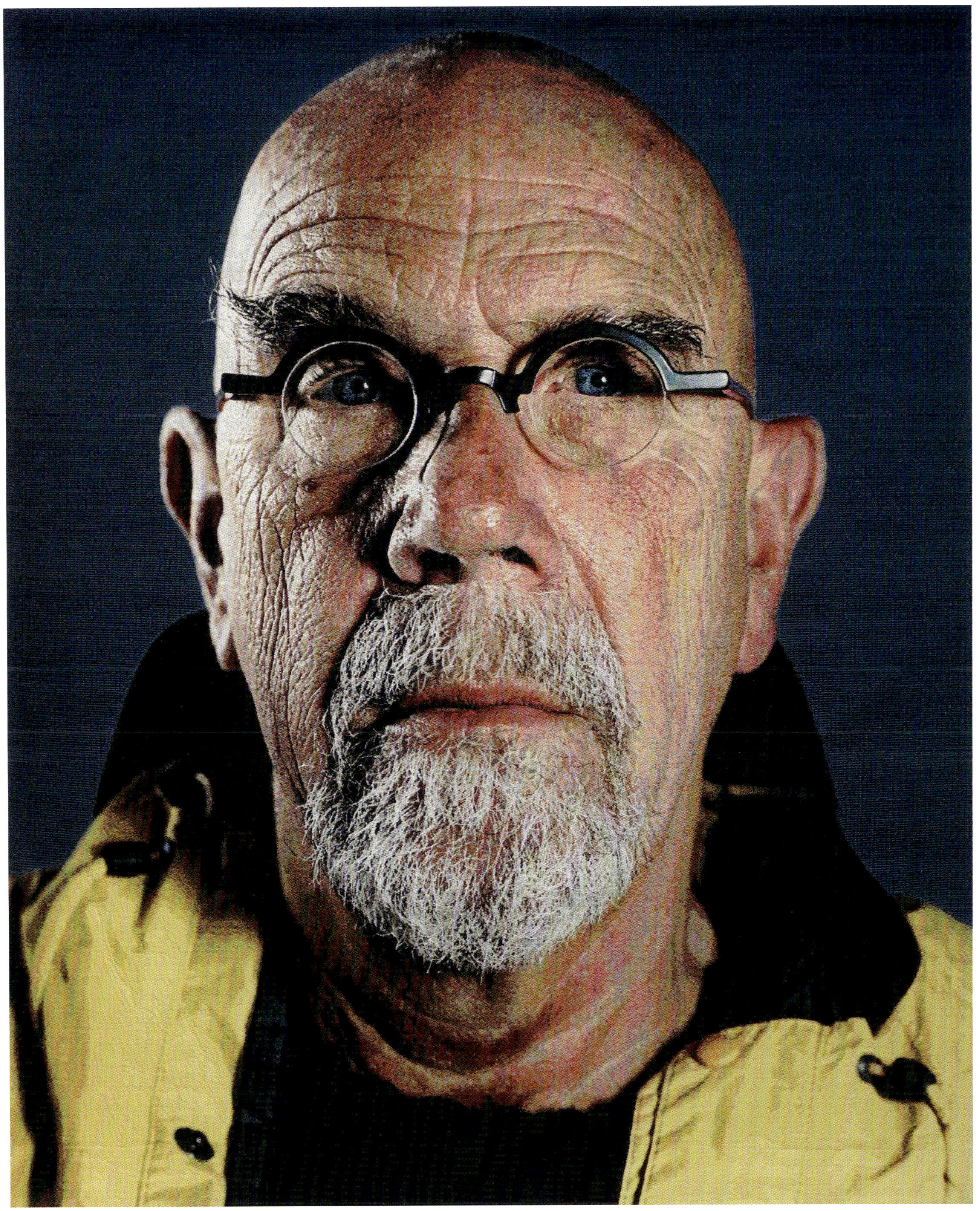

PLATE 35

87

VALERIE **HEGARTY** (b. 1967)

Born in Burlington, Vermont, Hegarty received her BA at Middlebury, her BFA from the Academy of Art College in San Francisco, and her MFA from The Art Institute of Chicago. She has lived in Brooklyn since 2003, has served on the National Advisory Board for the preservation of Olana since 2010, and had a Yaddo Residency in Saratoga Springs in 2011. Her unique dialogue with past art involves meticulously re-creating famed American artworks from the nineteenth century, then despoiling them through fire and manhandling, making it appear as if they have been through a conflagration, or storm, or fusillade, or attacked by animals. She has shown her works at Marlborough Chelsea and in other gallery spaces, but they achieve an added potency when seen in museums, as in the period rooms at the Brooklyn Museum in 2013, or in a historic house such as Olana. In *Picnic with Downy Woodpecker* and *Table and Chair with Pileated Woodpecker*, Hegarty engages with a consistent theme: "the cyclical nature of the world's fortunes, in which nations rise and fall."[1] But as in Cole's and Church's ruminations on faulty human endeavor, Hegarty's work is about the possibility of rebirth amid destruction, though not necessarily a rebirth involving people. *Picnic* is Hegarty's garish acrylic reproduction on canvas of Cole's meditative *A Pic-Nic Party* (1846, Brooklyn Museum) treated with an intensified Thomas Kinkade palette, and here frame and canvas are seemingly shot full of holes in an arc rising from lower left to upper right. But then the culprit is revealed, at left, in the form of a faux-taxidermical downy woodpecker that is poking at the fake foam-core and papier mâché frame in its endless quest for insects. In the furniture piece, a crow-size pileated woodpecker, also native to the Hudson River Valley but threated with extinction, goes to town on a mahogany card table, as if these mechanical beings from nature itself are taking their revenge on human intervention into the environment and transformation of natural materials. In Hegarty's work, often the materials of art, changed for human aesthetic delectation, are in chaotic and melancholy ways attempting to return to their natural state—frames transform into branches, metals return to ores in the form of rust, animals assist in this resilient process. The environs of the Hudson Valley, modern issues of conservation, and the art made in the region, have been key for Hegarty in developing these potent themes of constructed destruction.[2]

---

1. Elyse A. Gonzales, *Ruins in Contemporary Art: The Stumbling Present* (Santa Barbara, CA: Art, Design & Architecture Museum, 2013), 104.

2. See *Autumn in the Hudson Valley with Branches*, a Jasper Francis Cropsey-inspired work installed on Manhattan's High Line in 2009–2010. http://art.thehighline.org/project/valeriehegarty/.

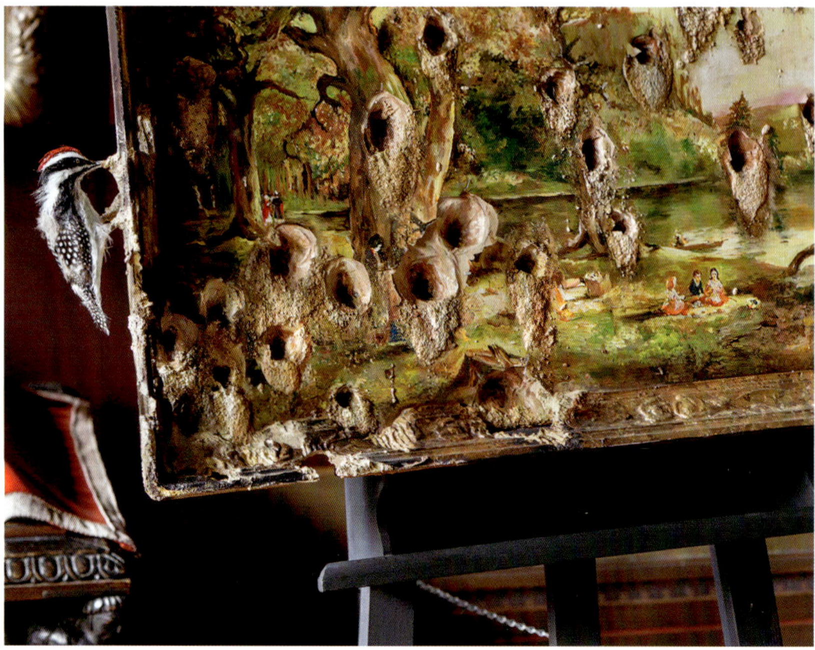

Detail of *Picnic with Downy Woodpecker*.

PLATE 36

Picnic with Downy Woodpecker, 2013. Canvas, stretcher, foam molding, acrylic paint, paper, glue, sand, gold foil, and feathers, 46 x 32½ x 5 in. (116.8 x 82.6 x 12.7 cm); and *Table and Chair with Pileated Woodpecker*, 2013. Table: foam-core, acrylic paint, paper, glue, sand, and feathers, 36 x 32 x 24 in. (91.4 x 81.3 x 61 cm); chair: 36 x 19 x 17 in. (91.4 x 48.3 x 43.2 cm). Collection of the artist.

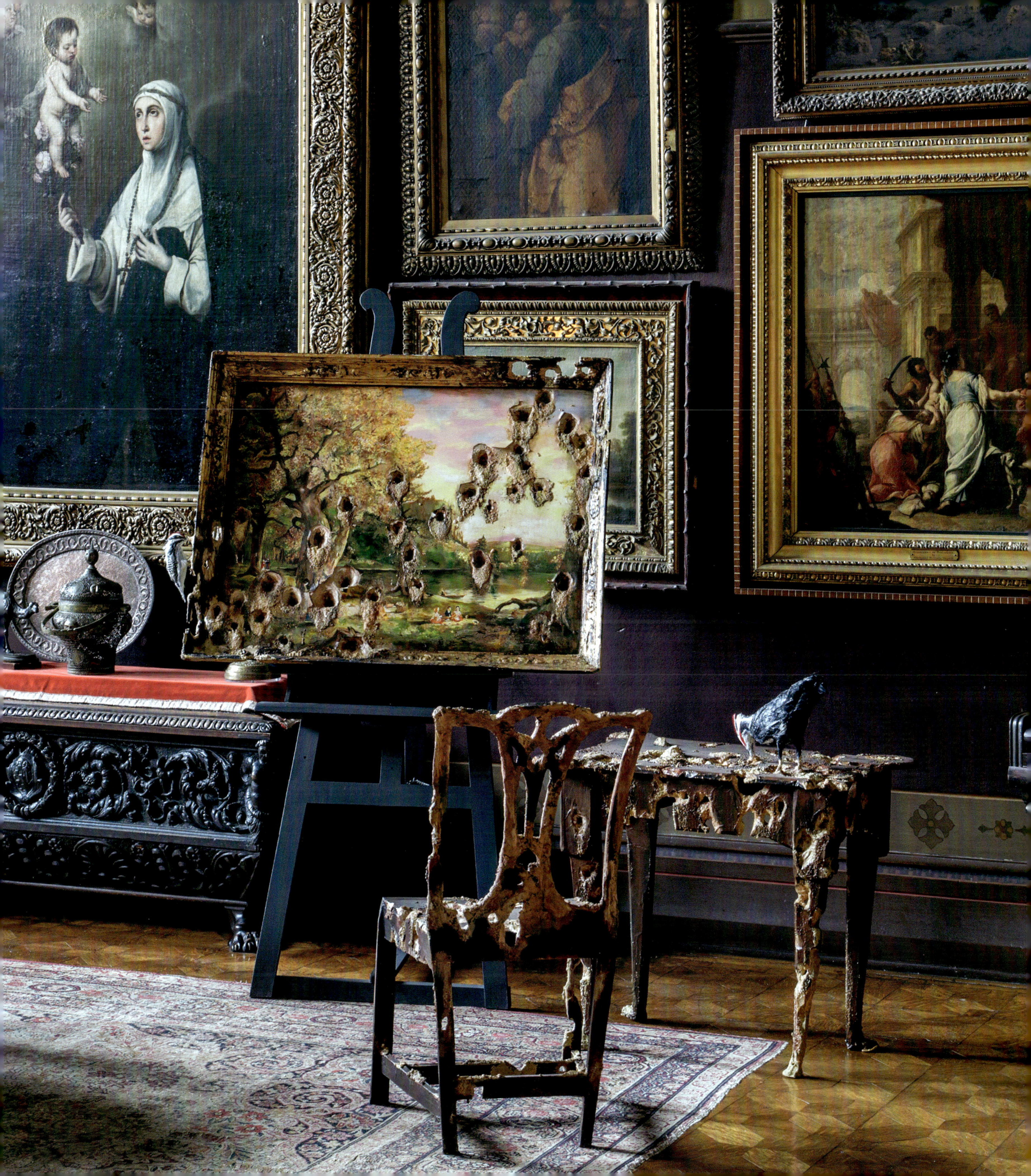

MARTIN **PURYEAR** (b. 1941)

Puryear was born and raised in Washington, DC, studied woodworking in Sierra Leone and Stockholm, Sweden, and earned an MFA from Yale University. He is one of the world's most eminent sculptors and has lived in the Hudson Valley for the past 25 years. His mother was a schoolteacher and his father a postal worker who was a handyman, someone who "would never have said he was an artist, [but] could build anything he needed."[1] This utilitarian impulse runs strongly through Puryear's art, a body of work free from slickness and thoroughly marked by sincerity. Puryear brought his father to Olana when he first visited the house, shortly after moving to the region. As discussed in "*River Crossings*: 'An unbounded capacity for improvement by art'" in this volume (pp. 12–21), Puryear's *Question* (plate 37), the work that serves as the directive theme of *River Crossings*, is consistent within his oeuvre in the sense that in John Elderfield's description, it "shows us the ordinary transforming into the extraordinary."[2] The work is richly organic—made of natural materials that have been evidently worked but are not visibly treated, stained, or polychromed, and with a bulbous base that resembles a germinated seed. The rippling cords of poplar burst from the pillowed orb base and stretch up—and here the subtleness of Puryear's exact placement of *Question* in the Court Hall at Olana (see cover and pp. 2–3) connects with the organic reading of the work, as the trunk cranes like a plant toward the sun, present in the form of the light filtering into the room from the vast southern window. The loop streams through space, reaches its apex at a little more than nine feet, and emphatically plunges down to intersect seamlessly with the floor, seemingly into the ground itself as if extending into Olana's lower level, its foundation, and then the earth of Sienghenberg, "Long Hill," on which the house sits. This connection to the environment is suggested, but the materials Puryear uses puts it into practice, and as in all his work, the making process is foregrounded. The various woods comprising *Question* absorb light into their smoothly worked surfaces and represent a variety of local growths. The huge and stately tulip poplar tree provided wood for the loop, the base is of eastern white pine, and the smaller joining shield between them is of hardwood ash, an arboreal species threatened in the area by the alien emerald ash borer insect, and a wood famous in applications from tool handles to the Morgan Sports Car frame to baseball bats. Remarkably, *Question* is built from the inside out and then sculpted—Puryear's mature and assured technique is both additive and subtractive, combining the two traditional approaches to the medium. For example, the loop is made of three combined elements: a middle section of poplar that is laminated with two thin layers that make the curve. These two cheek pieces are solid on either side and go up and follow the curvature of the loop, and then they are carved by hand into a "cross-sectional square." The entire sculpture is put together with wood connector splines and glue, no metal. However, *Question* does exist in a few bronze formats and in a related bronze titled *Lock* (2010), in addition to this single wood iteration. Here, the wood is tool worked, with no sandpaper, such that every pass of the woodworking implement leaves a facet for light, like Auguste Rodin (1840–1917) using his fingers in clay to develop his expressive surfaces, so that Puryear creates a subtle kind of sculptural facture. This approach is emblematic of the artist's continued dedication to simplified forms and consummate craft, in whatever medium he chooses to work in, and it sits well and harmoniously in Frederic Edwin Church's similarly handmade house.

---

1. Material for this entry derived from conversations with the artist, July 14 and 31, 2014 and April 28, 2015.

2. John Elderfield, "Martin Puryear: Ideas of Otherness," in *Martin Puryear* (New York: The Museum of Modern Art, 2007), 30.

Question, 2010–2014. Tulip poplar, pine, and ash, 90 x 109¼ x 34½ in. (228.6 x 277.5 x 87.6 cm). Collection of the artist. © Martin Puryear. Photograph courtesy of Matthew Marks Gallery.

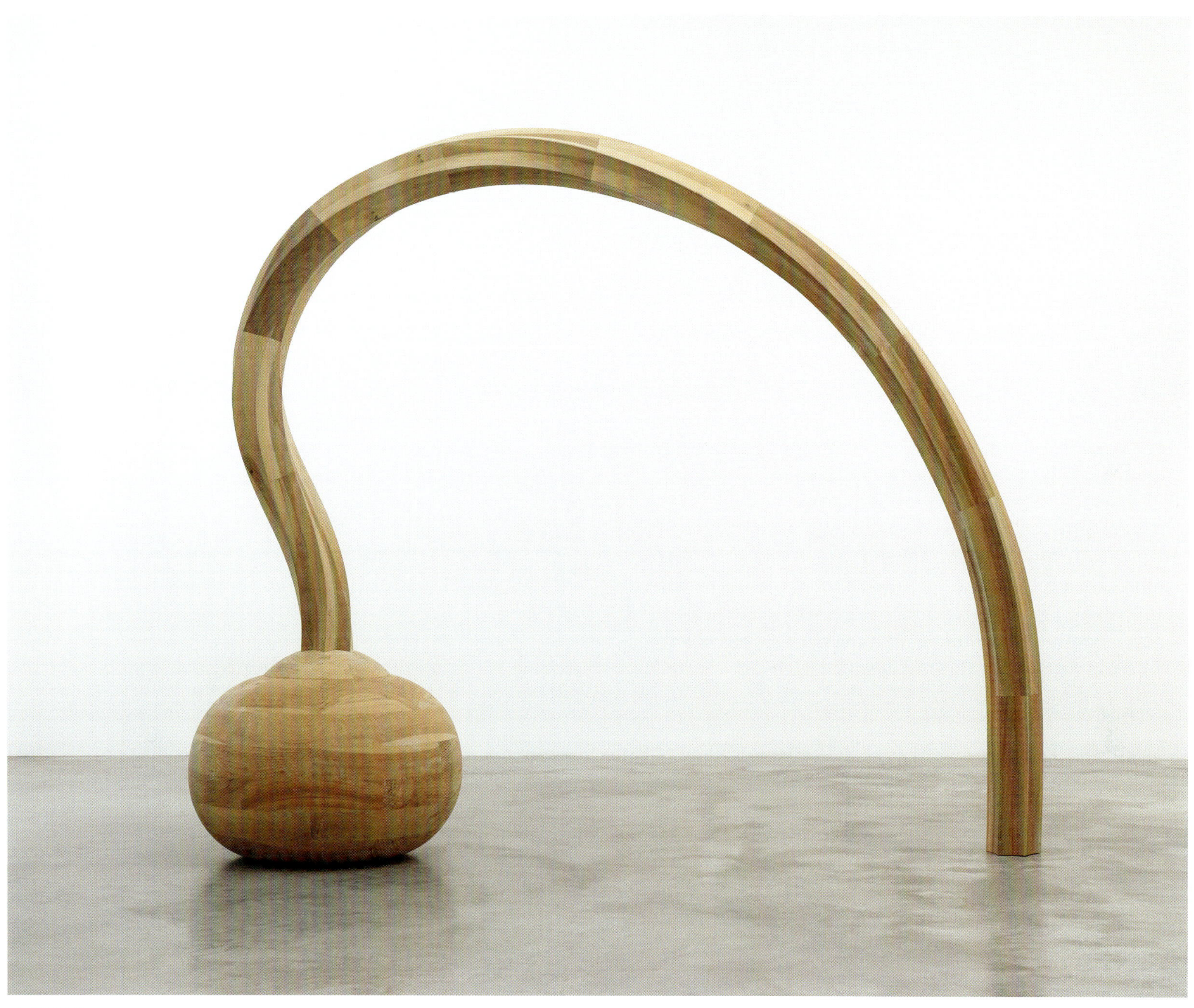

PLATE 37

LYNN **DAVIS** (b. 1944)

Photographer Davis received her BFA from the San Francisco Art Institute, apprenticed under Berenice Abbott (1898–1991), and now lives and works in Hudson, New York. Water is a consistent motif in Davis's large-format photographs, and the subject of her numerous solo exhibitions. Inspired by the themes and immersive sizes of Church's paintings, Davis has pursued a project of visiting the sites of the artist's travels and subjecting them to her own perspective and technical approach. Unlike Church, Davis works in a square format, and lets the natural scenery expand within these controlled proportions. In *Horseshoe Falls, Ontario, Canada* (plate 39), one of several images she has made around Niagara, Davis adopted her characteristically head-on position, avoiding the vertiginous aerial views of some of Church's paintings, or the worm's-eye view from terra firma of street photographers frequently adopted by Abbott. Imposing and timeless in their monochromatic stateliness, rigorously formatted in square compositions, Davis subjects the panoramic to the monumentally schematic, in works wherein perceptual proximity and scale are dissociated, spray renders the left and bottom edges incomprehensible, and the massive wall of water at right is blurred, its constituent shocks of foam unrecognizable. This work and her image *Iceberg 29, Disko Bay, Greenland* (plate 38) are installed in the East Parlor at Olana, the room best suited to hanging art in the house, and seen in collaborative company amidst Church's sketches of his favorite motifs.

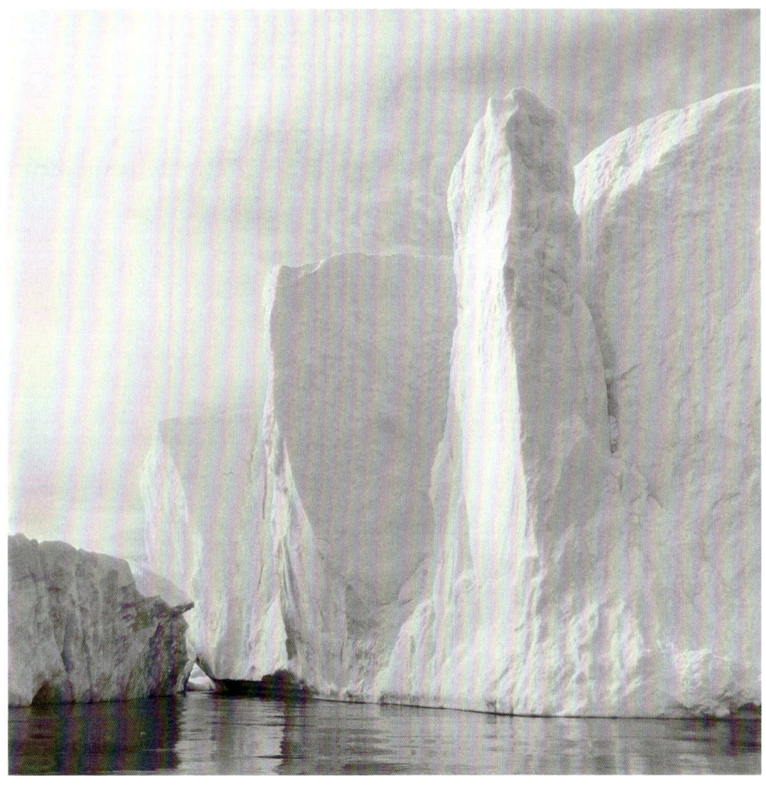

PLATE 38

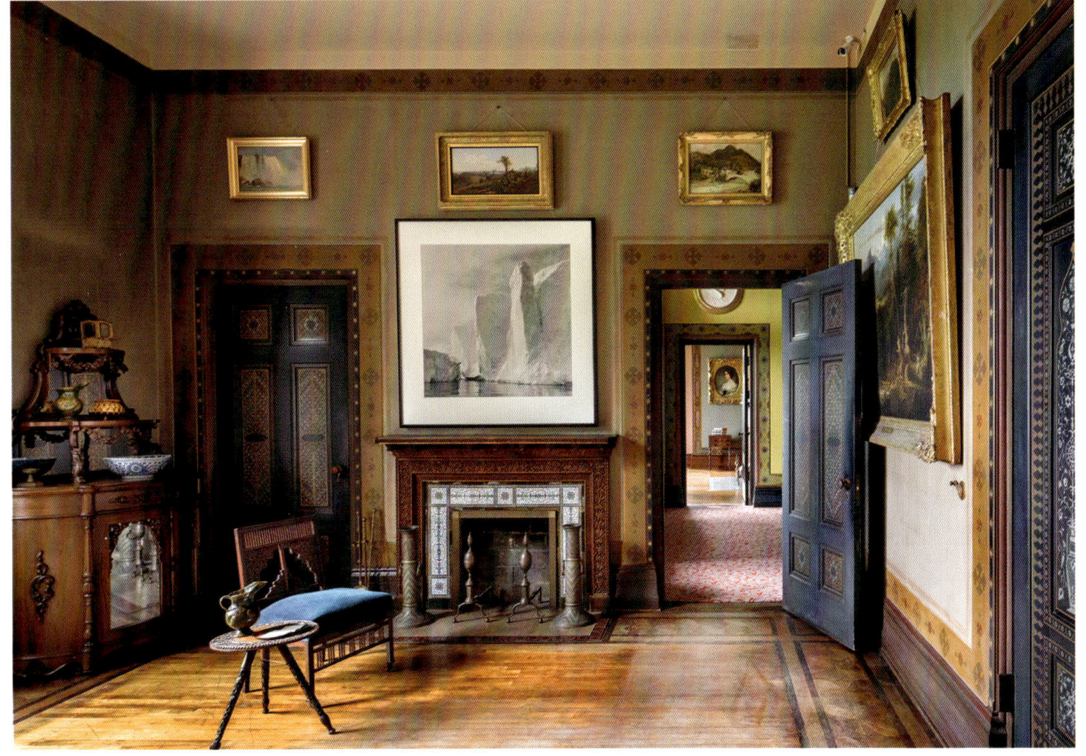

Lynn Davis, *Iceberg 29, Disko Bay, Greenland*, 2000 (plate 38) in the East Parlor.

Iceberg 29, Disko Bay, Greenland, 2000. Silver gelatin print, 40 x 40 in. (101.6 x 101.6 cm), framed. Collection of the artist. © Lynn Davis.

Horseshoe Falls, Ontario, Canada, 1992. Silver gelatin print, 45 x 45 in. (144.8 x 147.3 cm), framed. Collection of the artist. © Lynn Davis.

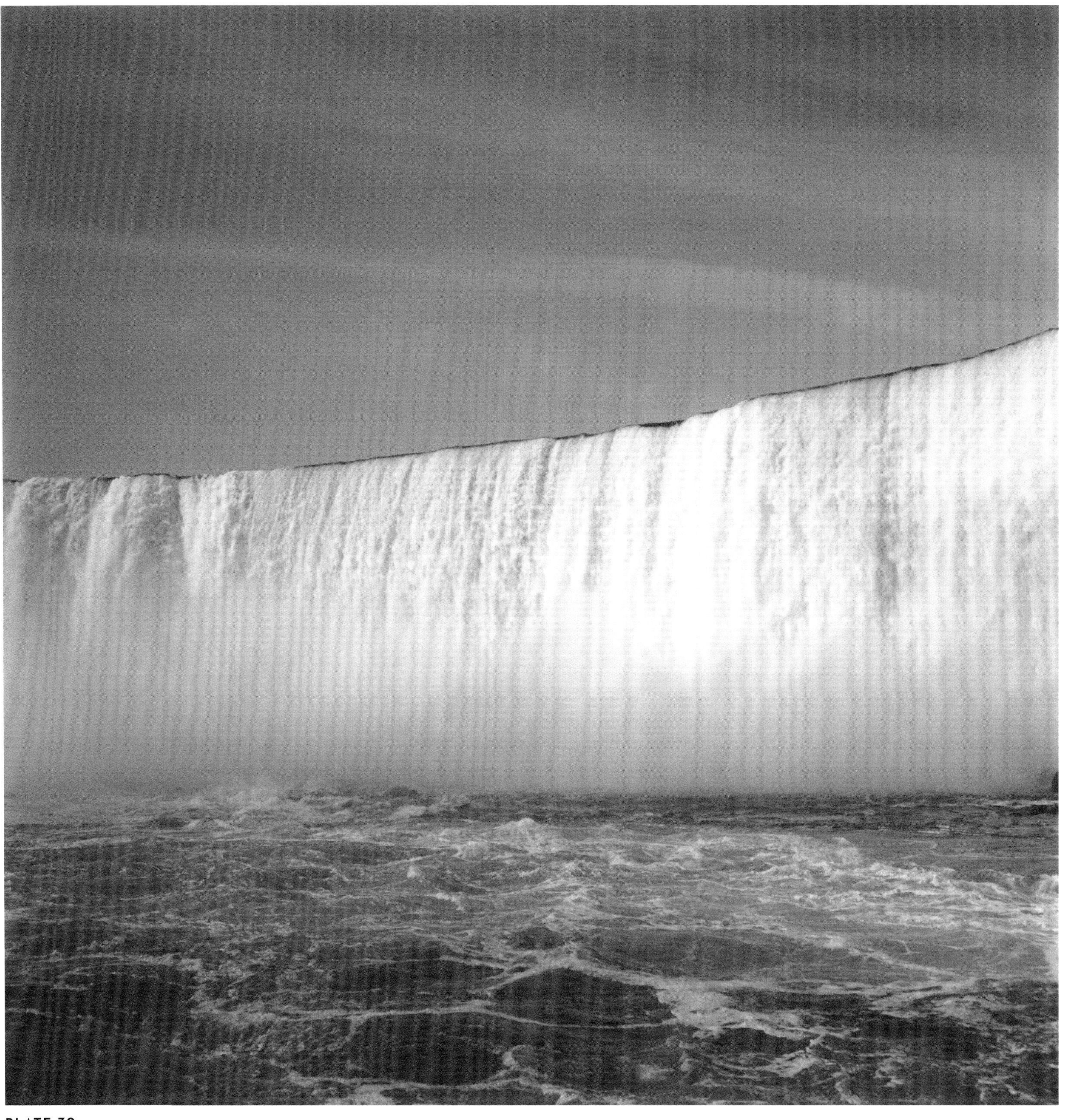

PLATE 39

MAYA **LIN** (b. 1959)

Architect and sculptor Maya Lin grew up in Ohio and studied at Yale University where, as an undergraduate, she won the national competition to design the Vietnam Veterans Memorial in Washington, DC (1982), a project that shifted the culture of such monuments in its successful combination of simplified form, formal rigor, and the ability to connect with a broad public. *Silver River–Hudson* (plate 40) in the Sitting Room at Olana, represents recent work concerned with documenting and aestheticizing the course of rivers, as discussed in my essay in this volume (see pages 12–21). Lin notes that "We have chosen where we live due to our access to major waterways—and these places were also where there was a historic abundance of biodiversity—over time one sees a severe degradation of these once amazing estuaries and waterways—I create these silver works while simultaneously researching the ecological history of each place—creating timelines that span from the earliest recorded accounts of those places to the present day—incorporating these into my final memorial, *What is Missing?* asking and inviting people to share their memorial of each place from an ecological perspective—following a river back in time."[1] Thus this piece is part of a larger project, ecologically based, and connected to the timeline of the Hudson stretching back to its earliest exploration, and then the influx of development that accompanied Cole, the Erie Canal, and Church upriver. Lin's silvered bas-relief map peters away at the top, at the waterway's origins at Lake Tear of the Clouds, and is redolent of the futility of Henry Hudson's quest for the Northwest Passage in the early seventeenth century. In the lower section, as if encouraged by gravity, the pooling metal stretches into New York Bay past the Verrazano Narrows and into the Atlantic, and out Long Island Sound as far east as Orient Point. The work's elegant, natural arabesques harmonize both with the craggy forms in *El Khasné, Petra* (1874) and the nonsensical scribblings meant to emulate Arabic script that Church painted in the decorative borders on the walls. If a line is traced from the underside of the top of the doorframe to the map, it falls onto the gentle curve of the Hudson to the south at Inbocht Bay and Silver Point, visible through the ornate neo-Persian window that Church included in the design of the room. Lin's sculpture, placed in this orientation vessel of a house (and with Church's compass in the floor of the piazza, just outside the Sitting Room), creates a moving sense of rootedness and calls to mind Thomas Cole's sonorous lines from a poem of 1833:

> "The Hudson lies below, a mirror'd heaven;
> Stainless, save where the joyous hills are given
> With grassy slope, dark rock, and breezy wood
> In purple beauty to the wooing flood—"[2]

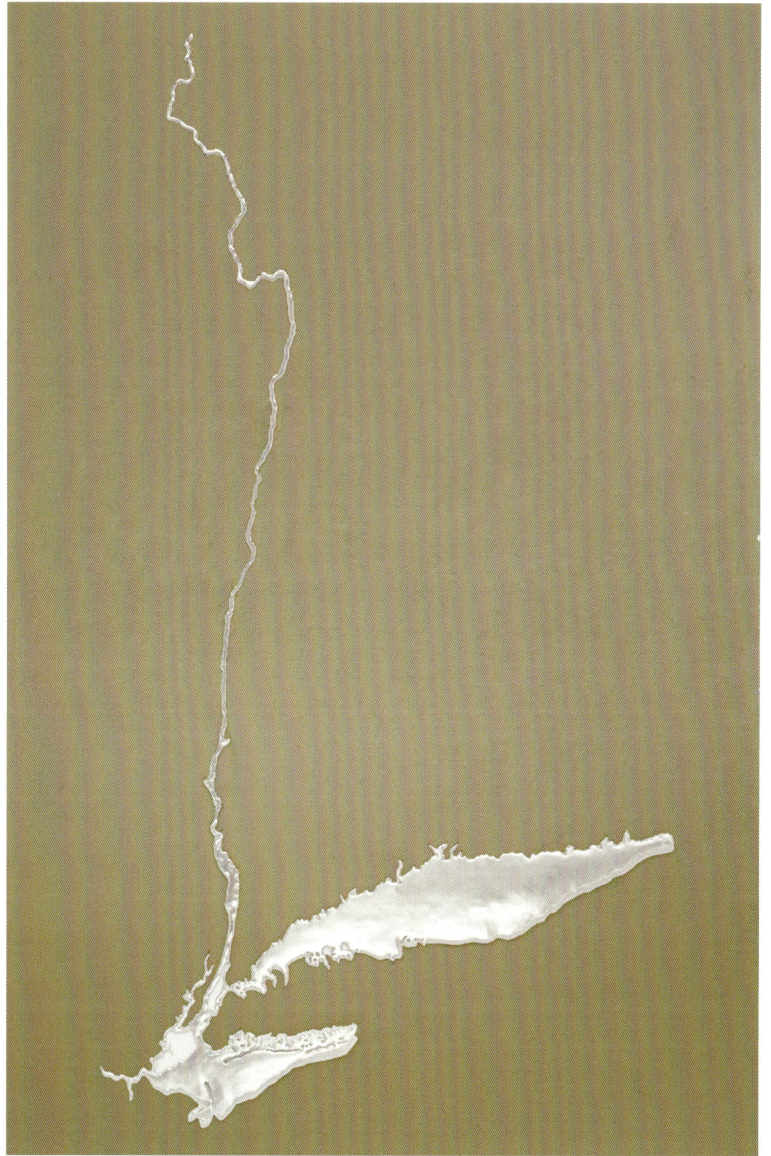

PLATE 40

---

1. Maya Lin, "Here and There," in *Maya Lin: Here and There* (New York: PaceWildenstein, 2013), 13.

2. "Lines Written after a Walk on [a] Beautiful Morning in November," dated Catskill, 1833. See Marshall B. Tymn, ed., *Thomas Cole's Poetry* (York, PA: Liberty Cap Books, 1972), 62.

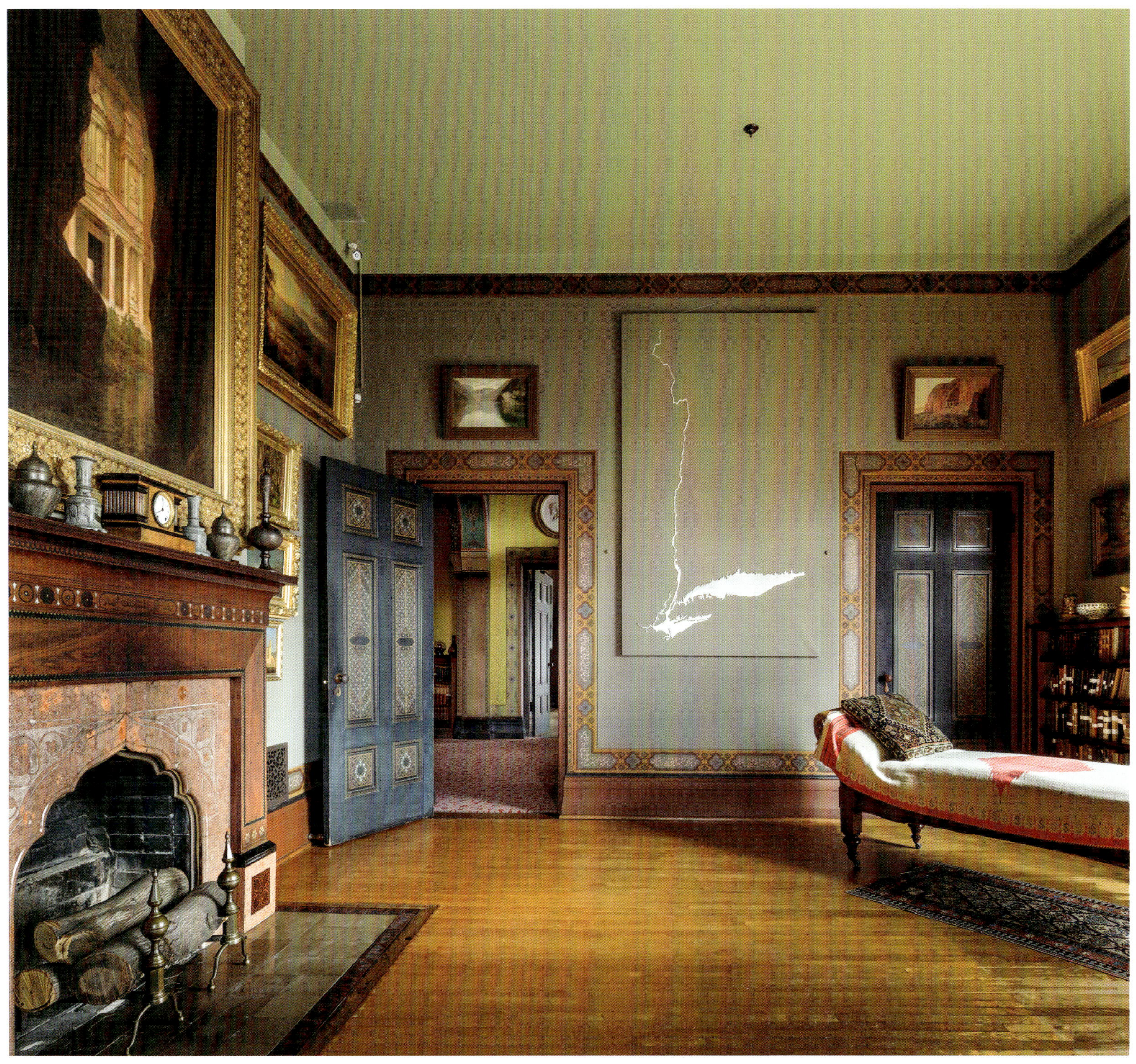

Maya Lin, *Silver River–Hudson*, 2011 (plate 40) in the Sitting Room.

Silver River–Hudson, 2011. Recycled silver,
81 x 45 x ¾ in. (205.7 x 114.3 x 1.9 cm), overall
installed. AP 2 of 2; edition of 3 + 2 APs. Collection
of the artist. © Maya Lin Studio. Photograph: Kerry
Ryan McFate, courtesy Pace Gallery.

ELIJAH **BURGHER** (b. 1978)

Born in Kingston, New York, and now living in Chicago, Burgher earned his degrees from Sarah Lawrence College and the School of The Art Institute of Chicago. His work was featured in the Whitney Biennial in 2014. Burgher has evolved a personal language in his art that communicates his interests in nature, sign-systems, gay identity, and color-coding. Such works based on tramps around Little Tonshi Mountain in Shokan, and the environs of the Ashokan Reservoir (plate 42), bear an intensity commensurate with the work supported by the English critic and champion of the English nineteenth-century Pre-Raphaelites, John Ruskin (1819–1900), whose writings also inspired Church and his generation of landscapists in New York and whom Church met in London. For Ruskin, an understanding of nature and a clear conceptualization of its forms would lead people to seek to better society and inspire a new generation of valued design, as bore fruit in the works of artists such as William Morris (1834–1896), Edward Burne-Jones (1833–1898), and Walter Crane (1845–1915). Burgher has developed a system of what he calls "sigils," rune-like forms that function as a personal language, though the etched elements on the large rock in *Sleep Has His House (for Antonio)* (plate 42) can be seen to resolve into his initials. As A.A. Bronson has written, "His process comes out of European ceremonial magic, and in particular uses the sigil technique of Austin Osman Spare, now standard in Chaos Magic."[1] The English artist and occultist Spare (1886–1956), from the generation after the Pre-Raphaelites, developed a psychologically and sexually engaged body of written and artistic work. And Burgher's meticulously drawn and ringingly colored works continue the focus of artists of this strain. Burgher's recent productions include large colorful drop cloths that bear such sigils and hang in the middle of rooms, like tapestries freed from a supporting wall, and let loose to flutter and communicate freely in the world.

---

1. "A.A. Bronson Selects Abstract Ceremonial Painter Elijah Burgher," last modified December 2014, http://www.hero-magazine.com/article/29217/ aa-bronson-selects-abstract-ceremonial-painter-elijah-burgher/.

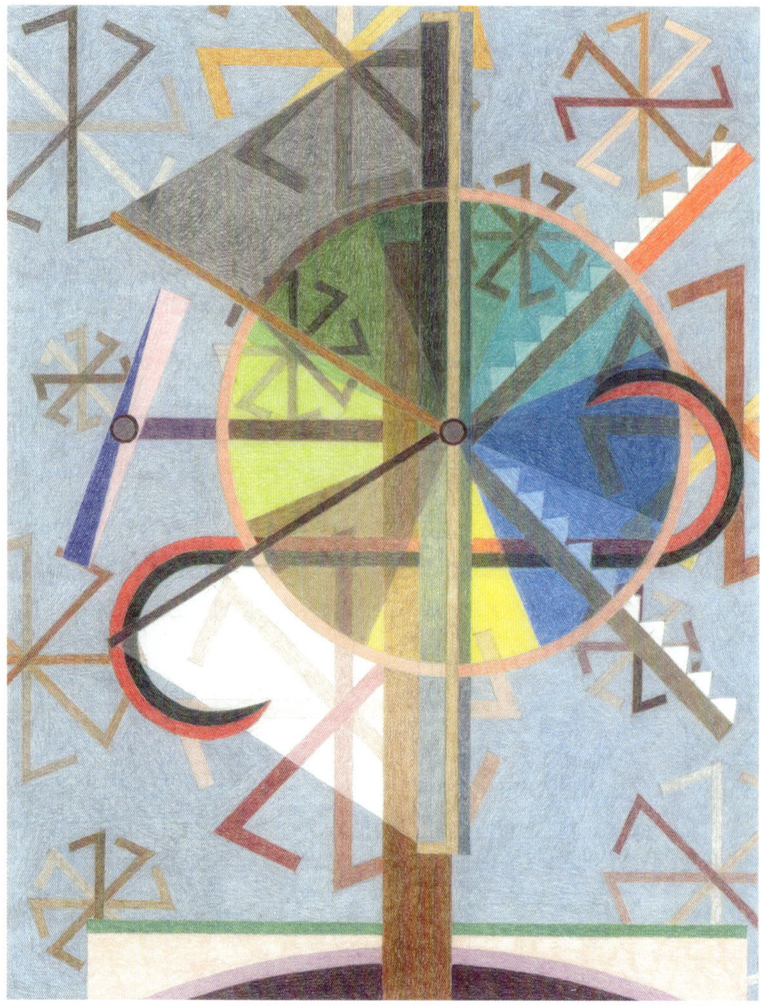

PLATE 41

Build Better Human Beings, 2012. Colored pencil and paper, 11 x 14 in. (27.9 x 35.6 cm). Collection of Jacob Meehan. Photograph courtesy of the artist and Western Exhibitions, Chicago, IL.

Sleep Has His House (for Antonio), 2012. Colored pencil and paper, 19 x 24 in. (48.3 x 61 cm). Pedro A. Guerrero Art Collection. Photograph courtesy of the artist and Western Exhibitions, Chicago, IL.

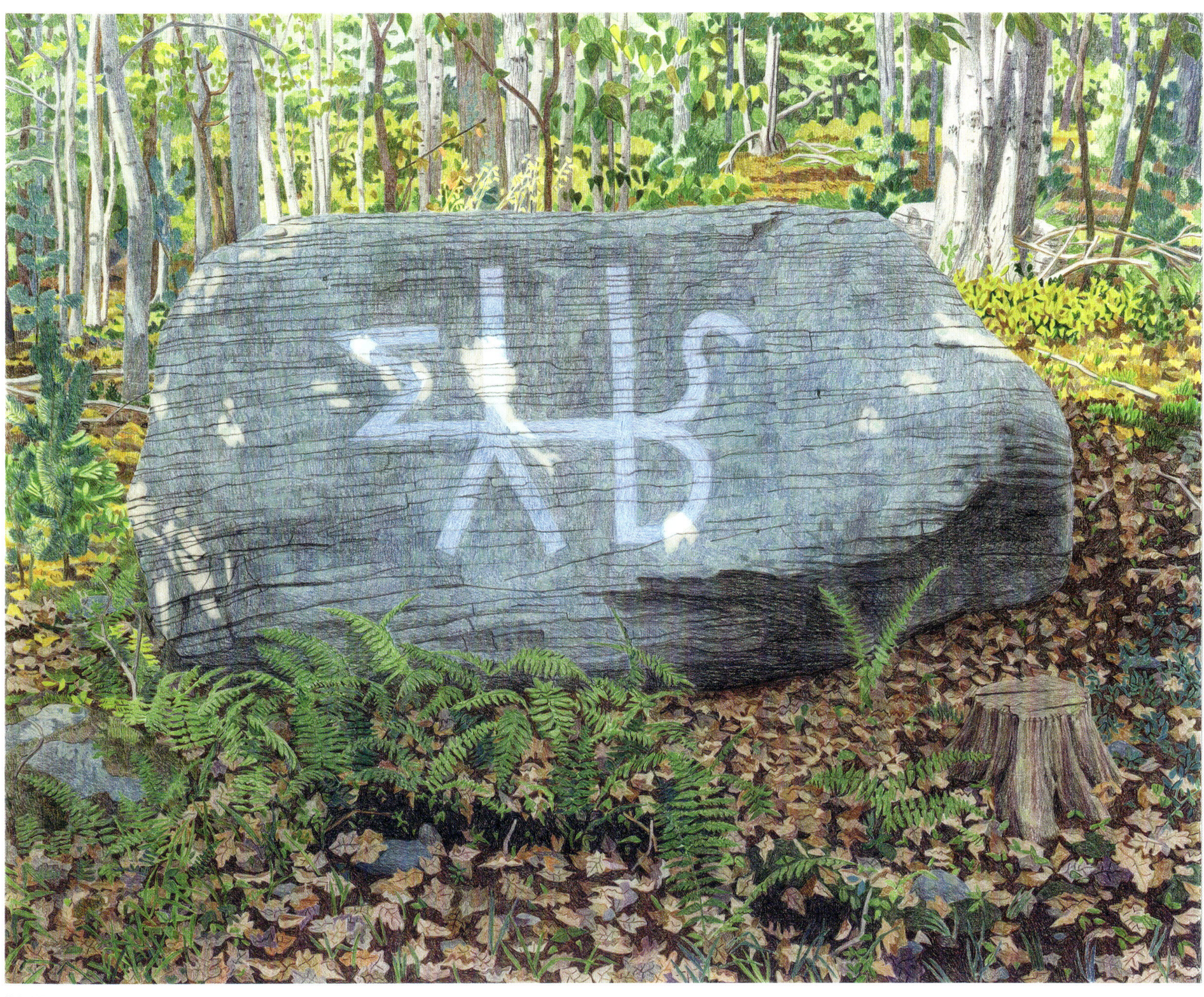

PLATE 42

LETHA **WILSON** (b. 1976)

Hawaiian-born Wilson has been a longtime resident of New York City and has more recently been working outside of Hudson, after having been an assistant to the local multimedia artist Jason Middlebrook (b. 1966). She studied at Syracuse University and Hunter College, New York. Wilson's work is based in photography but expands that medium's parameters both in terms of imagery and fabrication. Wilson's pieces, located in the studio alcove at Olana, engage Church and his practice in conversation, forming a dialogue that seeks to place works within the space so that they become one with the environment, and take up the nineteenth-century painter and traveler's exploratory spirit. She has been using concrete in her work for approximately the past five years, and her recent pieces can weigh up to 400 pounds. Wilson's photographs are typically folded into a mold and backed with concrete, in a reverse of the traditional method of fresco painting, a technique she worked in during a residency at the Skowhegan School of Painting and Sculpture in Maine in 2009. Thus photography, whether in a rare example of a tondo of folded and collaged Kodak C-prints, as in *Storm Cloud Circle Fold (Colorado)* (plate 43), or prints with concrete backing, as in *Rock Hole Punch (Utah Canyon)* (plate 44), assumes the condition of sculpture, and the works hang on walls as reliefs.[1] But instead of incorporating photography into sculpture, as Robert Rauschenberg (1925–2008) pursued from the 1950s in his combines, or as in the photographs applied to geometric sculptural surfaces in the work of Polish artist Szymon Rogiński (b. 1975),[2] Wilson's shots become symbiotically bound to concrete supports, or their emulsion is used in a transfer technique, wherein the photographic image is imprinted onto the concrete. The titles incorporate general geographical notations—part of her practice is to shoot landscape features while hiking, traveling, and camping in the American West, where her family lives. She seeks out sites that still bear an uninhabited sense of vastness, as if they have not yet been explored or mapped. *Rock Hole Punch* incorporates a photograph shot in a canyon in Utah that remains unnamed. Like nineteenth-century artists Albert Bierstadt (1830–1902) and Thomas Moran (1837–1926) before her, who accompanied missions to map, document, and photograph the farthest reaches of the nation, and who translated what they saw for avid audiences on the heavily developed East Coast, Wilson seeks to commune with the undiscovered and difficult to access spaces of this well-traversed nation in pursuing her exploratory and focused art.

---

1. See Carol Squires, *What is a Photograph?* (New York: Delmonico Books and KP, 2013).

2. Concepts first explored in curator Peter Bunnell's touring exhibition that originated at MoMA in April 1970 titled *The Photographic Object*. https://www.moma.org/momaorg/shared/pdfs/docs/press_archives/4438/releases/MOMA_1970_Jan-June_0035_36.pdf?2010.

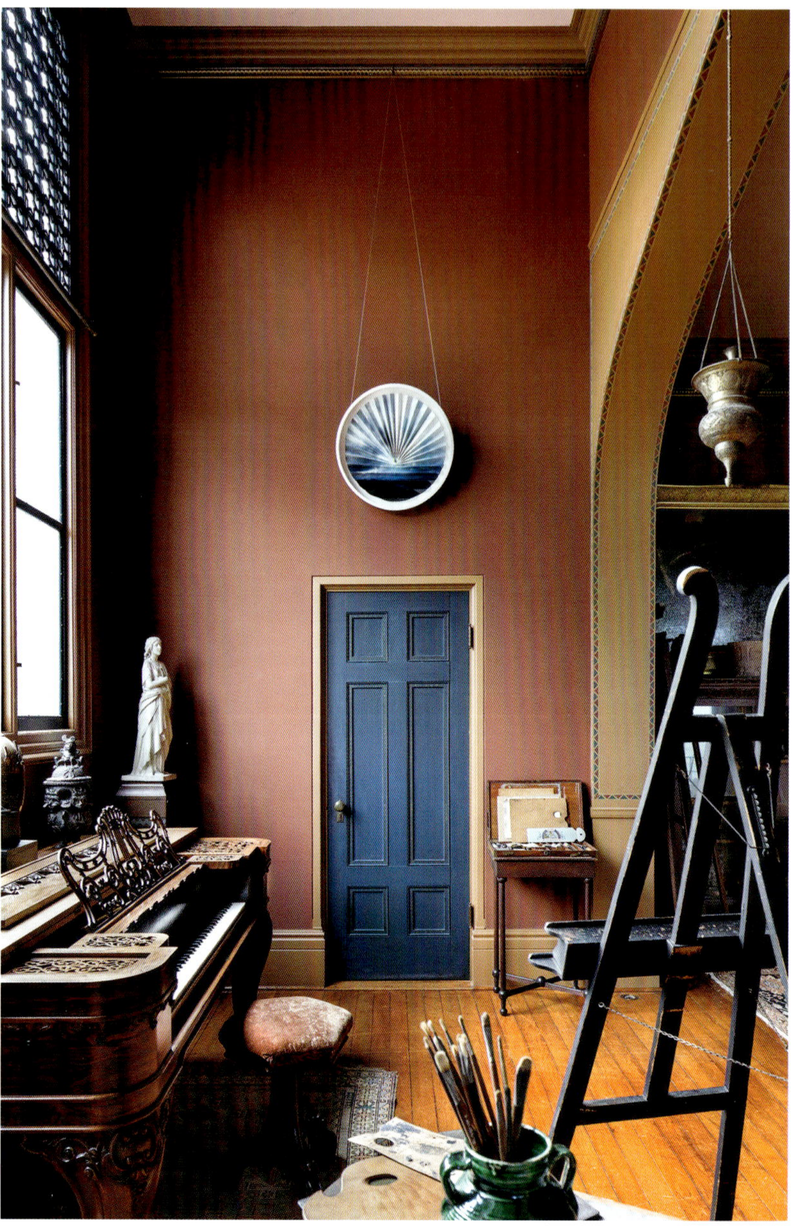

Letha Wilson, *Storm Cloud Circle Fold (Colorado)*, 2012 (plate 43) in the Studio.

Storm Cloud Circle Fold (Colorado), 2012. Unique C-prints on museum board, 21 x 21 x 2½ in. (53.3 x 53.3 x 6.4 cm) tondo. Collection of Marian and Stephan Loginsky.

Rock Hole Punch (Utah Canyon), 2014. Unique C-print and concrete, 20 x 16 x 2 in. (50.8 x 40.6 x 5.1 cm). Collection of the artist, Brooklyn, NY.

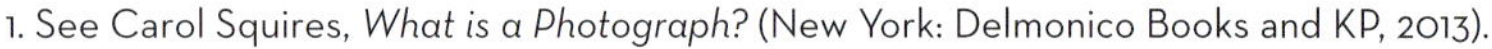

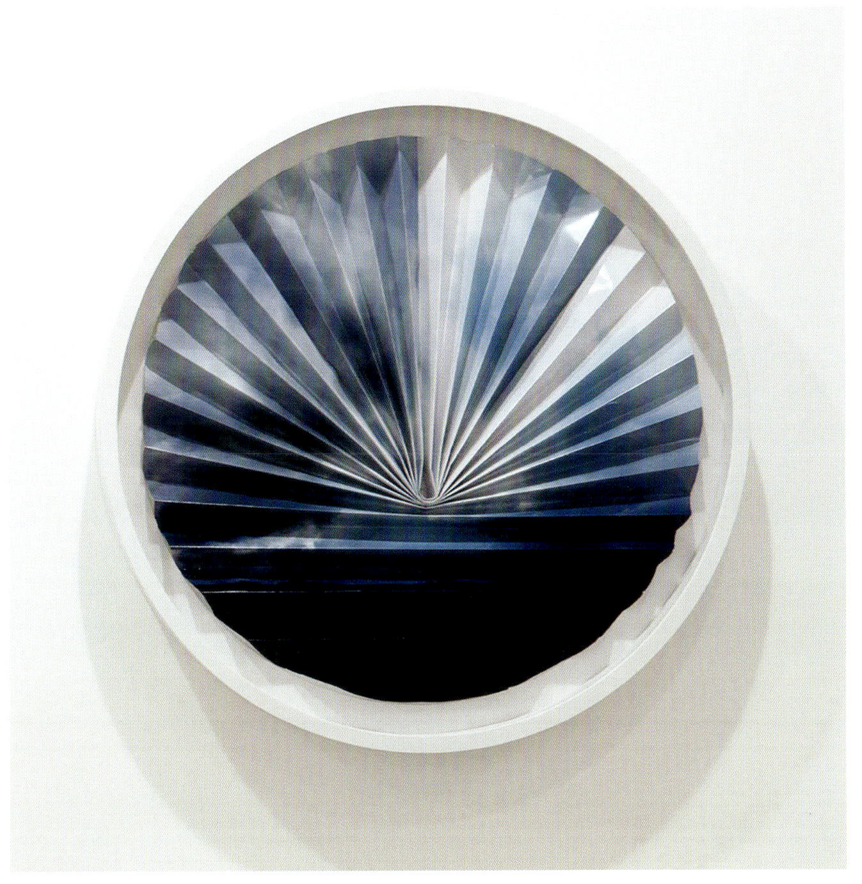

PLATE 43

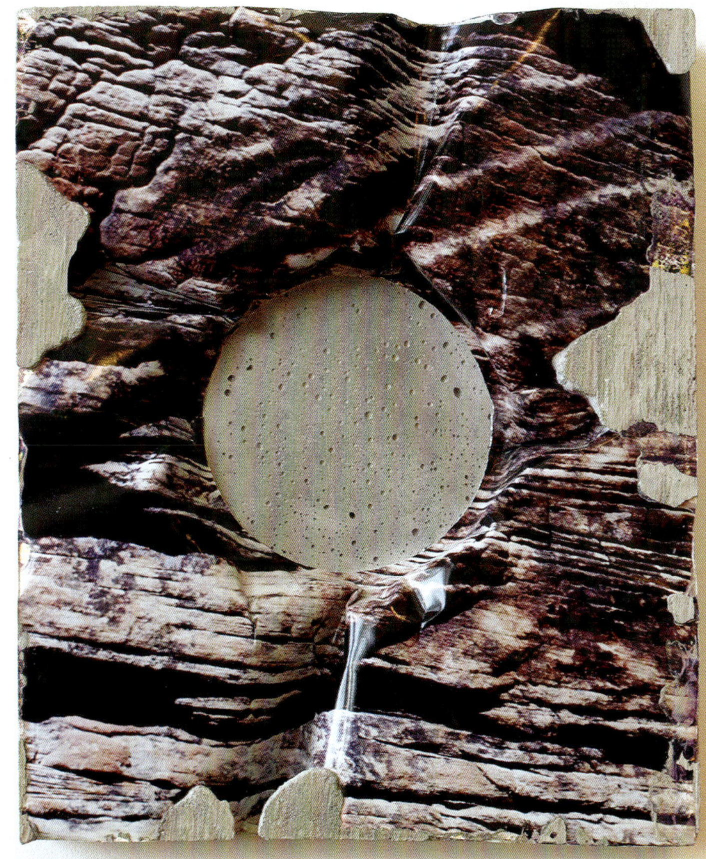

PLATE 44

WILL **COTTON** (b. 1965)

Cotton grew up in the Hudson Valley and has said that early experiences at Olana communicated to him that artists "could live in a total fantasy world of their own making." This freeing revelation has played out in his art. After studying at Cooper Union and New York Academy of Art, he evolved a painting style wherein landscapes are formed of confections and baked creations, and are interspersed with people. Like the English painter Thomas Gainsborough (1727–1788) in the late-eighteenth century, who built miniature landscape dioramas in his studio using twigs, glass, pebbles, grasses, and broccoli for trees that he then transformed into paintings, Cotton bakes the materials that he then uses in his paintings. The results, carefully painted but with a slight blur, as if seen through clouded glass, are not the trite subject matter of chocolate boxes, but rather grand style portraits such as the one on view in the corridor at Olana, hanging across the doorway to the studio from Charles Loring Elliott's (1812–1868) portrait of Church (1865). With its tenebrist background and eruptive chapeau of macaroons, Cotton's portrait (plate 45) bears a striking likeness to Baroque works from Europe and also Spanish and Portuguese colonies in America, wherein sitters would often be festooned with textured clothing and headgear, leavened with witty doffs of the cap to the performative samba-style aesthetic of Carmen Miranda.

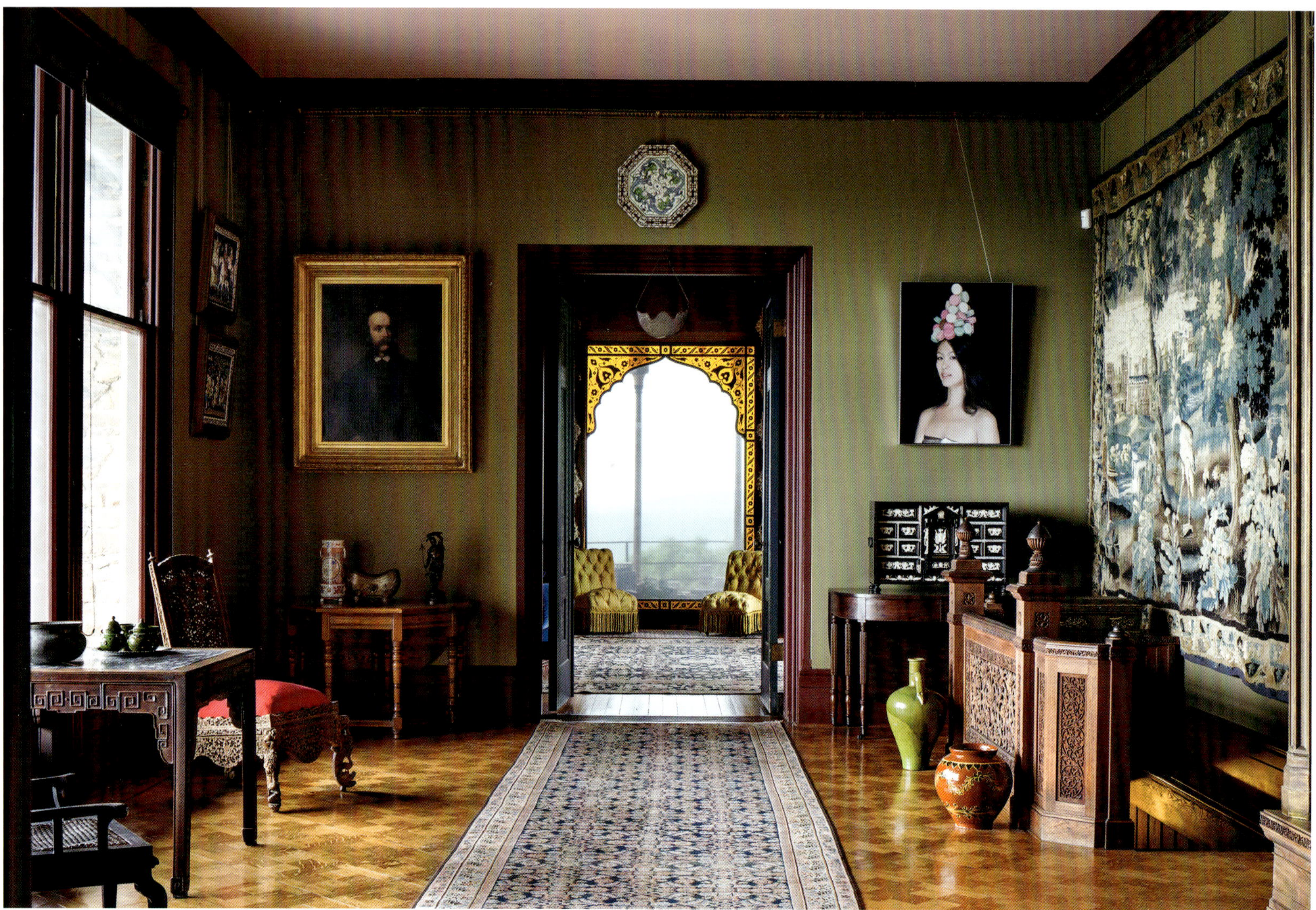

Will Cotton, *Untitled*, 2014 (plate 45) in the Corridor.

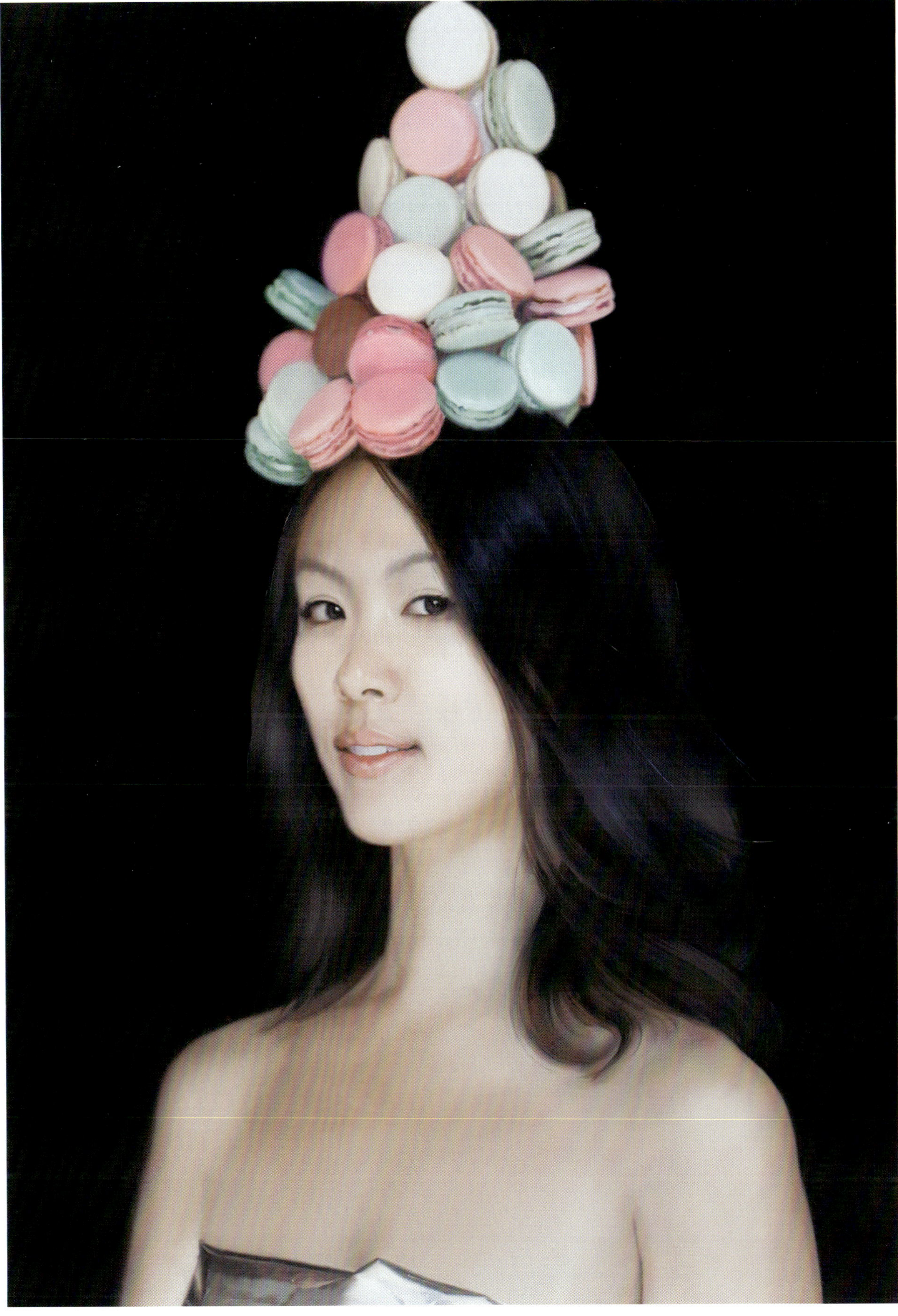

Untitled, 2014. Oil on linen, 34 x 24 in. (86.4 x 61 cm). Private collection. Photograph courtesy Mary Boone Gallery.

CHARLES LeDRAY (b. 1960)

LeDray's art displays, like that of Cole and Church, a deep sense of place and history, as discussed in *"River Crossings:* 'An unbounded capacity for improvement by art'" in this volume (pp. 12–21). The direct associations in *Empire* (plate 46), the site-specific sculptural installation that LeDray has made for the Round Verandah outside Church's studio at Olana, are clear: bricks were a key industry for the region, made of clay from along the Hudson's banks. And the imprint on these reads "Empire," a reference to the Empire Brick & Supply Company in Stockport, New York, Albany County, whose brickyard closed in 1940. *Empire* is visible through the large and slightly murky studio window, which affords a view of the Hudson and the Catskills through a misty scrim, like the effects of a Romantic-era Claude glass, giving the overall scene a painterly quality. In *Empire*, the bricks surround the bases of the columns, and the eight different types of cinderblocks rise to cover the lower part of the Round Verandah walls, as if the building itself is being bricked in. References are many: from Cole's *The Architect's Dream* (1840, Toledo Museum of Art) to Carl Andre's (b. 1935) *Manifest Destiny* (1986, Judd Foundation, 101 Spring Street) with its tower of eight gently listing real Empire bricks, to Alexander Calder's (1898–1976) intricately constructed *Circus* (1926–1931, Whitney Museum

of American Art) and similarly made of decidedly non-luxe materials. *Empire* links also to the irreverent spirit of Robert Smithson's (1938–1973) *Line of Wreckage* established in Bayonne in 1968, and composed of the detritus found amidst a defunct naval terminal, including rocks and cement and rebar.[1] There is a shrunken wood pallet at left that serves as a key to the piece: it displays a brick and one of each of the different miniaturized cinderblocks used in the work. Other features combine to collapse time in their references, from an Acropolis-like structure in the rear left, to a series of upright cinderblock forms in a row that resemble the Agency Buildings on Albany's modernist Empire State Plaza (the subject of Angie Keefer and Kianja Strobert's installation at Cedar Grove (plate 24). Crumbling brick pylons resembling the temple complex at Karnak, Egypt, stretch to the right. And a section in the front center of bricks laid on the floor mimics the paved driveway at Olana.

---

1. The related *Non-site* is in the collection of Milwaukee Art Museum. http://collection.mam.org/details.php?id=12826.

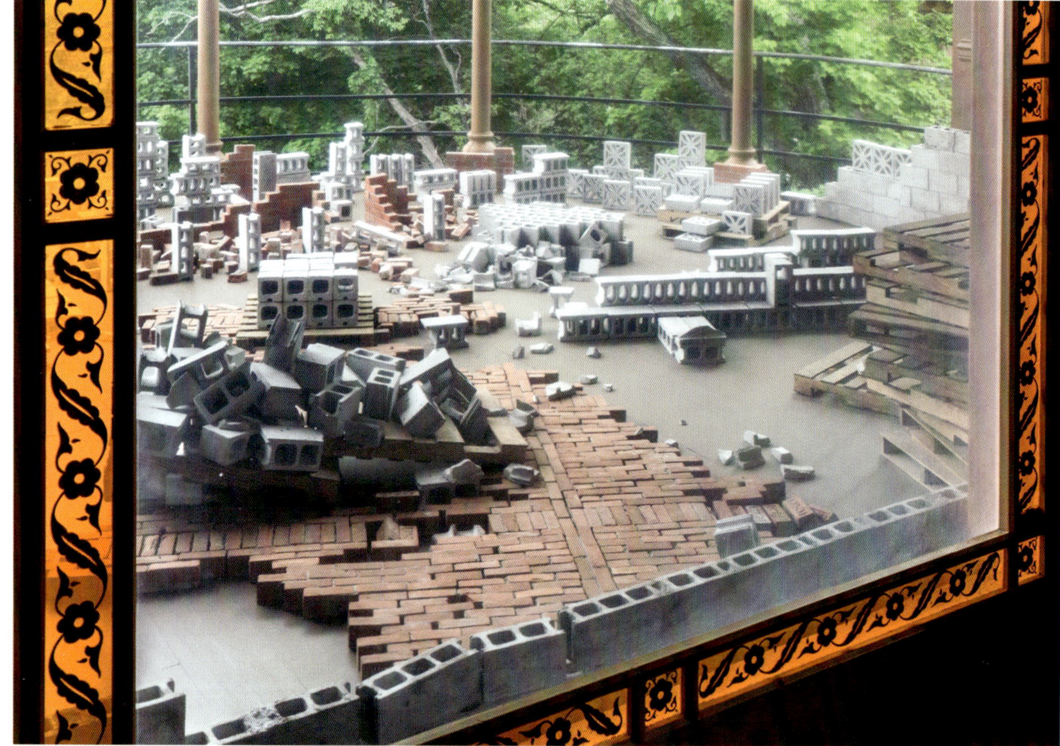

Detail of *Empire*.

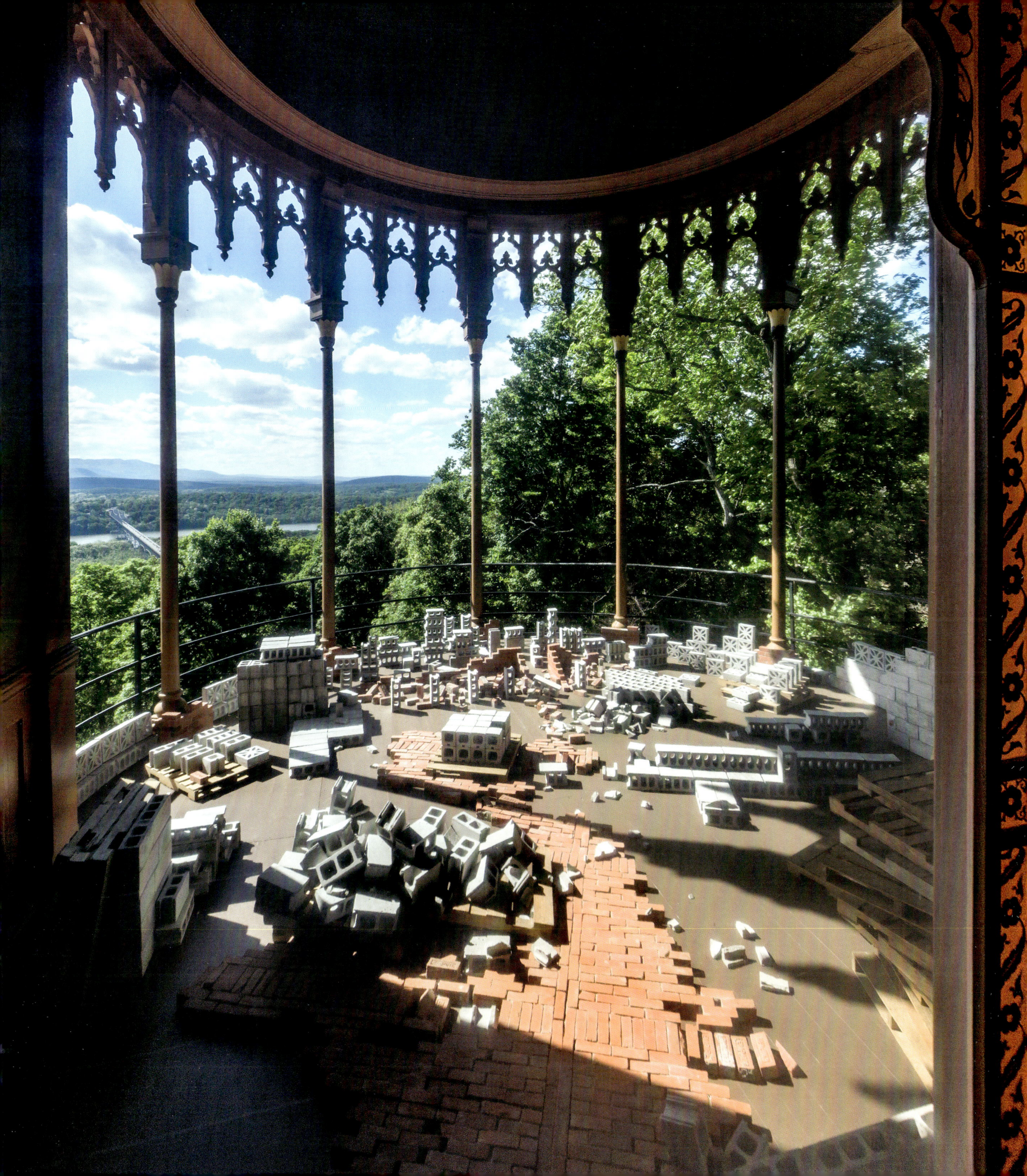

DON **GUMMER** (b. 1946)

Unlike Gummer's twinned sculptures at Cedar Grove that lead visitors straight across the property (plates 33 and 34), at Olana his four works encourage a more circuitous perambulation, along the touring road that Church built in the forest and around the lake (plates 47–50). They are positioned so that strollers may unexpectedly come upon them in the rolling woodlands, designed with curves and changes in elevation derived from English Georgian-era garden design. While their forms seem to echo the verticality of the multiple turrets of the Church house, Gummer has placed them within the woods so that Olana is difficult see through the branches of the trees when they are in full leaf. But less obscured views are possible in late autumn, when the trees are bare. The sculptures swirl and spin like tops, tornadoes, or waterspouts on their concrete or metal bases. The multicolored *Uniting Blue and Red* (plate 50) resembles a Fernand Léger (1881–1955) *Contrast of Forms* painted geometric abstraction come to vivid plastic life, with its translucent red-and-blue-stained panels, elevated by twisting strands of alternately solid and perforated rectangular bronze boxes. *Spanish Guitar* (plate 49) expands the play of solid and void that Pablo Picasso (1881–1973) first assayed in his similarly themed wall-relief sculptures of 1912–1914, while the shimmering water, foliage, and sunlight play through its shard-like punched-out elements. In a similar vein, at almost seven feet tall, *House of Music* (plate 47) is a just under half-size model for a commissioned monument outside the Hibicki Concert Hall in Kitakyushu, Japan (1993). Its Cubo-Furturist spiraling and curving forms on firm vertical supports may call to mind the evocative gestures of a conductor, and a physical sense of tones, mixed with the openwork designs of Russian Constructivism, such as Vladimir Tatlin's (1885–1953) ambitious and soaring design for a *Monument to the Third International* (1919).

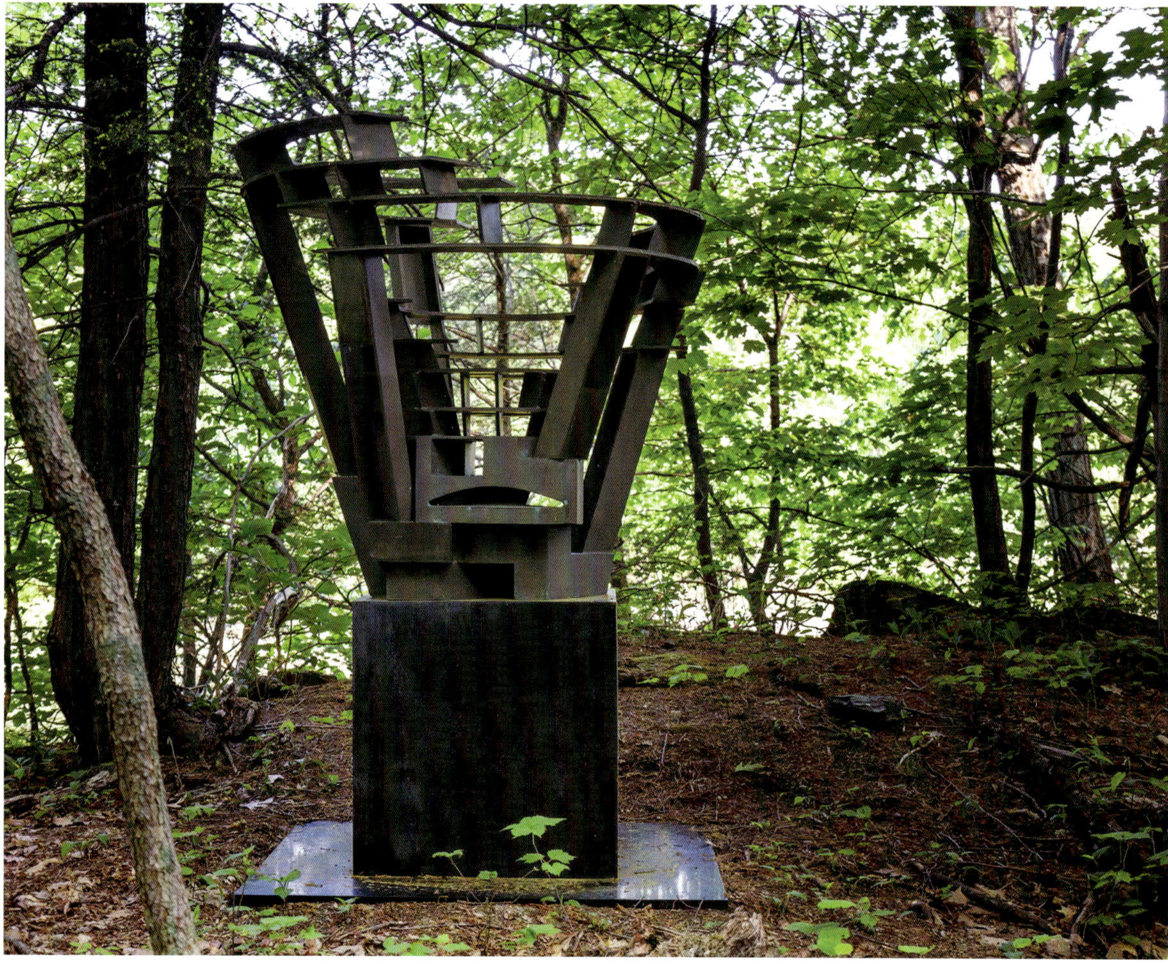

House of Music (model), 1993. Cast bronze on concrete base, 80 x 56 x 52 in. (203.2 x 142.2 x 132.1 cm). Collection of the artist. Courtesy Don Gummer.

PLATE 47

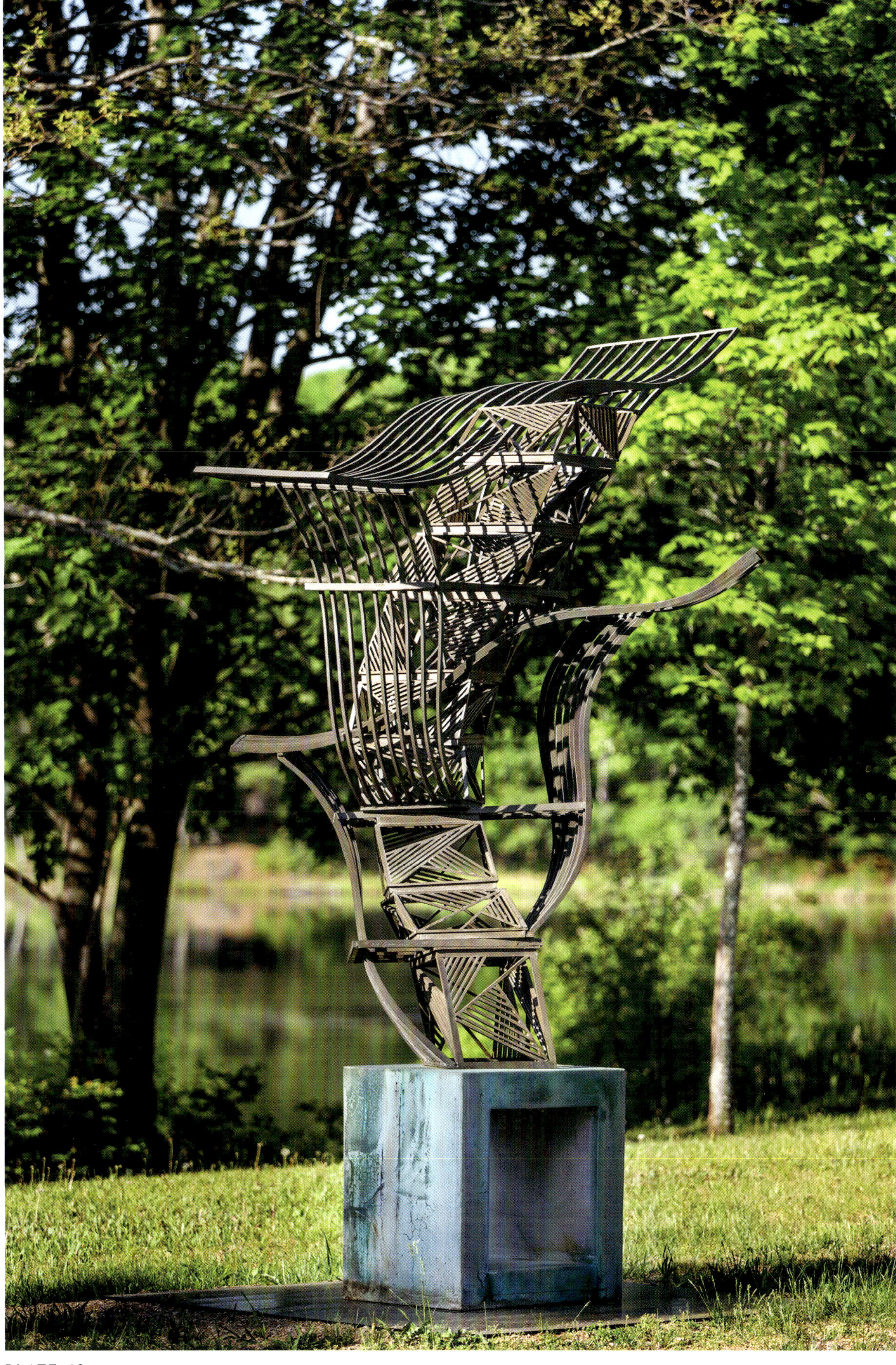

Passage, 1993. Cast bronze on concrete base, 106½ x 66 x 56 in. (270.5 x 167.6 x 142.2 cm). Collection of the artist. Courtesy Don Gummer.

PLATE 48

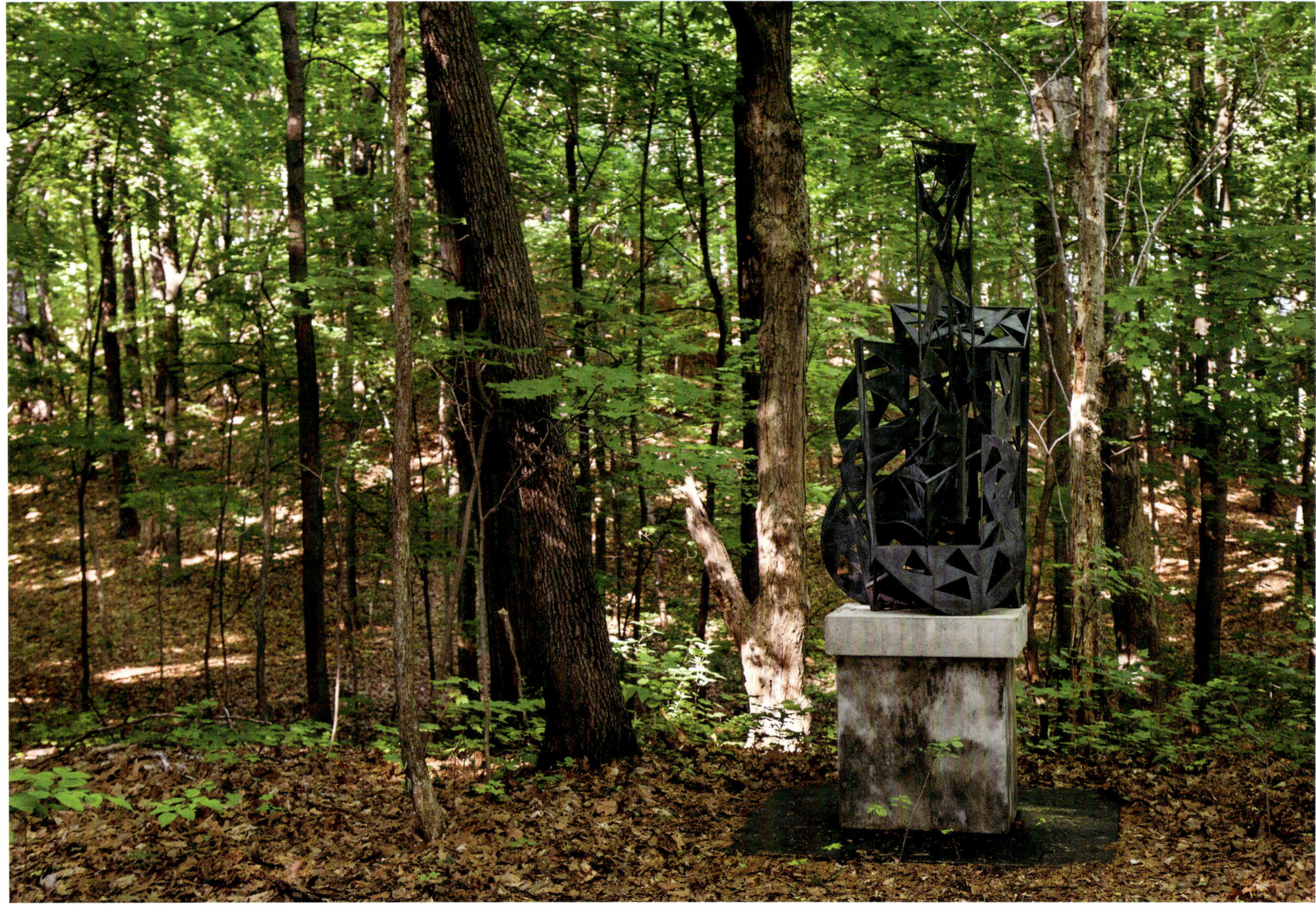

PLATE 49

Spanish Guitar, 1992. Cast bronze, 108 x 35½ x 32 in. (274.3 x 90.2 x 81.3 cm). Collection of the artist. Courtesy Don Gummer.

Uniting Blue and Red, 1999. Cast bronze, 93 x 56 x 29 in. (236.2 x 142.2 x 73.7 cm). Collection of the artist. Courtesy Don Gummer.

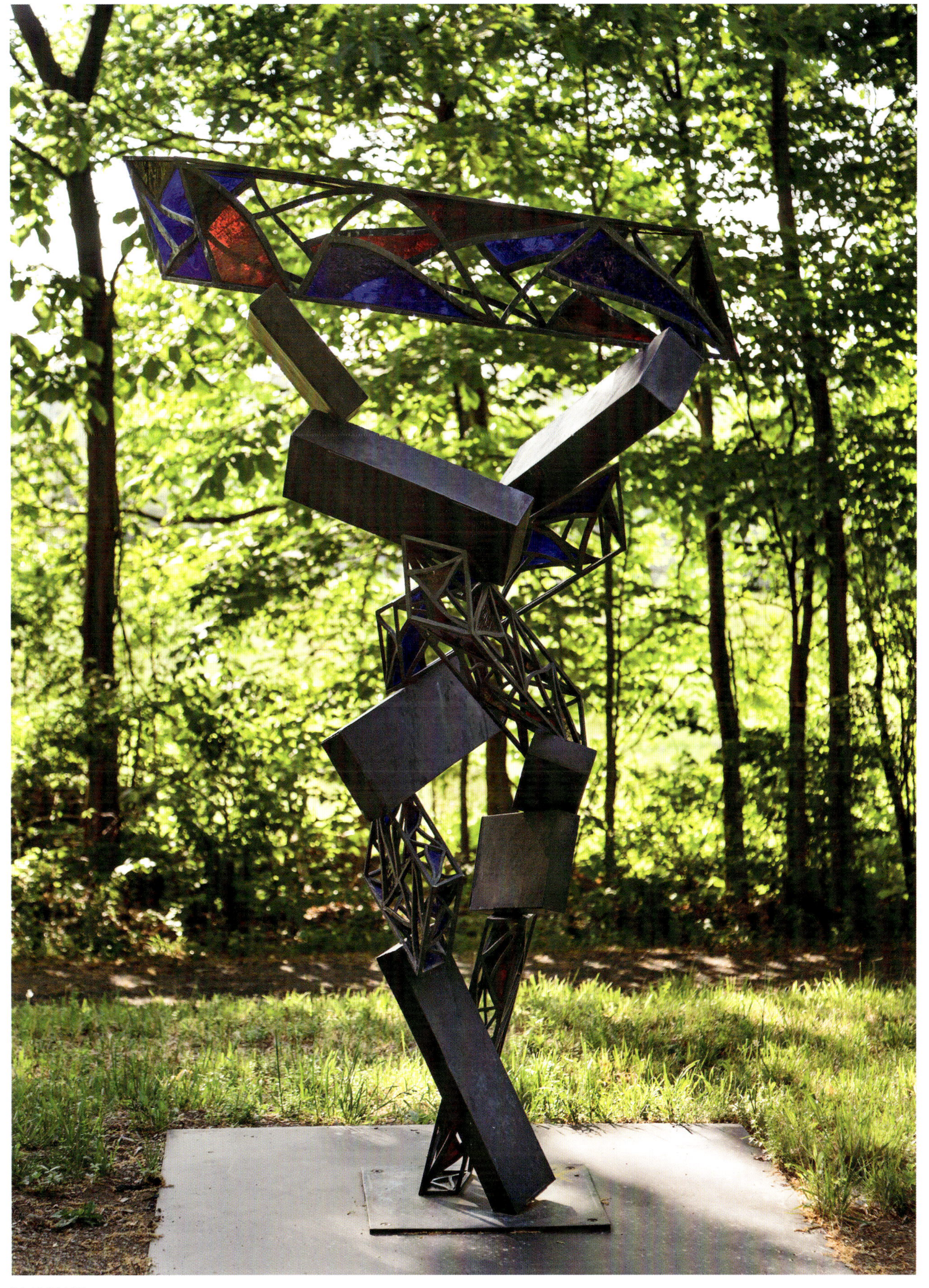

PLATE 50

A sculptor known for large-scale public works, Zimmerman's conceptual project for *River Crossings*—Church's *Olana: Observing the Site/Sights*—envisioned four platforms at sites around the property at Olana affording views either of the house or of the vistas spreading out in three directions across the broader valley (plates 51–54). In her scheme, the wood platforms would be laid with tiles in patterns inspired by the designs of the roof slats at Olana, or after drawings Church made on his travels through the Mediterranean region. The project highlights not only Church's visionary project of erecting a monument atop this hill in Hudson that is a tribute to a limitless view of the landscape, but also the great success of The Olana Partnership and its conservation allies in the region and in New York State that have created the Olana viewshed (the natural environment that is visible from one or more viewing locations) to preserve these vistas from development in perpetuity.

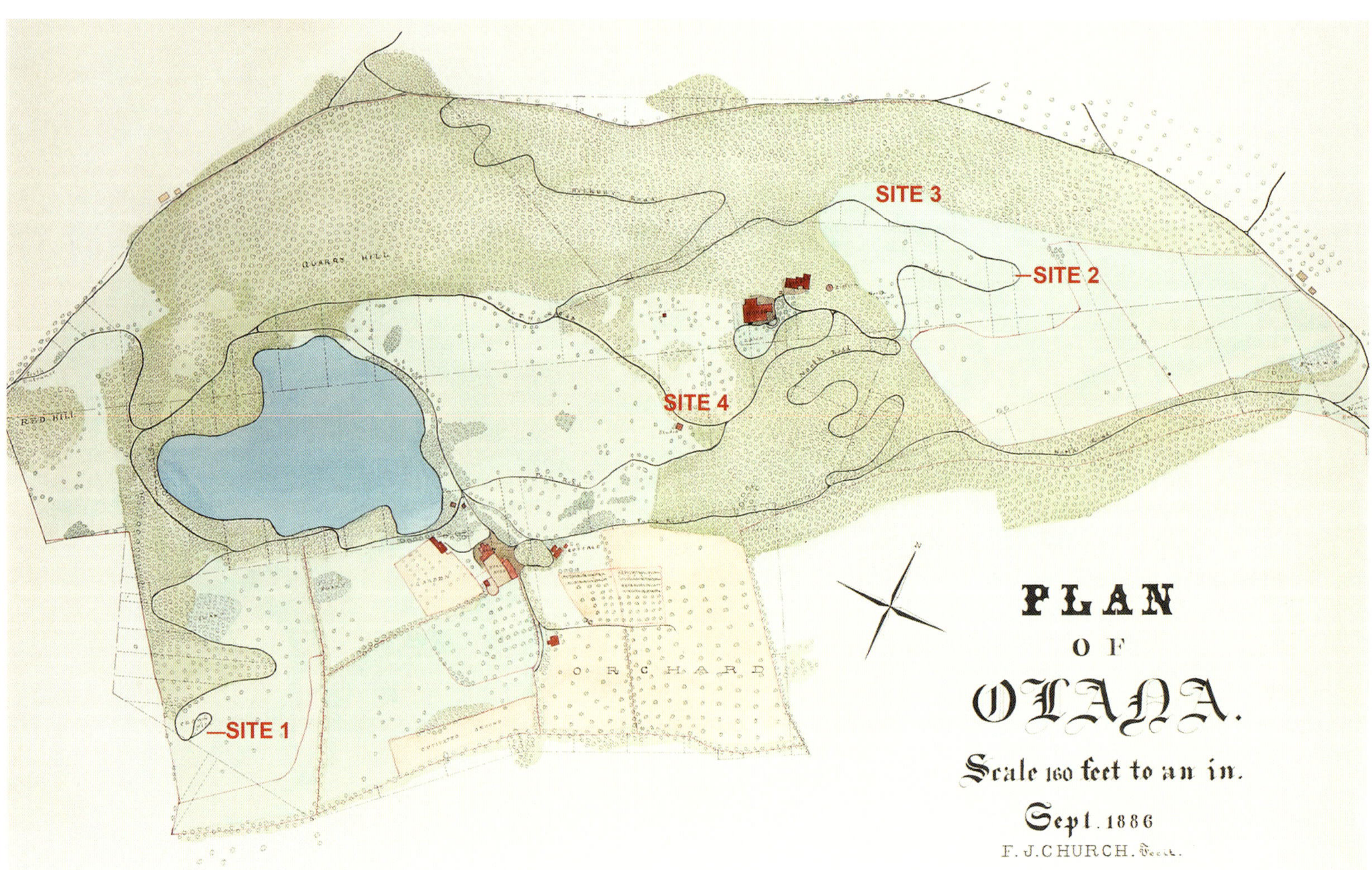

Frederic Joseph Church, *Plan of Olana*, September 1886. Ink and watercolor on paper, 22⅛ x 36¼ in. (56.2 x 92.1 cm). Collection Olana State Historic Site.

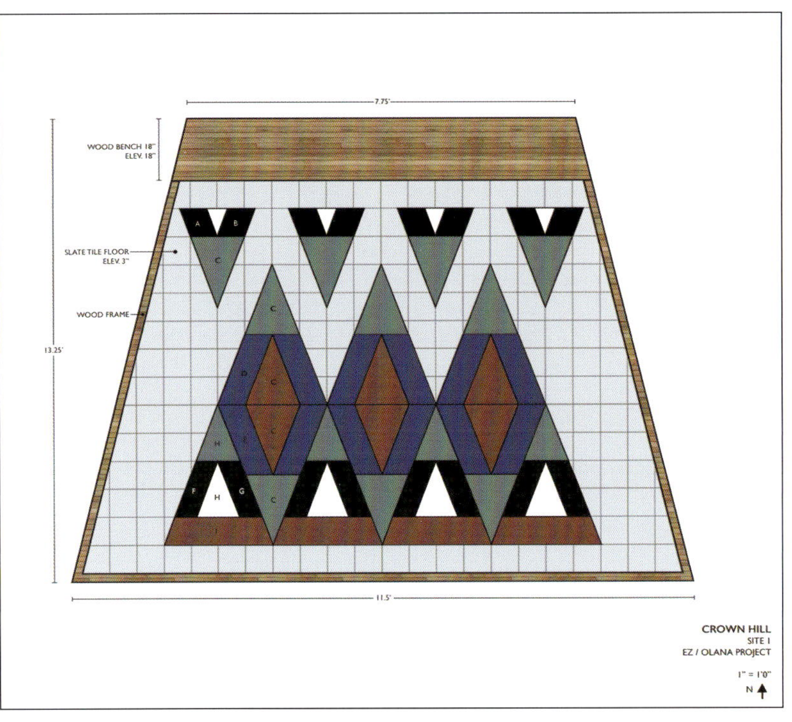

PLATE 51

Crown Hill (Site 1). Proposed materials: pressure-treated wood and Sheldon slate, trapezoid, 9 feet wide at top x 8½ feet from top to bottom x 11 feet wide at bottom in plan x 18 in. maximum bench height (2.7 x 2.6 x 3.4 m x 45.7 cm). Collection of the artist. Site-specific installation.

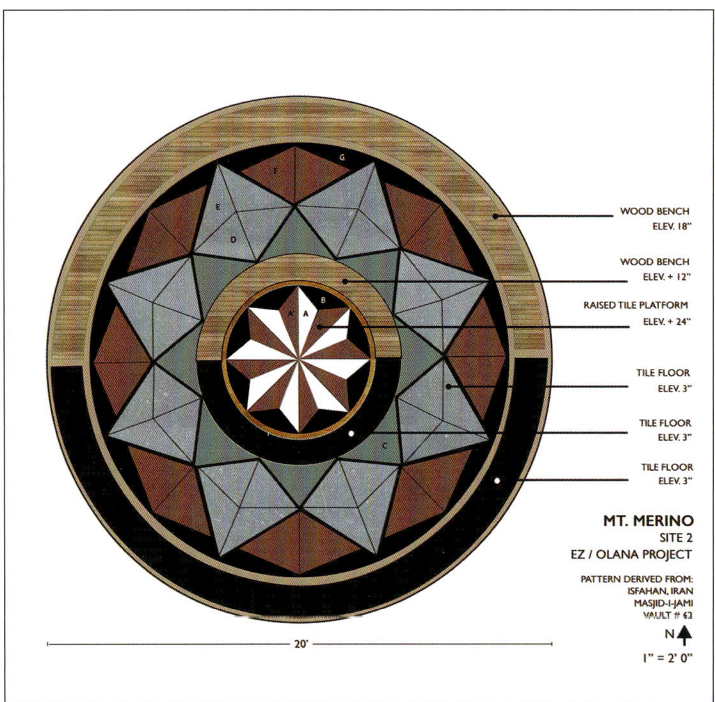

PLATE 52

Mount Merino (Site 2). Proposed materials: pressure-treated wood and Sheldon slate, circle, 20 feet in diameter in plan x 18 in. maximum bench height (6.1 m x 45.7 cm). Collection of the artist. Site-specific installation.

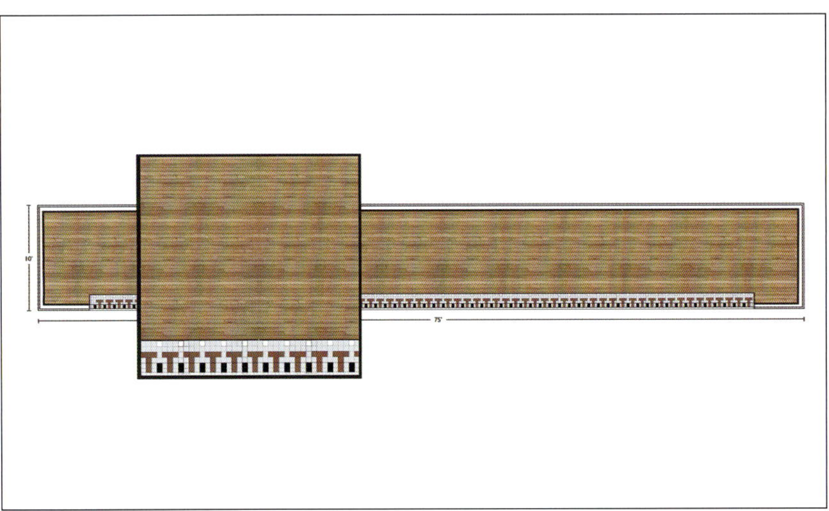

PLATE 53

River View (Site 3). Proposed materials: pressure-treated wood and Sheldon slate, 75 x 10 feet in plan x 18 in. maximum bench height (22.9 x 3 m x 45.7 cm). Collection of the artist. Site-specific installation.

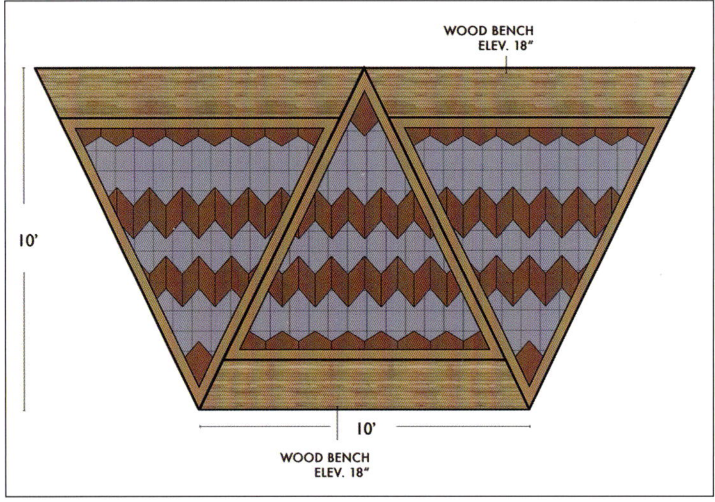

PLATE 54

The Old Studio (Site 4). Proposed materials: pressure-treated wood and Sheldon slate, trapezoid with three irregularly tilted triangular sections, 10 feet wide at top x 10 feet from top to bottom x 20 feet wide at bottom in overall plan x 18 in. maximum bench height (3 x 3 6.1 m x 45.7 cm). Collection of the artist. Site-specific installation.

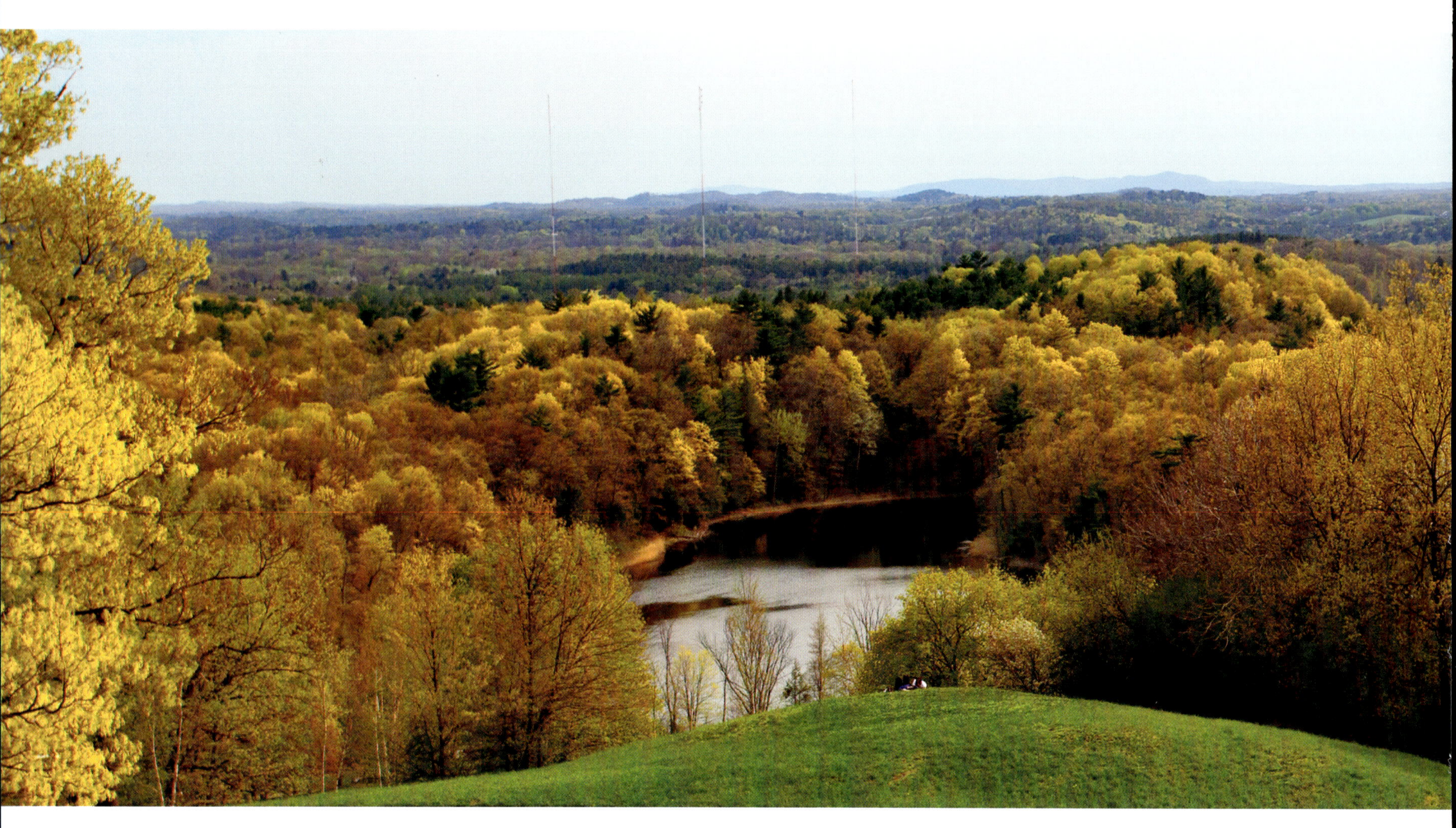

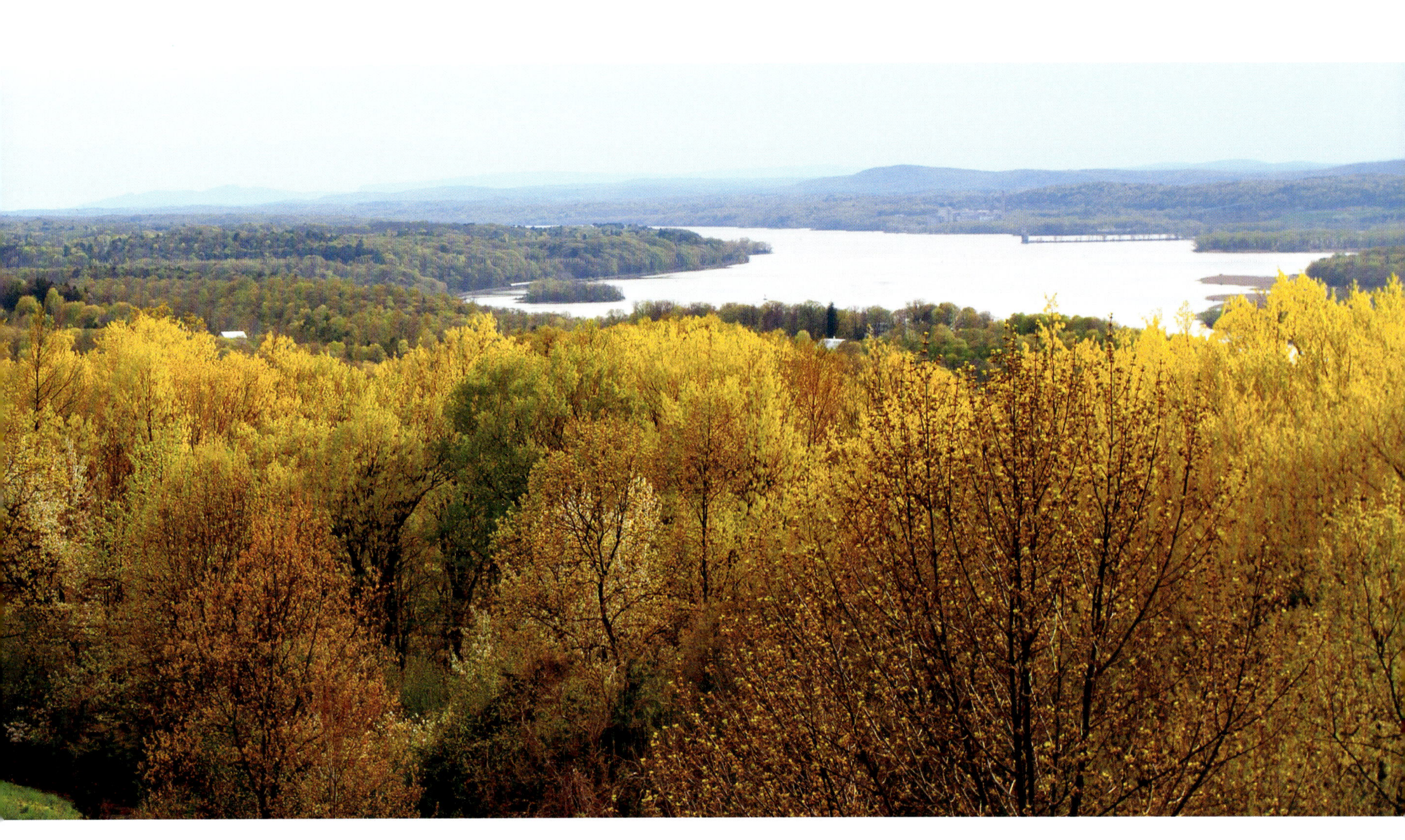

ACKNOWLEDGMENTS

River Crossings: Contemporary Art Comes Home marks the first collaborative exhibition between the Thomas Cole National Historic Site and The Olana Partnership at the Olana State Historic Site. It has been a thrill for all of us at both organizations to work with so many dedicated and accomplished collaborators throughout the complex process of organizing and mounting this exhibition. The staff and trustees would like to express their profound thanks to the many people who have made this project possible.

River Crossings stems from Stephen Hannock's extraordinary vision, and we are forever in his debt for conceiving of this exhibition and pulling out all the stops to make it happen. He and his tireless co-curator, Jason Rosenfeld, have selected artists of the highest artistic merit and have created an exhibition that is both unprecedented and inimitable. We thank them from the bottom of our hearts for giving so much of their time, passion, and dedication.

We are extremely grateful to all of the artists who participated in the exhibition. The artists include Romare Bearden, Elijah Burgher, Chuck Close, Will Cotton, Gregory Crewdson, Lynn Davis, Jerry Gretzinger, Don Gummer, Kara Hamilton, Duncan Hannah, Stephen Hannock, Valerie Hegarty, Angie Keefer, Charles LeDray, Maya Lin, Frank Moore, Elizabeth Murray, Rashaad Newsome, Thomas Nozkowski, Stephen Petegorsky, Martin Puryear, Cindy Sherman, Sienna Shields, Kiki Smith, Joel Sternfeld, Kianja Strobert, Letha Wilson, and Elyn Zimmerman. We have been inspired and humbled by your creativity and enthusiasm for this unique presentation.

In addition to the artists, numerous collectors, galleries, and museums have also generously loaned artworks for *River Crossings*. For the loaned artwork, the related arrangements, and photography we thank Andrea Fisher-Scherer at the Artists Rights Society; Elizabeth A. Carpenter, Anne Collins Goodyear, and Frank H. Goodyear III at the Bowdoin College Museum of Art; The Brooklyn Museum; Beth Zopf, studio manager, Chuck Close Studio; Rebeccah Johnson, studio manager, Lynn Davis Studio; Russell Williams at DG Studio; Jeanne Englert, personal assistant to Martin Puryear; Putri Tan at Gagosian Gallery; Bruce Barnes, Sara Evans, Lisa Hostetler, and Joe R. Struble at The George Eastman House International Museum of Photography and Film; The Murray-Holman Family Trust; Patrick Lloyd at Higher Pictures; Maria and Conrad Janis; David Lachman; Stephan and Marian Loginsky; Alexandra Ferrari and Caroline Burghardt at Luhring Augustine; Matthew Marks Gallery; Heather Russell and Bruce Kriegel at Marlborough Gallery; Mary Boone Gallery; James Cabot Ewart at Maya Lin Studio; Pedro Antonio Guerrero Art Collection; Margaret Zwilling and Michael Plunkett at METRO Pictures; Elizabeth Moore; David Goerk, Raina Mehler, Lindsay McGuire, Britta Nelson, and Nancy Rattenbury at PACE Gallery; Jacob Meehan; Alex Schneider and Eileen Jeng at Sperone Westwater; Colin Stair and Stair Galleries; Thelma Golden, Whitney Snyder, and Gina Guddemi at The Studio Museum in Harlem; Sydney Weinberg; Scott Speh, owner and director, Western Exhibitions; Brittni Zotos, studio manager, Will Cotton Studio; and L. Lynne Addison, Pamela Franks, Lisa Hodermarsky, Rachel L. Mihalko, Jock Reynolds, and David Whaples at Yale University Art Gallery.

We would like to thank the wonderful professionals who helped make this exhibition a reality: Carla Rozman for graphic design; Goodman Media for public relations; AdWorkshop for digital outreach; and Peter Aaron for site photography. We would also like to thank Robin Key Landscape Design, George Lagonia Jr. Inc., Cherie Miller Schwartz, and Robert Silman Associates for ensuring the success of landscape installations. We would like to thank Mike Prudhomme and Patrick Terenchin for their astute help with installation at the Cole site, and photographers Michael Fredericks and Chad Kleitsch for their meticulous photographic work. For this excellent publication, we thank Leslie Pell van Breen and The Artist Book Foundation.

We wish to recognize the support of Governor Andrew M. Cuomo; New York State Office of Parks, Recreation and Historic Preservation Commissioner Rose Harvey; Deputy Commissioner for Historic Preservation Ruth Pierpont; Regional Director, Taconic Region, Linda Cooper; Director of the Bureau of Historic Sites Mark Peckham; Capital Facilities Manager, Taconic Region, Garrett Johnson; Olana Site Manager Kimberly Flook; Interpretive Programs Assistant Paul Banks; and Park Supervisor Tim Dodge. We are grateful to the New York State Office of Parks, Recreation and Historic Preservation staff: Collections Manager Ronna Dixson and her staff members Hajime Stickel and Mary Zaremski; Furniture Conservator David Bayne; Paintings Conservator Mary Betlejeski; Senior Historic Sites Restoration Coordinator Chris Flagg; Decorative Arts Conservator Heidi Miksch; Grants Administrator, Taconic Region, OPRHP, Erin O'Neil; Paper Conservator Michele Phillips; Frames Conservator Eric Price; Michael Roets, scientist (archaeology); Textile Conservator Deborah Trupin; and Assistant Frames Conservator Abby Zoldowski.

We are thankful to all of the staff of both institutions who worked together to bring this exhibition to fruition. In particular we would like to acknowledge the curatorial staff who went beyond the call of duty to bring all of the disparate pieces together in the most professional manner: Kate Menconeri, Curator at the Thomas Cole National Historic Site and The Olana Partnership's Curator Evelyn Trebilcock and Landscape Curator Mark Prezorski. There are many staff who coordinated the colossal marketing and logistics efforts, including Development and Marketing Communications Manager Melanie Hasbrook and Thomas Cole Director of Education Melissa Gavilanes.

This work was only possible with vital support from Olana Associate Curator Valerie A. Balint, Thomas Cole Retail Manager Marie Spano, Thomas Cole Program Manager Alice Tunison, Thomas Cole Museum Educator Erin Dinan, Olana Archivist/Librarian Ida Brier, Olana Curatorial Assistant Andrea Nero, Thomas Cole Curatorial Assistant Kellan Rohde, Olana Curatorial Maintenance Robert Hills, and Caretakers Peter and Tone Noci. We thank Olana Development Consultant Tim Runion, Olana Head of Education Amy Hufnagel, Thomas Cole Executive Assistant Sheri DeJan, and Olana Executive Assistant Julia Thomas. Finally, we acknowledge Sara Johns Griffen, former President of The Olana Partnership, for shepherding *River Crossings* through its initial stages.

The *River Crossings* exhibition and the companion publication were made possible by the generous support of many donors. Major funding for *River Crossings* was provided by The Moore Charitable Foundation, the New York State Council on the Arts, New York State's Empire State Development and the I ❤ NY Division of Tourism under Governor Andrew Cuomo's Regional Economic Development Council Initiative, Tiger and Caroline Williams, and The Bay & Paul Foundations. Additional support is provided by Ed Herrington, Inc., the Hudson River Valley National Heritage Area, the Village of Catskill, the County Initiative Program of the Greene County Legislature administered by the Greene County Council on the Arts, the Columbia County Tourism Department, Jennifer Krieger, and Chas Miller. The companion book and related public programs were funded by Tiger and Caroline Williams, Furthermore: a program of the J. M. Kaplan Fund, and the National Endowment for the Arts.

Elizabeth B. Jacks, Executive Director
Thomas Cole National Historic Site, Catskill, New York

Rena Zurofsky, Interim President
The Olana Partnership, Hudson, New York

April 2015

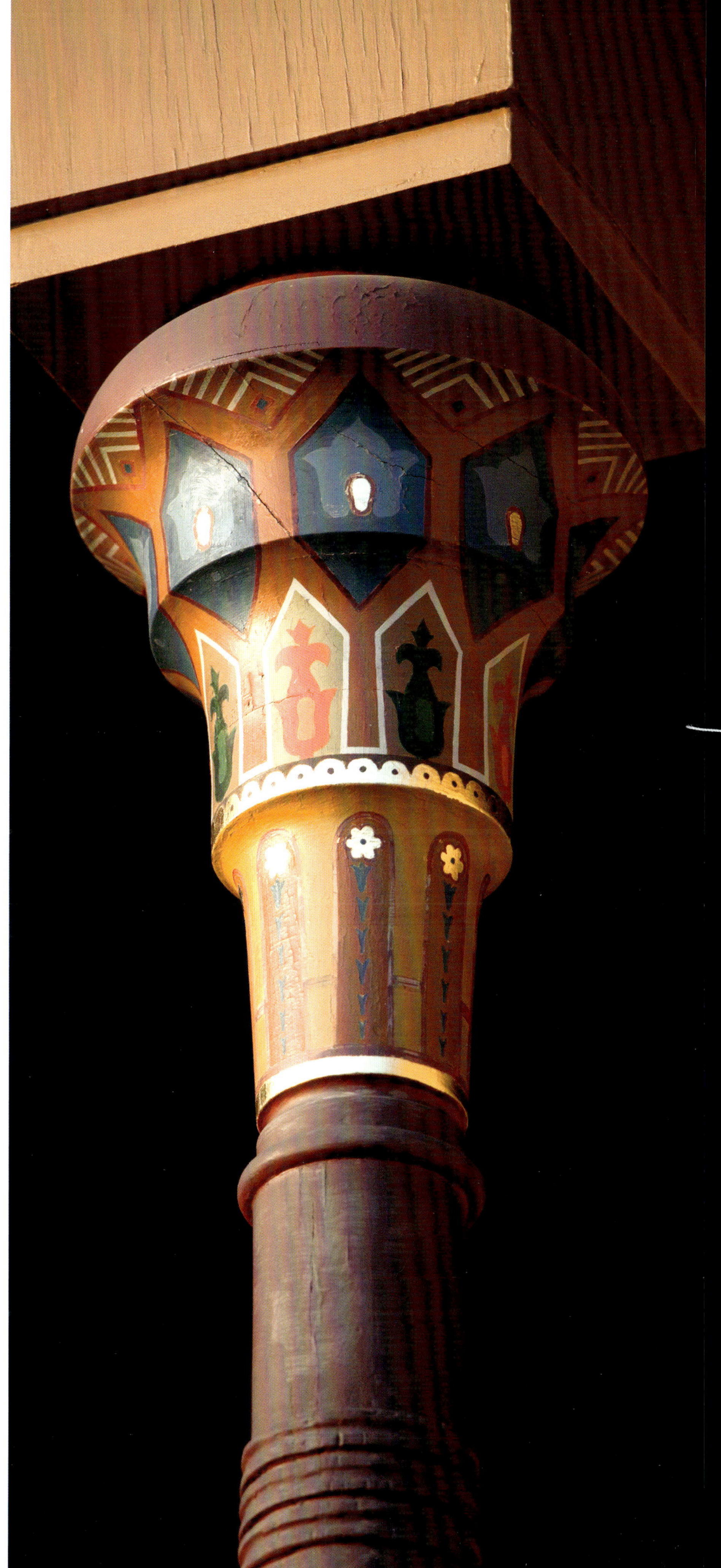

Olana architectural detail

CHECKLIST OF ADDITIONAL WORKS BY SITE: FREDERIC EDWIN CHURCH, THOMAS COLE, AND OTHER ARTISTS

CHURCH PAINTINGS CURRENTLY ON DISPLAY ON THE FIRST FLOOR OF THE HOUSE AT OLANA

EAST PARLOR

Frederic Edwin Church, *The Catskill Creek*, c. 1845. Oil on beveled pine panel, 11⅞ x 16 in. (30.2 x 40.6 cm). OL.1980.1873, Olana Collection.

Frederic Edwin Church, study for *Under Niagara*, c. 1858. Oil on paper mounted on canvas, 11¾ x 17½ in. (29.8 x 44.5 cm). OL. 1981.51, Olana Collection.

Frederic Edwin Church, *Mount Chimborazo at Sunset*, c. 1857. Oil on academy board mounted on canvas, 12 x 21⁷⁄₁₆ in. (30.5 x 54.5 cm). OL.1980.1884, Olana Collection.

Frederic Edwin Church, study for *The Heart of the Andes*, 1858. Oil on canvas, 10¼ x 18¼ in. (26 x 46.4 cm). OL.1981.47, Olana Collection.

Frederic Edwin Church, *Scene in the Blue Mountains, Jamaica*, 1865. Oil on paper mounted on academy board, 10⅝ x 17¾ in. (27 x 45.1 cm). OL.1981.69, Olana Collection.

Frederic Edwin Church, *Apple Blossoms at Olana*, 1870. Oil on canvas, 11⅝ x 18¼ in. (29.5 x 46.4 cm). OL.1981.23, Olana Collection.

Frederic Edwin Church, *The Hudson Valley in Winter from Olana*, 1866–1872. Oil on academy board, 11¾ x 18¼ in. (29.8 x 46.4 cm). OL.1980.36, Olana Collection.

Frederic Edwin Church, *Twilight Among the Mountains (Catskill Creek)*, 1845. Oil on canvas, 18½ x 24 in. (47 x 61 cm). OL.1981.25, Olana Collection.

Frederic Edwin Church, *Sunset, Bar Harbor*, c. 1854. Oil on paper mounted on canvas, 10⅛ x 17¼ in. (25.7 x 43.8 cm). OL.1981.72, Olana Collection.

Frederic Edwin Church, *The Bridge at Ponte Grande, Italy*, 1868. Oil on paper mounted on canvas, 13⅛ x 20⅛ in. (33.3 x 51.1 cm). OL.1981.24, Olana Collection.

Thomas Cole, *Solitary Lake in New Hampshire*, 1830. Oil on canvas, 45 x 63¼ in. (114.3 x 160.7 cm). OL.1981.19, Olana Collection.

SITTING ROOM

Frederic Edwin Church, *Moonrise (The Rising Moon)*, 1865. Oil on canvas, 10 x 17 in. (25.4 x 43.2 cm). OL.1981.11, Olana Collection.

Frederic Edwin Church, *Sunset, Jamaica*, 1865. Oil on paper mounted on canvas, 12⅛ x 18⅛ in. (30.8 x 46 cm). OL.1981.26, Olana Collection.

Frederic Edwin Church, *The Urn Tomb, Silk Tomb, and Corinthian Tomb, Petra*, 1868. Oil on paper mounted on canvas, 13 x 20⅛ in. (33 x 51.1 cm). OL.1981.52, Olana Collection.

Frederic Edwin Church, *Konigssee, Germany*, 1868. Oil on paper mounted on canvas, 13 x 20 in. (33 x 50.8 cm). OL.1981.42, Olana Collection.

Frederic Edwin Church, *El Khasné, Petra*, 1874. Oil on canvas, 60½ x 50¼ in. (153.7 x 127.6 cm). OL.1981.10, Olana Collection.

Frederic Edwin Church, *Sunset*, 1856–1865. Oil on paper mounted on rag board and panel, 11⅝ x 18¼ in. (29.5 x 46.4 cm). OL.1980.1633, Olana Collection.

Frederic Edwin Church, *Catskill Mountains from the Home of the Artist*, 1871. Oil on canvas, 22⅛ x 36⅜ in. (56.2 x 92.4 cm). OL.1981.13, Olana Collection.

Frederic Edwin Church, *Mount Katahdin from Upper Togue Lake*, 1877–1878. Oil on academy board, 8⅛ x 20 in. (20.6 x 50.8 cm). OL.1981.70, Olana Collection.

Frederic Edwin Church, *Wood Interior near Mount Katahdin*, c. 1877. Oil on paper mounted on canvas, 12⁵⁄₁₆ x 17¹⁄₁₆ in. (31.3 x 43.3 cm). OL.1980.1871, Olana Collection.

Frederic Edwin Church, *Olive Trees, Athens*, 1869. Oil on paper mounted on canvas, 13⅛ x 20⅛ in. (33.3 x 51.1 cm). OL.1980.1892, Olana Collection.

Frederic Edwin Church, *Church of the Tercer Orden de San Francisco, Cuernavaca, Mexico*, 1896. Oil on academy board, 9½ x 14 in. (24.1 x 35.6 cm). OL.1980.1893, Olana Collection.

CORRIDOR

Frederic Edwin Church, *Rainbow near Berchtesgaden, Germany*, 1868. Oil on paper mounted on canvas, 8³⁄₁₆ x 11¹⁵⁄₁₆ in. (20.8 x 30.3 cm). OL.1980.1883, Olana Collection.

Frederic Edwin Church, *Campfire near Mount Katahdin*, c. 1877. Oil on paper mounted on canvas, 12⅜ x 20⅜ in. (31.4 x 51.8 cm). OL.1980.1916, Olana Collection.

Frederic Edwin Church, *Goldfish Pond*, 1875–1880. Oil on paper mounted on canvas, 12⅜ x 14⅜ in. (31.4 x 36.5 cm). OL.1981.44, Olana Collection.

Frederic Edwin Church, *Autumn Scene, Vermont*, 1865. Oil on paper mounted on canvas, 12⁷⁄₁₆ x 20½ in. (31.6 x 52.1 cm). OL.1980.1886, Olana Collection.

Charles Loring Elliott (1812–1868), *Frederic Edwin Church*, 1865. Oil on canvas, 34 x 27 in. (86.4 x 68.6 cm). Collection of Olana State Historic Site, OL.1981.4

STUDIO

Frederic Edwin Church, *Ira Mountain, Vermont*, 1850. Oil on canvas, 40⅝ x 61⅝ in. (103.2 x 156.5 cm). OL. 1981.49, Olana Collection.

Frederic Edwin Church, *Mexican Forest—a Composition*, 1891. Oil on canvas, 14⅛ x 20⅞ in. (35.9 x 53 cm). OL.1980.1925, Olana Collection.

Frederic Edwin Church, *Christian on the Borders of the "Valley of the Shadow of Death," Pilgrim's Progress*, 1847. Oil on canvas, 40½ x 60½ in. (102.9 x 153.7 cm). OL.1981.50, Olana Collection.

Frederic Edwin Church, *Ruins at Baalbeck*, c. 1868. Oil on paper, mounted on canvas, 13 x 20 in. (33 x 50.8 cm). Private collection.

Frederic Edwin Church, *Mountain Lake, Twilight*, 1850–1856. Oil on academy board, 5¼ x 9¼ in. (13.3 x 23.5 cm). OL.1981.40, Olana Collection.

Frederic Edwin Church, *Mountain Lake*, 1851. Oil on academy board, 6⅝ x 10¾ in. (16.8 x 27.3 cm). OL.1981.41, Olana Collection.

CHECKLIST OF WORKS BY THOMAS COLE, SARAH COLE, AND OTHER ARTISTS BY ROOM AT TCNHS

West Parlor

Thomas Cole, *Catskill Mountain Landscape*, n.d. Oil on canvas, 12½ x 15½ in. (31.8 x 39.4 cm). On loan from Richard Sharp.

Sarah Cole, *Untitled English Landscape*, c. 1846. Oil on board, 13⅛ x 15 in. (33.3 x 38.1 cm). Thomas Cole National Historic Site, gift of Edith Cole Silberstein and the Greene County Historical Society.

Sarah Cole, *Landscape with Church*, 1846. Oil on board, 11⅞ x 13⅞ in. (30.2 x 35.2 cm). Thomas Cole National Historic Site, gift of Lynne Hill Bosnack.

Thomas Cole, *Landscape, Sunrise in the Clove*, n.d. Oil on canvas, 5½ x 8½ in. (14 x 21.6 cm). Thomas Cole National Historic Site, gift of Edith Cole Silberstein and the Greene County Historical Society.

Thomas Cole, *On the Mountaintop*, n.d. Oil on board, 7⁷⁄₁₆ x 9½ in. (18.9 x 24.1 cm). On extended loan to the Thomas Cole National Historic Site, Drs. Matthew and Maria Brown and Questroyal Fine Art, LLC.

Thomas Cole, *American Lake Scene*, n.d. Oil on canvas, 11½ x 16 in. (29.2 x 40.6 cm). Estate of the Price Family.

Second-Floor Gallery

Thomas Cole, *Prometheus Bound*, c. 1846. Oil on canvas, 29¾ x 44½ in. (75.6 x 113 cm). On loan from the Catskill Public Library, gift of Florence Cole Vincent as a memorial to her grandfather, the artist.

Sketch box with interior oil painting of Sicily by Thomas Cole, *Girgenti*, 1835–1845. Hinged mahogany box, oil paint, and brass, closed: 2½ x 18 x 14 in. (6.4 x 45.7 x 35.6 cm); interior painting: 13¼ x 15¼ in. (33.7 x 38.7 cm). Greene County Historical Society.

Thomas Cole, *Untitled (Landscape/Italian Ruins)*, n.d. Unfinished, oil on board in reproduction frame, 12½ x 15¾ in. (31.8 x 40 cm). Thomas Cole National Historic Site, gift of Edith Cole Silberstein and the Greene County Historical Society.

Thomas Cole, *Study of Mountain Crags*, n.d. Oil on canvas, 17 x 22 in. (43.2 x 55.9 cm). On loan from Richard Sharp.

Thomas Cole, *On Catskill Creek*, 1836. Oil on canvas, 19½ x 14¾ in. (49.5 x 37.5 cm). On extended loan to the Thomas Cole National Historic Site, Drs. Matthew and Maria Brown and Questroyal Fine Art, LLC.

Thomas Cole, *A Sketch: Catskill Landscape*, 1845–1847. Oil on wood pulp paperboard, 10¾ x 7⅞ in. (27.3 x 20 cm). Thomas Cole National Historic Site, gift of Seattle Art Museum.

Thomas Cole, *Untitled sketch*, n.d. Graphite on paper, 8 x 12¼ in. (20.3 x 31.1 cm). Thomas Cole National Historic Site, gift of Edith Cole Silberstein and the Greene County Historical Society.

Thomas Cole, *Ruined Castle*, c. 1830. Watercolor on paper, 6 x 8½ in. (15.2 x 21.6 cm). On loan from Richard Sharp.

Thomas Cole, *Hudson Highlands*, n.d. Pencil on paper, 6¼ x 9½ in. (15.9 x 24.1 cm). Thomas Cole National Historic Site, gift of Edith Cole Silberstein and the Greene County Historical Society.

Thomas Cole, *Reflection*, n.d. Oil on canvas, 13 x 11 in. (33 x 27.9 cm). On loan from Richard Sharp.

Thomas Cole, *Untitled (portrait)*, n.d. Oil on canvas, 9 x 8 in. (22.9 x 20.3 cm). Thomas Cole National Historic Site.

Thomas Cole, *Untitled sketch (Autumnal Sunset)*, n.d. Graphite on paper, 2 x 3½ in. (5.1 x 8.9 cm). Thomas Cole National Historic Site, gift of Edith Cole Silberstein and the Greene County Historical Society.

Thomas Cole, *Tower by Moonlight*, c. 1838. Oil on canvas, 16¾ x 20½ in. (42.5 x 52.1 cm). Thomas Cole National Historic Site, gift of David and Laura Grey.

North Room

Thomas Cole, *Diagram of Contrasts*, 1834. Oil on panel, 23½ x 35 in. (59.7 x 88.9 cm). On loan from Richard Sharp.

Additional works on view in the Cole house / first-floor hallway

Reproduction copy detail of Frederic Church, *Portrait of Thomas Cole*, 1846. Pencil and ink on paper, 7 x 9⁵⁄₁₆ in. (17.8 x 23.7 cm). National Portrait Gallery, Smithsonian Institution.

Reproduction copy of Thomas Cole, *Portrait of the Artist's Wife*, 1836–1848. Graphite on paper, 12½ x 9⁵⁄₁₆ in. (31.8 x 23.7 cm). Museum of Fine Arts Boston.

Charles Herbert Moore, *Thomas Cole's Studio*, 1868. Oil on canvas mounted on board, framed: 5⅞ x 9¼ in. (14.9 x 23.5 cm). Thomas Cole National Historic Site, Gift of Edith Cole Silberstein and the Greene County Historical Society.

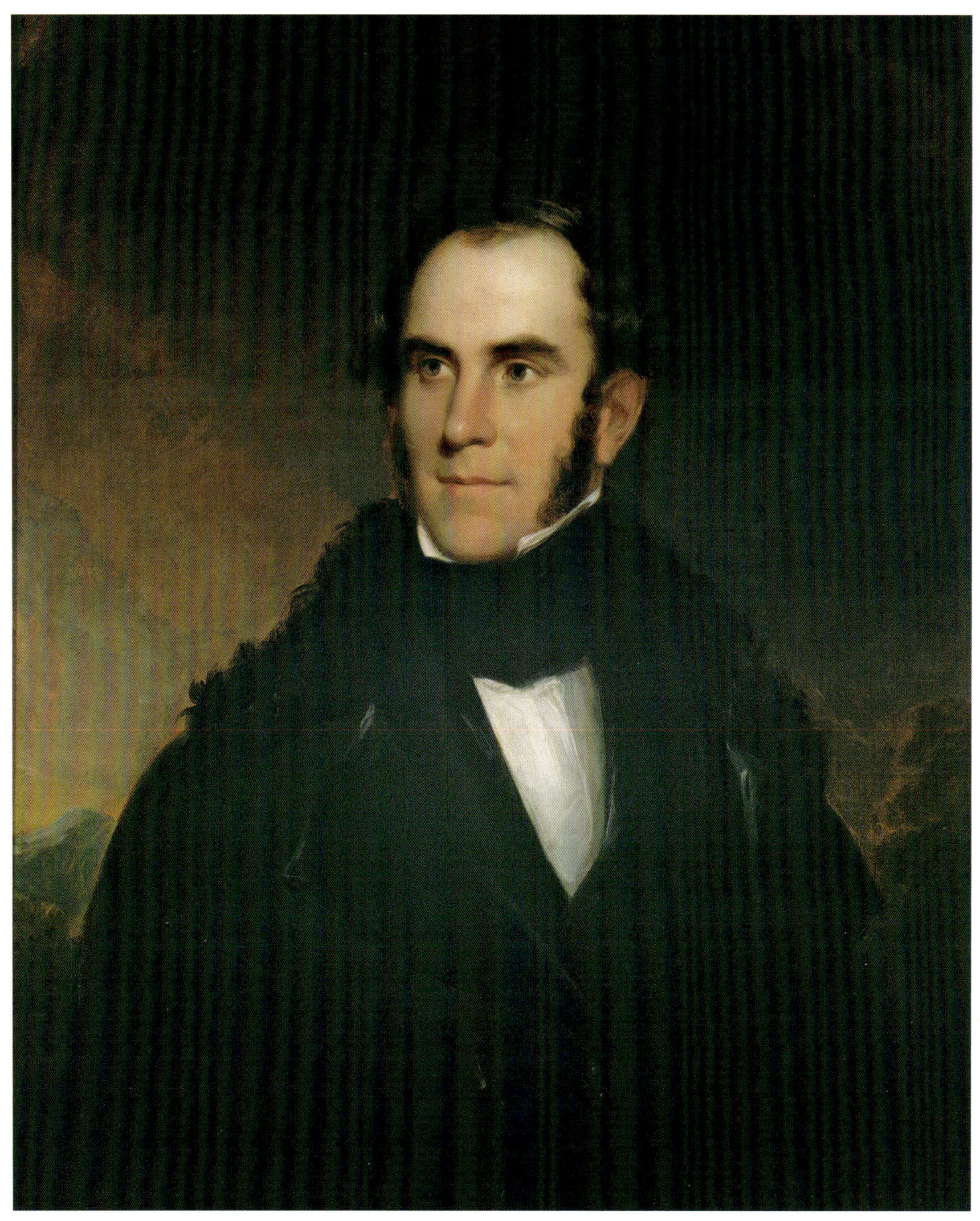

Asher B. Durand, *Portrait of Thomas Cole*, 1838. Oil on canvas, 29½ x 24½ in. (74.9 x 62.2 cm). Gift of Zenas Crane, 1917.13, courtesy of the Berkshire Museum, Pittsfield, Massachusetts , USA.

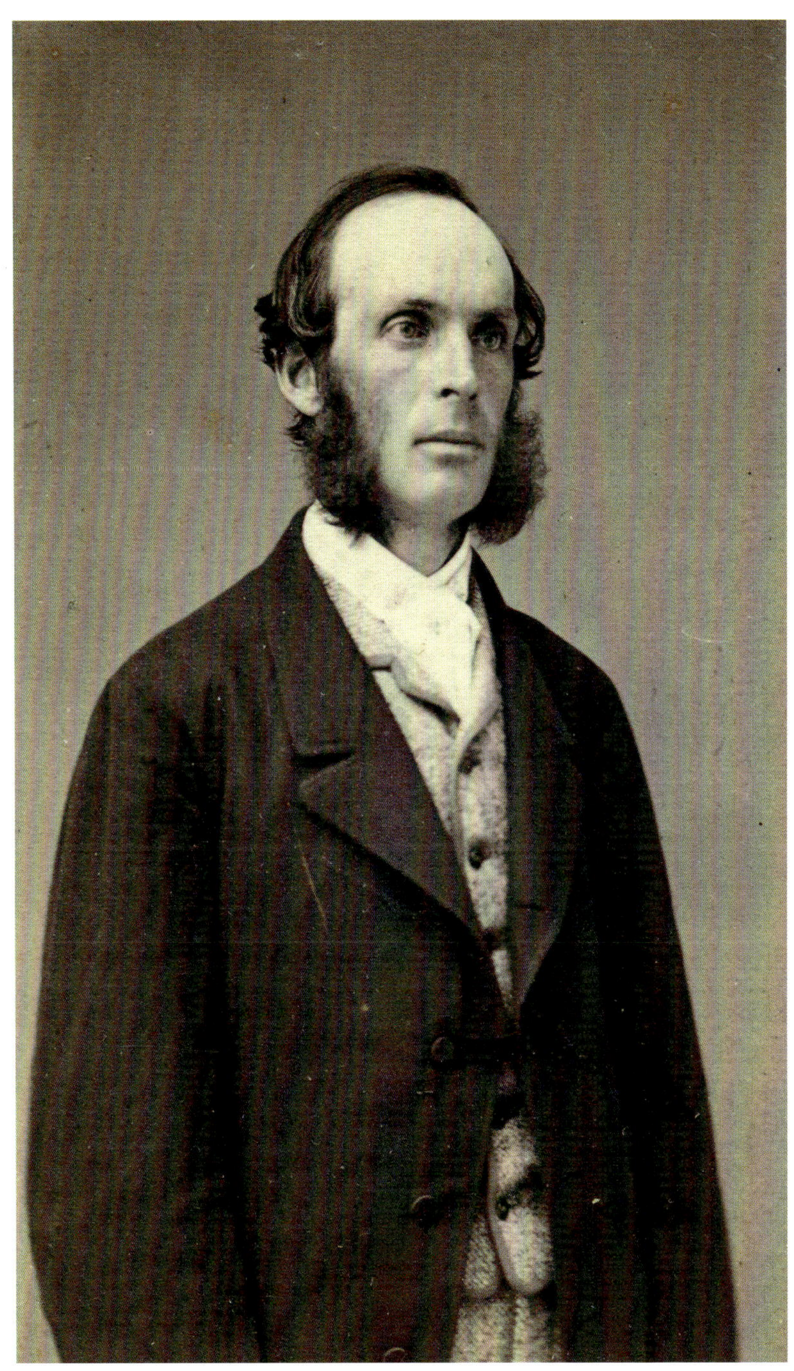

Thompson Studio (Albany, NY), *Frederic Edwin Church*, c. 1862. Carte-de-visite, 3⅞ x 2⅜ in. (9.8 x 6 cm). Collection of Olana State Historic Site, OL.1986.628.

Published on the occasion of the landmark exhibition *River Crossings: Contemporary Art Comes Home*,
on view at Olana State Historic Site, Hudson, New York, and Thomas Cole National Historic Site, Catskill, New York,
from May 3 to November 1, 2015.

Photographer Peter Aaron is gratefully acknowledged for his generous contribution of time and expertise
in the gift of his photography for this unique presentation, in two iconic venues, for the accompanying publication.
Unless otherwise noted, all installation, exterior, and landscape photographs are © Peter Aaron.

Published in the United States by The Artist Book Foundation
115 East 57th Street, 11th floor, New York, New York 10022

Distributed in the United States, its territories and possessions, and Canada by
ARTBOOK LLC D.A.P. | Distributed Art Publishers, Inc.
www.artbook.com
Distributed outside North America by ACC Distribution
www.accdistribution.com/uk

Publisher and Co-founder: Leslie Pell van Breen
Co-founder: H. Gibbs Taylor, Jr.
Production Manager: David Skolkin
Design: Christopher Kuntze
Editor: Marisa Crumb
Proofreader: Deborah Thompson
Printed and bound by Friesens

Manufactured in Canada

ISBN 978-0-9888557-9-3

LIBRARY OF CONGRESS CATALOGING-IN-PUBLICATION DATA

River crossings (2015)
 River crossings : contemporary art comes home / By Jason Rosenfeld ; Preface by
Stephen Hannock ; Foreword by Ken Burns ; Essays by Marvin Heiferman, Maurice
Berger. — First Edition.
    pages cm
 "Published on the occasion of the landmark exhibition River Crossings:
Contemporary Art Comes Home, on view at Olana State Historic Site, Hudson,
New York and Thomas Cole National Historic Site, Catskill, New York from May 3
to November 1, 2015."
 Includes index.
 ISBN 978-0-9888557-9-3
 1. Art, American—21st century—Exhibitions. 2. Art, American—Hudson River Valley
(N.Y. and N.J.)—Exhibitions. I. Hannock, Stephen, 1951- writer of preface. II. Burns,
Ken, 1953- writer of foreword. III. Rosenfeld, Jason. River crossings. IV. Heiferman,
Marvin. Changing nature of nature's image. V. Berger, Maurice, 1956- Ghosts of the
Hudson Valley. VI. Olana State Historic Site (Hudson, N.Y.), host institution.
VII. Thomas Cole National Historic Site (Catskill, N.Y.), host institution. VIII. Title.
 N6512.7.R58 2015
 709.73'07474737—dc23   2015029355

Front cover: Martin Puryear, *Question*, 2010–2014 (plate 37) in the Court Hall at Olana.

Back cover: Jerry Gretzinger, *Jerry's Map*, 1963 to present (plate 13) in the Second-Floor
Hallway at the Thomas Cole National Historic Site.

Title page: Martin Puryear, *Question*, 2010–2014 (plate 37) in the Court Hall and Chuck
Close, *Self-Portrait (Yellow Raincoat)*, 2013 (plate 35) on the Stair Hall wall at Olana.

Opposite contents: Detail of map of Hudson River from *Hudson by Daylight*, by William
F. Link (New York: Day Line Steamers, 1878); includes map from New York Bay to the
Head of Tide Water, with noted location of Cole's Grove and Thomas Cole house, 6 x 5 x
¼ in. (15.2 x 12.7 x 0.6 cm). Thomas Cole National Historic Site Archives, gift of the artist's
family and the Greene County Historical Society.

Spread (pp. 32–33): Exterior view of the Thomas Cole National Historic Site house,
Catskill, NY, 2013.

Spread (pp. 82–83): View of Olana in the summer from the lake, Hudson, NY, 2010.

Spread (pp. 110–111): Panoramic view across the Hudson River from the south steps
at Olana, Hudson, NY, 2010.

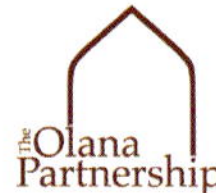
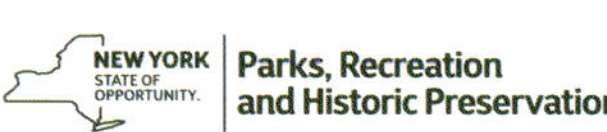
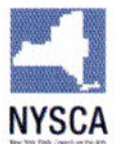
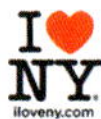
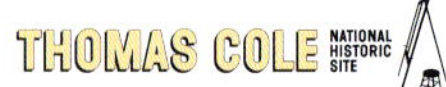
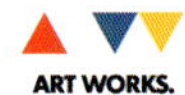
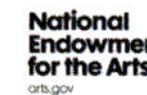
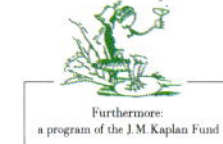